D

NOV 19 2003

Profile of an Americanized Danube Swabian *Ethnically Cleansed Under Tito*

By

Jacob Steigerwald, Ph. D.

Translation & Interpretation Svc
Littleton, Colorado 80123

In Memory of
Yugoslavia's Indigenous
Ethnic-Germans Who Fell Victim to
"Ethnic Cleansing" Under Tito, 1944-1948

ISBN 0-9615505-4-6

Library of Congress Control Number: 2001116229

PUBLISHED AND DISTRIBUTED BY:
Translation & Interpretation Service
5960 South Estes Street
Littleton CO 80123 U.S.A.

Printed in the U.S.A. by
Morris Publishing
3212 East Highway 30
Kearney, NE 68847
1-800-650-7888

Table of Contents

IX. REFERENCES

Acknowledgements and Preface

To all persons who contributed toward drafting and crafting this opus, I want to express my sincere thanks. Above all, my wife Marie merits recognition for encouraging me to write this book as a bequest to our family and for concerned widely scattered descendants of Danube Swabians whose collective experiences as members of an arbitrarily dispersed ethnic group happen to be reflected in my life, too. Readers are familiarized with applicable events in East Central Europe and attendant consequences right up to the aftermath of WW II. As a voice against recurrent genocide, the biography should also add to the limited coverage in English regarding this exceptionally adaptable minority whose values are said to include "portable roots" (cf. Katherine Stenger Frey). In essence, efforts of group members to substantiate their contributions to society can be regarded as a common trait fittingly illustrated by my own motivation to do well.

Marie also deserves credit for identifying passages in the manuscript that needed to be rounded out or tidied up. For her valued practical review with helpful suggestions toward improvements in form and structure, I wish to express my gratitude to Shirley Meier whose own literary achievements include works about Germans from Russia in the U.S.A.

In chapter 1, an historic overview is given concerning the origin of the ethnic minority whose members came to be known as Danube Swabians. Their disconnected former locations in multi-national settings along the middle Danube had the makings of a kind of "melting-pot" also, but divisive chauvinism still prevalent in Southeastern Europe kept assimilation from ever coming to bounteous fruition. WW II and its ultimate stages resulted in the group's large-scale dispersal from Hungary, Romania, and Yugoslavia. While over a half million managed to get off to fresh starts in Germany and Austria as time went on, tens of thousands eventually emigrated to far-flung places like Argentina, Australia, Brazil, Canada, France, the U.S.A., and other countries.

Quite a few Danube Swabian ancestors hailed from French as well as German-speaking areas in Lorraine, including several of my maternal forefathers as indicated in chapter 2. During the 18th Century, the proverbial "Spessartnot" (indigence) mentioned in chapter 3 had also prompted emigration to overseas destinations along with migrations to other parts of

Europe. Among others who settled in Hungary, some of my paternal ancestors were traced to Franconia as well.

Perceptions of my childhood in a Danube Swabian environment are provided in chapter 4 with due reference to my mother's premature death at age 39, which was attributable to the resolve of AVNOJ to get rid of Yugoslavia's remaining ethnic-Germans after WW II. Tito's vengeful partisans saw to it that no medicine was "wasted" on members of the country's unwanted Germans. Ways to achieve the minority's elimination resembled what became known as "ethnic cleansing" a half century later. Today, the very phrase sends shivers down the spine of considerate folks including President George W. Bush, as indicated in a personal statement reprinted by the German-American weekly *Eintracht*, Jg. 79 - Vol. 8 (Oct 21, 2000), p. 3.

Chapters 5 and 6 describe my April 1945 confinement to a Yugoslav concentration camp for members of the country's ethnic-German minority. Detained group members in over seventy camps of three types were subjected to varying degrees of maltreatment - all too often with fatal results. Fortunately, I ended up among compatriots who managed to flee to neighboring countries from where most of us eventually wound up in Austria or Germany - in many cases just for a while, until other options materialized.

It took years, before opportunities for group emigration presented themselves. As shown in chapters 7 and 8, I was one of over forty thousand who immigrated to the United States of America in the 1950's. Upon initially working and living in Chicago, Illinois, my acclimation was further enhanced through service in the U. S. Army. Chapter 9 recounts my naturalization and rapport with fellow soldiers as well as general educational achievements plus marriage and employment. Family growth and additional schooling to attain a professional status are covered in chapter 10. Chapter 11 describes extensive job searches and our family's relocation from Ohio to Minnesota where I found employment as a foreign language professor at Winona State University.

The enduring struggle for survival in academe is focused upon in chapters 12 and 13. Chapter 14 deals with the wrongful death of our only daughter Ellen and difficulties in coping with it. Chapter 15 portrays our relocation from Minnesota to Colorado for family and other reasons. In chapter 16, the impact of Americanization upon Danube Swabian thinking is reviewed. Insights gained by examining tenets held not only deepen understanding but they also suggest how Danube Swabian attributes enriched their host countries worldwide.

Appendix A provides an overview of Danube Swabians in America. Appendix B consists of a treatise I wrote in 1986 concerning fifty-three years of foreign language instruction at Winona State University in Minnesota. Appendix C lists my personal earnings from the time of my arrival in the U. S. until retirement. The inflation rate for each of the corresponding forty-two years is also denoted.

An annotated bibliography concludes the volume to which access is facilitated by means of an Index. Subject areas dealt with or touched upon can be categorized under headings as follows:

1. BIOGRAPHY
   a) 023 Autobiography
2. EDUCATION AND GUIDANCE
   a) 065 Adult Education
   b) 069 Education - General
   c) 081 Occupational and Educational Information
   d) 084 Personality Development
   e) 086 Tests - Achievement
3. GOVERNMENT AND POLITICAL SCIENCE
   a) 451 Civil Rights
   b) 105 Current Events
   c) Current World Affairs
   d) 462 Minority Group Studies
4. HISTORY
   a) Americana
   b) Continental Europe
   c) World (Incl. WW I and WW II)

5. LANGUAGE ARTS
   a) 174 Communications
   b) 188 Linguistics
6. LANGUAGE - FOREIGN
   a) 205 Modern Language Study
   b) 207 French
   c) 209 German
   d) 219 Spanish
   e) 221 Other Languages
7. LITERATURE (incl. Poetry)
   a) 232 Continental European
8. PHILOSOPHY
   a) 299 Ethics and Logic
   b) 300 Philosophy
9. SOCIOLOGY
   a) 368 Crime and Criminals
10. VOCATIONAL EDUCATION
   a) 399 Agriculture
   b) 402 Building Trades

Jacob Steigerwald, Ph.D.

vii

Clarification of Terminology

AVNOJ - acronym denoting the Serb equivalent of Anti-fascist Council for the National Liberation of Yugoslavia.

Backa/Bacska - geographic area bounded by Hungary in the North, by the Danube west and south, and by the Tisza River in the East, now constituting part of the Vojvodina.

Banat - region of East Central Europe in the Danube basin between the Tisza and Mures rivers and the Transylvania Alps (see map on p. 2).

Baranya - triangular area of the Vojvodina W of the Danube, S of Hungary, and NE of Croatia

BRD - acronym for the German equivalent of Federal Republic of Germany, the political entity that emanated from the occupation zones of the Western allies after WW II.

CMH - Community Memorial Hospital at Winona, Minnesota

DDR - acronym for the German equivalent of German Democratic Republic, which had evolved from the post-war Russian zone of occupation encompassing the central part of former Germany, west of the Oder-Neisse Line. Territories east of this line were seized by Poland and the USSR. As of 1990, the *DDR* became incorporated into the *BRD*, under Chancellor Helmut Kohl (*1930).

DP - displaced person.

Franconia - German region in NW Bavaria.

Hauptschule - upper primary school

Lorraine - former duchy in NE France around the Moselle and the Meuse rivers, also includes territory between the Rhine and the Scheldt rivers.

Magyarization - efforts by the dominant group of Hungary to assimilate indigenous members of other nationalities.

Tolonc-ház - main compound for transient DPs at Budapest.

USSR - Union of Socialist Soviet Republics, also called Soviet Union.

Vértesacsa - community in the Bakony forest, SW of Budapest.

Vojvodina - includes the Southern Baranya, the Backa, and the Western third of the Banat.

I. ANCESTRAL HERITAGE AND EARLY ENVIRONMENT

1. Background of Childhood Setting

The geographic coordinates of my birthplace Banat-Topola (postal code YU-23315) are 4540 2028. The village is situated 57.6 miles north of Belgrade, Serbia. It was founded in 1791 at the edge of a drained marshy area in old Hungary, about one kilometer east of a now extinct hamlet named Novo Selo whose initial inhabitants used to be Serbs followed by Hungarians. In the 18th Century, families from German-speaking immigrant enclaves in the Banat, whose descendants became known as "Danube Swabians," took up residence there also. My great-great-grandfather Josef STEIGERWALD (1816-1890) and his wife Margaretha Magdalena, née LEUTNER (1818-1882) moved to Banat-Topola from Heufeld (Hungarian name: Nagytószeg, Serbian name: Novi Kozarci), Banat, shortly after they got married in 1837.

The inaugural name of my birthplace was Torontáltopolya. "Torontál" identified the county in which the new habitat was situated and the Hungarian derivation "topolya," from the Serbian word "topola" (poplar), referred to a local landmark consisting of a group of towering trees that could be seen from afar in the flat terrain.

As part of extensive redistricting in Hungary, the village name was changed to "Töröktopolya" in 1908, since it was no longer within Torontál County. "Török" means Turk in Hungarian, though it is unclear how that related to this particular locale. After WW I, the village wound up in what became the Kingdom of Yugoslavia, whence it has been officially known as Banatska Topola. Along with its district capital of Kikinda, it is now part of the Vojvodina, which extends north from Belgrade to the Hungarian border. Romania is east and Croatia west of the area in question. In 1989, the semi-autonomous multi-ethnic Vojvodina province was annexed to Serbia without a plebiscite.

Upon the tripartite division of the Banat in accordance with the Treaty of Trianon after WW I, only the District of Szeged was left within drastically decimated Hungary. The Banat is comparable in size to the country of Belgium. The area is bounded by the Maros River in the North, the Tisza in the West, the Danube in the South, and the Carpathian foothills in the East. Romania took possession of about two-thirds of the territory in 1919. The Western third including my birthplace became part of the Kingdom of Serbs, Croats, and Slovenes,

1

known as Yugoslavia after 1929. The name "Banat" was derived from a Persian word that signified lord, or master. The Avars introduced the term to Europe where it came to designate a frontier province or a district under military governance. The Banat has rich, fertile soil plus coal and ore deposits in some of its southern sections.

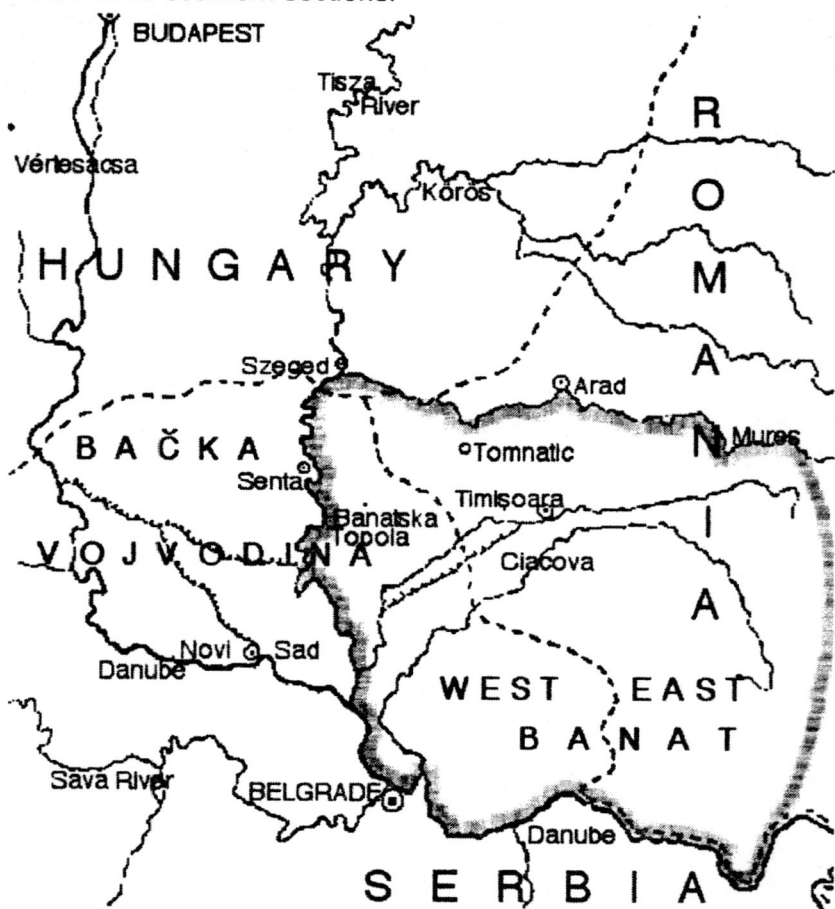

The tripartite division of the Banat after WW I

Hungarians as well as descendants of French and German immigrants were among the founders of Banat-Topola. The elders of the latter had been called upon to settle in certain relatively unpopulated regions of former Hungary that had been gradually liberated by Austrian and allied Christian armies, after more than 150 years of Ottoman domination. The treaty whereby the Banat came under Austrian jurisdiction was concluded at Pozarevac in 1718. Count Claudius Florimund Mercy of Lorraine became the territory's first governor.

In trying to determine the reasons for the ancestors' migrations, many factors need to be taken into account. To begin with, most were still obliged to contend with feudalistic social conditions in their respective traditional areas of residence, which proved rather restrictive, to say the least. In stark contrast to that, imperial Habsburg recruiters held out prospects of land and real estate ownership along with attractive tax concessions to enterprising workers who were willing to relocate to desolate and inhospitable, sparsely populated regions of liberated Hungary. The aim was to convert uncultivated and partially inundated, malaria-infested marshy areas into productive farmland. Relocation alternatives in pursuit of improved living conditions included emigration to distant foreign colonies overseas in slow, inadequately equipped sailing ships or overland migration to remote areas in Russia under the auspices of Catherine II (1729-1796), the Great Empress (1762-1796). Often, decisions concerning destinations were also influenced by a desire to remain under Austrian jurisdiction where imperial authorities could be dealt with in German, a language in which a large percentage of the colonists were conversant.

Prior to their intended departure, most emigrants had to petition their respective overlords for permission to leave, which was not always readily granted and usually involved payment of required fees for being released from feudal tenure. Consequently, some determined individuals chose to leave secretly; but doing so, generally amounted to forfeiture of their eligibility for state assistance and guidance from official re-population agencies. However, since a lot of enterprising independent land owners in Hungary were also interested in finding good workers, jobs were not too difficult to come by, but living conditions on most local private estates, as compared to state-sponsored settlements, continued to be rather feudalistic for some time to come.

Austrian authorities in charge of the 18th Century re-population projects in liberated parts of Hungary wanted to achieve a number of goals. The overall objective was to broaden the tax base. That was accomplished by getting freed enterprising former bondsmen and serfs, along with relatively indigent peasants, craftsmen, artisans and former soldiers from different areas of the extended Habsburg domains encompassing the Holy Roman Empire of the German Nation, to settle at scattered locations in the Danube basin. By serving as agricultural role models among indigenous multi-ethnic populations, overall productivity was notably raised. The "pioneers," as the new colonists or settlers were called, also had a stabilizing influence upon the nomadic lifestyle of local herdsmen that were accustomed to moving around to greener pastures almost at will. The presence of strategically interspersed German-speaking settlements also proved to be of benefit to Austrian authorities insofar as they served to strengthen the region's defense posture while facilitating persecution of marauding lawbreakers.

As time passed, one might have expected more intermarriages and increasing interpersonal relations between the different ethnic groups; instead, they tended to perpetuate their particular lifestyles, as manifested by their adherence to traditional customs and the retention of their respective ancestral language. Unlike in the United States where becoming Americanized is viewed as a move beyond dogmatic nationalism, assimilation in many parts of Europe tended to be regarded as tantamount to deviation from rectitude! It usually resulted in selective ostracism of individuals and families by biased persons among groups concerned. From another perspective, it was indicative of a broader, more open-minded disposition and a lot of self-confidence when descendants adopted the ways of a different local population group and blended them with their own. Among those whose ethnic identity eventually changed in the Banat were descendants of French-speaking settlers of whom most became Germanized. Spanish-speaking groups around Becskerek (now called Zrenjanin) who introduced silkworm breeding in the area largely chose to relocate to other Habsburg lands where the climate was more to their liking.

In the cities, there was a greater tendency for people to become assimilated because of greater economic and social interaction. In contrast to that, the ethnic mosaic of the rather self-sufficient villages proved to be quite durable until after WW II. Nationalization of farmland and commercial properties following the post-war communist takeover in East Central Europe generally deprived minorities along with other entrepreneurs of their respective bases of self-reliant existence and made everyone collectively dependent upon the state. Under the socialist maxim, each person was to receive benefits based on his or her needs and in return, everyone was to contribute to society according to his or her abilities to work. It evidently took quite a few decades for most advocates of such an unrealistic system to learn that a) there are never enough resources to satisfy everyone's needs and b) productivity tends to drop when few

4

incentives of enduring personal advantage are offered for people to optimize their productive capacities.

The 1931 census confirmed the presence of no less than fourteen (14) different nationality groups with substantial representation in the fledgling Kingdom of Yugoslavia, which had come into existence as a political entity only twelve years earlier. Therefore, it should have been generally realized that NOT all persons born within that realm were Slavs any more than everyone born in historic Hungary or in expanded Romania was of corresponding nationality. Far from it! Contrary to expectations of President Woodrow Wilson (1856-1924) and other well-intentioned Americans, the new boundaries of the successor states could not be drawn along gerrymandering ethnic demarcation lines everywhere when the multi-ethnic Austro-Hungarian monarchy was carved up after 1918. Lobbying efforts of the lesser WW I allies paid off handsomely in terms of extra territorial concessions that they were granted by the major Western powers. The size of Romania was increased quite a bit for example at the expense of Hungary, which lost nearly two-thirds of its former realm!

Although the resultant political realities in Europe would have been inconceivable without direct U. S. involvement in WW I, very few Americans took time to inform themselves about the consequent ramifications. The average person's lack of awareness was clearly demonstrated by the reaction of a fellow GI who inquired about my nationality. In response to my answer, he spontaneously exclaimed: "How can you be German if you were born in Yugoslavia?" To me, this question was similar to asking a Hispanic American 'how can you be Mexican, if you were born in the United States?' Like millions of others here as well as abroad, the GI obviously did not realize that the socio-ethnic environment at my birthplace and in other multi-national villages throughout the Banat, the Backa, and the Baranya for instance, had remained quite Austro-Hungarian. People did not automatically become Slavs when former boundaries were re-drawn to include various multi-ethnic areas in a newly created state!

At Banat-Topola, half of the inhabitants happened to be Hungarians and the other half Swabians. To the latter's inadvertent sorrow, that situation changed radically in April 1945 when Yugoslavia's remaining German minority was summarily confined to forced labor and starvation death camps. The massive uprooting was decreed by the anti-fascist council for the liberation of Yugoslavia (AVNOJ) in a resolution passed on November 21, 1944 at Jajce. New Yugoslav officials seem ready

5

to acknowledge the implementation of genocidal proceedings involved. The criminal process was never accorded due coverage in non-German media either. Since the occurrence constituted an early manifestation of what became known as "ethnic cleansing" about fifty years later, condemnation of the reprehensible action in the world press might have averted subsequent similar events in Bosnia-Herzegovina and Kosovo.

The garish Yugoslav treatment of the country's Swabians hardly ever registered in world consciousness since acts of hostility committed AGAINST German people at the time tended to be viewed as expectable reactions to Hitler's excesses. It did not matter that, as citizens of Yugoslavia, the country's ethnic-Germans obviously were neither responsible for Hitler's rise to power nor of his abuse of it. It has also been conveniently overlooked that the misguided dictator had high-handedly exploited the minority itself! - In a memorable statement during the O. J. Simpson trial on August 15, 1995, which was broadcasted over CNN-TV for example, Judge Lance Ito fittingly shed some light on this phenomenon in human affairs. He observed that it is the *appearance* of partiality or impartiality that matters and not so much whether actual guilt was incurred. Along lines of such thought, merely being ethnically German was sufficient "reason" for a person to be regarded as culpable; it was rather immaterial whether random Swabian individuals had personally harmed anyone at all.

What constituted an older prevalent motive for wanting to get rid of the German minority was the long-standing desire of plenty of South-Slavs to come into possession of minority members' hard-earned real estate and land holdings and to attain extra living space for themselves. Toward the end of WW II and in the aftermath, Tito and his partisans resolved to carry out "ethnic-cleansing" without soliciting the consent of the Western allies. On December 7, 1997, an applicable article appeared in the weekly *Der Donauschwabe,* vol. 47, No. 49, p. 5, entitled "Das Schicksal der Donauschwaben" (The Fate of the Danube Swabians). It was written by a group of researchers called Arbeitskreis Dokumentation in der Donauschwäbischen Kulturstiftung. The authors identified a number of reasons why Yugoslav communist leaders wanted to get rid of the country's German minority. Related factors revolved around a) nationalism, b) ideology, c) power politics, d) psychological differences, and e) other topics. Specific criteria included the following:

1) Serbs wanted to "cleanse" their habitat areas ethnically.

2) The entrepreneurial indigenous ethnic-Germans would have resisted collectivization.

3) Terrorization of the respected ethnic minority discouraged others from opposing communism.

4) Confiscated personal possessions of the Swabian population proved useful in rewarding Yugoslav partisan paupers.

5) Indigent members of other groups generally envied the Swabians for being better off economically.

6) The German invasion of Yugoslavia in 1941 elicited rancor against local Swabians also.

Important representatives of Tito's nationalistic communist ideology included Eduard Kardelj, Moshe Pijade, Milovan Djilas, and Aleksandar Rankovic. - The eventual autocratic annexation of the Vojvodina to Serbia and the abrogation of Kosovo's autonomous status in 1989 represented other important milestones along expansionist aspirations among the former Yugoslav federation's dominant group. Due to the heavy influx of so-called "Krajina" and other Serbs to the Vojvodina, particularly in 1995, remaining indigenous Hungarian and other minority groups came under renewed assimilation pressure.

Ethnic intolerance was among the main factors that led to the dissolution of Austria-Hungary after WW I. Unfortunately, it continued to be a problem in the successor states as well. This turned out to be true even though President Woodrow Wilson had exacted concessions from governments concerned, regarding favorable accommodations of ethnic minorities within their respective realms. In Yugoslavia, the implementation of minority rights remained rather sketchy right up to WW II. Representatives of minority groups were often confronted with undue delays or outright interference as they tried to serve the interests of their respective group. Recalcitrant and obtrusive conduct by bureaucrats tended to alienate the minorities as much as the latter's claims to particular rights antagonized the majority group at large, which happened to consist of Serbs.

From lessons learned in having demanded and achieved concessions under the Austro-Hungarian regime, Yugoslav officials were quite touchy about this subject, which had ruinously plagued the dual monarchy. - Just as there are many Americans, for instance, who feel that speakers of Spanish in the U. S. should also be conversant in English, Yugoslav patriots expected the country's ethnic minorities to become proficient in the use of a Slavic language, too. Many seemed to have forgotten that earlier, bitterly decried historic Magyarization efforts to achieve assimilation in Hungary had largely served to strengthen the resolve of different ethnic groups, including Slavic ones, to maintain their particular ethnic identity!

What the ethnic minorities continued to want, was the right to self-perpetuation through provisions involving cultural autonomy. The German minority's attitude found expression in the terms "volkstreu und staatstreu;" in other words, they aimed to be loyal citizens of their respective host country while striving to maintain their ethnic identity. Conflicts in trying to adhere to this goal became evident when a determined Yugoslav political faction decided in 1941 that war was preferable to a pact with Germany. When Hitler's invasion of Yugoslavia became imminent in April that year, civil authorities in the Vojvodina precipitately took prominent members of the country's German minority into custody as hostages for bargaining purposes. Many Swabian captives were told that they would be executed. The swift conquest of Yugoslavia spared these men from conceivable greater harm and personal suffering at the time.

Numerically speaking, the most extensive forced relocation of a nationality group, which constituted "ethnic cleansing" on the largest scale yet, was carried out with the concurrence of representatives of Great Britain, the Soviet Union, and the United States. Some details can be found in protocols issued mainly by the Soviet Union at Potsdam in July and August 1945. In accordance with procedural stipulations over fifteen million (15,000,000) Germans were subsequently unceremoniously expelled from Czechoslovakia (3 million), Hungary (221,000), and the new Poland (12 million), which was given large territorial areas of former Germany. It is estimated that a couple of million German expellees and refugees lost their lives in the relocation process. Alfred M. de Zayas described the historic event in his books a) *Nemesis at Potsdam: The Anglo-Americans and the Expulsion of the Germans* (London: Routledge & Kegan Paul, 1977) - now in its 10th edition, and b) *A Terrible Revenge: The Ethnic Cleansing of the East European Germans, 1944-1950*. Translated from German by John A. Koehler (New York: St. Martin's Press, 1994).

The number of German expellees turned out to be so high, because Poland and the Soviet Union moved their respective state boundaries westward whereby Poland lost extensive eastern territories to the USSR while Germany lost nearly one-fourth of its pre-WW II domain (1937 boundaries) to Poland and the USSR. Sadly, the millions of Germans who used to live in the severed regions for centuries were expelled along with others from scattered enclaves farther east. - While Germans had long been talking about eastward expansion of their living space (Drang nach Osten), the way things turned out they lost over 24 percent of their former territorial area as part of the price they had to pay for aggression. Ironically, among reasons for starting WW II, there was a desire "to right" wrongs imposed on Germany in the aftermath of WW I at Versailles, mostly by England and France. Even some Western historians conceded that these countries usurped some of the Wilson-inspired terms of the armistice on the basis of which the Germans had laid down their arms in November 1918.

As mentioned earlier, Yugoslavia did not solicit consent for the expulsion of the country's Germans at the end of WW II. Tito (1892-1980) and his fellow communists had already indicated on November 29, 1943 that they planned to get rid of them. Their resolve was triggered by Heinrich Himmler's (1900-1945) unabashed decision to induct members of the minority group into regular German army and SS units. This self-serving policy was contrary to established international laws since the conscripts were citizens of an enemy country. In an effort to make their consignment to German military units appear legal, Nazis falsely claimed that the draftees were "volunteers!" Ringleaders also demonstrated their arrogance and lack of concern for others by having the inductees serve with military units that were stationed in Yugoslavia; thus, indigenous ethnic-German and Slavic neighbors ended up facing each other in area battles! Contention between indigenous Slavic groups compounded situations even further where Serbs fought Croats and Tito's communists fought royalists led by Draza Mihajlovic, etc. Ultimately, it would have been better for ethnic-Germans too, if Yugoslav leaders had opted for non-incriminating ways to solve problems concerning divergent constituent groups.

Regarding Yugoslavia's German minority, the allies would have most likely preferred orderly population transfers over gradual attrition through starvation and maltreatment in barbed-wire-enclosed former Swabian village neighborhoods. Conditions in most areas of confinement were reminiscent of the pernicious environment in nazi concentration camps. Places of large-scale genocide like Auschwitz, Buchenwald, etc., have been covered extensively and repeatedly in world media, but sites where Danube Swabians perished en mass as victims of discrimination on the basis of nationality are rarely spoken of at all outside of German and Austrian circles. Whatever may account for the international community's selective silence, long overdue homage to those who perished warrants commemorative mention of the most notorious Yugoslav death camps for the country's ethnic-Germans. Among the seventy or so internment camps in which minority group members were confined under Tito, there were three (3) types:

I. Concentration camps
II. Forced labor camps
III. Extermination camps

Eight (8) locations in the latter category were as follows:

a) In the Vojvodina (Banat and Backa):

1. Knicanin (also called Rudolfsgnad, Rezsöháza, and Knicaninovo) postal code YU-23265.
2. Molin (also called Molidorf and Mollyfalva; now extinct, because of flooding).
3. Backi Jarak (also called Schönhausen, Jarek, Tiszaistvánfalu, and Jármos) postal code YU-21234.
4. Gakova (also called Gakowa, Gaumarkt, Gádar and Gádor) postal code YU-25282.
5. Krusevlje (also called Kruschiwl, Birndorf, Bácskörtés, and Körtés).

b) In Syrmia:

6. Sremska Mitrovica (also called Mitrowitz, Syrmisch-Mitrowitz, and Mitrovicza located on the Sava River) former postal code YU-22000.

c) In Slavonia:

7. Krndija (also called Kerndia).
8. Valpovo (also called Walpach and Walpowo) former postal code YU-54550.

Most of the burial sites have yet to be identified with appropriate markers. Like the mass graves of unwanted indigenous folks near Ljubija, Prijedor, Srebrenica, and at other locations in Bosnia as well as in Kosovo, the final "disposal" sites of Danube Swabian victims were not meant to come to anyone's attention outside the country.

According to best calculations, nearly two-fifths of Yugoslavia's ethnic Germans came under Tito's communist jurisdiction as of October 1944 since they were unable or unwilling to flee westward before the Red Army reached their areas of habitation in the Vojvodina and elsewhere. Between July 1941 and October 1944, partisans had killed about 1,500 German minority members in raids on their villages within Yugoslavia. About 9,500 imprisoned ethnic group members including my uncle Michael STEIGERWALD (1896-1944) fell victim to uncountable acts of vengeance by individual partisans, which included torturous bodily disfigurement and execution-style shootings as of autumn 1944. By May 1945, the remaining minority members had all been evicted from their hereditary homes and were placed in forced labor and starvation camps until 1948 where many more succumbed to beatings, shootings, starvation, and illnesses like dysentery, typhus, and malaria.

Of the approximately 167,000 group members confined, roughly 51,000 met with death. Another 2,000 or so perished in the Soviet Union where about 8,000 women and 4,000 men were taken as forced laborers around Christmas 1944. All in all, Yugoslavia's residual German minority was decimated by nearly one-third between 1944 and 1948. No one ever had to answer for this criminal process of "ethnic cleansing!" In view of matching occurrences in Bosnia-Herzegovina and in Kosovo, one cannot help but wonder whether the equally deplorable recent firebrands would have come about at all if Tito and his partisans had been called on the carpet for their analogous crimes in the *aftermath* of WW II. - For more related factual data, see Georg Wildmann, Hans Sonnleitner, Karl Weber et al. *Verbrechen an den Deutschen in Jugoslawien 1944-1948: Die Stationen eines Völkermords*. Munich: Donauschwäbische Kulturstiftung, 1998. 358 pp., including maps, charts, chronology, bibliography, and a place index. A compendium in English has the title *Genocide of the Ethnic Germans in Yugoslavia 1944-1948* (Chicago, IL 60639: Award Printing Corp., 2001).

When the attrition camps were finally abolished after March 1948, the released former captives who could still work were placed under 3-year contracts with state-run collective enterprises at low wages. In 1951, Yugoslav citizenship was re-conferred upon them without providing the option to leave the country instead. Younger men including my half-brother Michael STEIGERWALD (1923-1956) were subsequently inducted into military units of the communist state. Ethnic-Germans who wished to emigrate first had to pay 12,000 Dinars for having their re-affirmed Yugoslav citizenship rescinded. It took some of them until 1958 before they could save enough money to buy themselves off and leave for Germany.

Most of the ethnic-German detainees in the forced labor and starvation death camps were women, children, and elderly men. What made their prolonged suffering even more tragic was the fact that most had remained in their respective domiciles hoping that they would be able to continue to live and let live since none of them had been personally involved in any wrongdoing. As things turned out though, they had to bear the brunt of the pent-up anger of vengeance-seeking partisans whose understandable hatred of Nazis made them lash out at anyone of kindred national descent. As one might have guessed, minority group members who had actually given aid and comfort to Hitler's accomplices were nowhere around in the end! They had fled the country in time to escape expectable reprisals; thus, quite a few of the indigenous meek did indeed wind up inheriting the earth, albeit six feet under in unmarked individual and mass graves.

In retrospect, this unpunished crime against humanity that Tito's partisans committed between 1944 and 1948 may have been viewed as generally conducive to national aims. It may well have been among factors that prompted a subsequent Yugoslav head of state to venture into new rounds of "ethnic cleansing." The new location of brutal eradication efforts regarding unwanted indigenous groups ironically turned out to be Bosnia where the resolution to expel Yugoslavia's Germans had been passed five decades earlier, namely at the City of Jajce. The apparent coincidence gave pause to ponder predictions made by persecuted, deeply religious Swabians who strongly felt that God's punishment for injustices committed would be inevitable. What happened in and to Serbia fifty years later may perhaps be regarded as a manifestation of the wrath of God also.

In the United States of America, public education is geared toward assimilating the diverse groups on an egalitarian basis. In former Austria-Hungary and the pre-WW II successor states, public education included special provisions for minorities. Diverse nationality groups were officially enabled to maintain their respective linguistic and cultural identity as a matter of state policy. Minority group children were entitled to attend lower primary school classes where they received instruction in the language of their parents at public expense. Starting in the third grade though, classes in the official state language were introduced and certain subjects like History and Geography had to be taught in that language so that interpretations and emphases would jive with accepted concepts of the preponderant group. The inner conflicts that such an approach to learning was certain to elicit among children of different ethnic backgrounds can be more readily visualized if one alternately tries to view world events from perspectives of other groups, too.

In the long run, ethnic minorities probably fare best under an umbrella of *laissez-faire* policies; however, upon having enriched the host society through infusions of meaningful variations, assimilation can be viewed as a natural solution to problems associated with a perpetual minority group status. It should be kept in mind though that minority group members who maintain their ancestral heritage in addition to becoming

12

proficient in the primary language of their host country do indeed amount to a more valuable manpower resource. Thus, a minority's elimination by forced relocation or abrupt annihilation also exacts an overall economic toll besides constituting human rights violations.

A Danube Swabian self-perception was that their ancestors were summoned to old Hungary as laborers, homesteaders, tradesmen, etc., to help rebuild the liberated ravaged country's neglected infrastructure and to cultivate desolate, swampy, and undeveloped land areas. Many of the initial immigrants succumbed to harsh prevailing conditions including periodic pestilence. Sustained efforts of successive generations eventually culminated in a veritable territorial breadbasket. Because of political developments beyond the range of the group's capacity to get decisively involved in, the minority wound up between historic grindstones that precipitated its doom. Though the undeserved fate of the descendants was not at all unprecedented in the annals of humankind, a better awareness of it might help deter similar future injustice.

Not unlike the soldiers commemorated by Abraham Lincoln on November 19, 1863 at Gettysburg, Pennsylvania, for having tendered their last measure of devotion to preserve government of, by, and for the people, the ancestors of the Danube Swabians distinguished themselves with plows rather than swords. They helped create better living conditions for everyone in their multi-national environment. Yet, the world took "little note" of and remembers even less concerning their momentous contributions! Adding insult to injury, their descendants were ultimately forced to yield the very ground their ancestors had tamed to unworthy communists at gunpoint.

All too often in the turn of events, right has to yield to might; however, instead of being totally dispirited by such occurrences, it is better to keep in mind that the noblest calling of memory is to accord honor its timeless due. The Nobel Peace Laureate Elie Wiesel had this advice: "Learn what human beings can do to other human beings. Learn the limits of humanity. Learn, and hope is possible. Forget, and despair is inevitable" (quoted on page iii in the February 1988 edition of the Directory of Holocaust Institutions).

2. Maternal Ancestry: From Lorraine to the Banat

In our part of the Banat, ordinary folks generally did not have middle names. Having more than one given name seemed to be a custom that sophisticated people had adopted from the nobility. My parents did not have middle names and neither have I. My mother's name was Elisabeth, née MARTIN (1906-1944). In the early 1770's, several of her ancestors including the Martins migrated from the Château Salins district in Lorraine to the Banat, which was an Austrian crown colony at the time. Empress Maria Theresa (1717-1780) and her son Joseph II (1741-1790) jointly ruled this Christian frontier territory after 1760.

Some of my mother's ancestors were among the founders of the tripartite Banat habitat of St. Hubert, Charleville, and Seultour, now collectively known as Banatsko Veliko Selo, Vojvodina. Currently, the constituents of the combined community are South-Slavs who moved into the dwellings of the founders' descendants after the latter's summary expulsion and confinement to forced labor and starvation death camps at the end of WW II. Yugoslavia's entire German-speaking minority was subjected to malicious "ethnic cleansing" between 1944 and 1948. Since Josip Broz(ovic) Tito (1892-1980) was a communist ally and not a tortuous Nazi, this crime against humanity received even less coverage in non-German world media than Joseph Stalin's liquidation of millions of USSR-citizens did or does.

Another place that was founded by French-speaking settlers in the Banat during the Eighteenth Century is located in Romania now. Its German-speaking inhabitants were not expelled after WW II; however, descendants of the original settlers from Lorraine tried in vain to be recognized as a French minority in Romania. The current name of the town concerned is Tomnatic. In German, it is called Triebswetter and in Hungarian, Nagy Ösz. Historians, demographers, genealogists, and others can find helpful information about Tomnatic in *Heimatbuch der Heidegemeinde Triebswetter im Banat*, by Anton Peter Petri and Josef Wolf (Tuttlingen, 1983). The origin and growth of Banatsko Veliko Selo is covered in *Heimatbuch der Banater Schwestergemeinden St. Hubert, Charleville, Soltur* by Nikolaus Hess and Michael Gross (Munich, 1981).

Among particular places in France from where several of my maternal ancestors hailed are Bidestroff, Juville, and Viviers in the Château Salins area of Lorraine. Some surnames are easily recognizable as French. Regarding others, the

14

spelling in older records is sometimes indicative of the bearers' language or nationality. The spelling "Marteng" for instance suggests a nasalized French pronunciation as far as the surname MARTIN is concerned. The family name RICHARD, though Germanic in origin, is spelled "Rischar" and "Risar" in some records, which conforms to a German and a Hungarian auditory rendition respectively if one takes into account that final "d" is silent in French pronunciation. Similarly, the surname MICHEL appears in the forms "Mischel," "Mischl," and "Misli" suggesting a French pronunciation also. The fact that our branch of the MARTIN family hailed from Lorraine can be verified by looking up part of my mother's lineage as follows: 1) parents, 2) grandparents, 3) great-grandparents, and 4) great great grandparents.

1) Johann MARTIN was born in 1875 at Banat-Topola, Austria-Hungary. He died there of double pneumonia in 1919. His wife Anna née SPRINGER was born in 1878 at Topola also. She died there of dropsy in 1920.
2) Anton MARTIN was born in 1829 at Charleville, Banat, Austria-Hungary; he died at Topola (date unknown). His second wife Susanna née MICHEL was born in 1851 at Deutsch-Zerne, Banat, Austria-Hungary; she died at Topola (date unknown).
3) Louis MARTIN was born in 1792 at St. Hubert, Banat, Austria-Hungary; the place and date of death are unknown. His wife Anna Maria ALOFF was also born at St. Hubert in 1792; the place and date of her death are unknown also.
4) Francois MARTIN was born in 1754 at Juville, Lotharingia Gallica; he died in 1815 at St. Hubert, Banat, Austria-Hungary. His wife Anna ADAM was born in 1759 at Vitjoncourt, Lotharingia; she died in 1830 at St. Hubert, Banat.

My mother's paternal grandmother Susanna MICHEL (*1851) was the second wife of her grandfather Anton MARTIN (*1829). When the couple got married, she already had a daughter named Susanna (1863-1945) who was an "illegitimate" child by another man. In those days, having a son or daughter out of wedlock ruined a girl's chances of getting a single guy to marry her; thus, my great-grandmother née MICHEL (1851) undoubtedly was a good catch as the second wife of my mother's widowed grandfather. To avoid confusion when talking about either Susanna, the elder was called 'tall' Susan and the young one 'hefty' Susan. The nicknames alluded to their respective shape. 'Hefty' Susan later married a farmer named SCHWARZ at Banat-Topola; the couple remained childless and eventually adopted Josef MARTIN (1912-1977), one of my mother's orphaned siblings. At the age of 82, 'hefty' Susan SCHWARZ née MICHEL was destined to become the first person to die in confinement at Banat-Topola after Tito's partisans rounded up the German-speaking minority as of April 18, 1945.

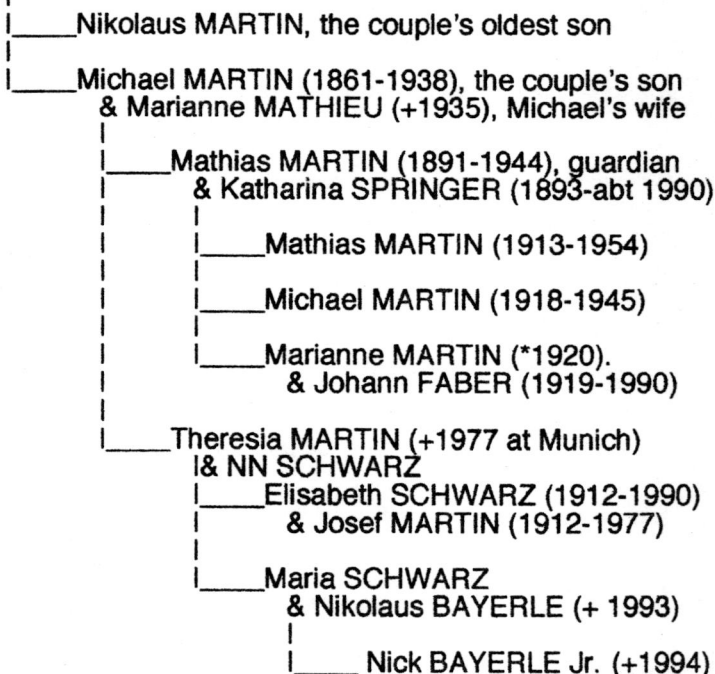

The first wife of my mother's paternal grandfather Anton MARTIN (*1829) was Barbara née LUTHIER. In the Banat, the spelling of her family name was shortened to "Lutje." The couple's grandson Mathias MARTIN and his wife Katharina née SPRINGER, who also happened to be an aunt of my mother, ended up playing important roles as guardians of my mother and her younger siblings.

Anton MARTIN (*1829) – my mother Elisabeth's paternal grandfather & Barbara LUTHIER (Anton's first wife – unrelated)
```
I
I____Nikolaus MARTIN, the couple's oldest son
I
I____Michael MARTIN (1861-1938), the couple's son
        & Marianne MATHIEU (+1935), Michael's wife
      I
      I____Mathias MARTIN (1891-1944), guardian
      I        & Katharina SPRINGER (1893-abt 1990)
      I        I
      I        I____Mathias MARTIN (1913-1954)
      I        I
      I        I____Michael MARTIN (1918-1945)
      I        I
      I        I____Marianne MARTIN (*1920).
      I            & Johann FABER (1919-1990)
      I
      I____Theresia MARTIN (+1977 at Munich)
          I& NN SCHWARZ
          I____Elisabeth SCHWARZ (1912-1990)
          I        & Josef MARTIN (1912-1977)
          I
          I____Maria SCHWARZ
              & Nikolaus BAYERLE (+ 1993)
              I
              I____ Nick BAYERLE Jr. (+1994)
```
The two children of my mother's paternal grandfather Anton MARTIN (*1829) and his second wife Susanna née MICHEL (*1851) were twins: Johann (1875-1919), my mother's father and his sister Theresa (*1875) who eventually married a man named Jacob MACK. The MACK family resided at Bocsár, Banat, when Jacob immigrated to the United States in 1911. Theresa and the couple's sons Frank (1894-1973), John (1908-

16

1978), and Jack (1911-1980) joined Jacob at Philadelphia in 1912. The family left Hamburg aboard the German steamship *President Grant* on April 25, 1912. Upon making scheduled stops at Boulogne, France and Southampton, England the ship arrived safely in New York.

At the time of the 1920 census, the Jacob MACK family was living at 1246 N. Caldwaller Place in Philadelphia, PA. The couple's youngest son Nicholas (1914-1991) was born at 1417 N. American Street in Philadelphia and christened on August 2, 1914 at St. Peter the Apostle Church, 1019 N. Fifth Street, Philadelphia PA 19123-1459. Unfortunately, contact between my great-aunt Theresa's family and relatives in Europe was not maintained. Records show that she was still alive during WW II but apparently had never learned how to write. It appears doubtful whether any of her four sons attempted to get in touch with us and we never got around to doing so either. From the Social Security Death Index, we eventually learned about the sons' respective demise.

My maternal grandfather Johann MARTIN (1875-1919) was nicknamed "Suss-Hans" in allusion to his mother's first name. Johann was literate and gained work experience in various occupations including farm and industrial labor. Eventually, he became an innkeeper. When he was twenty-four years of age, he married Anna SPRINGER (1878-1920), the oldest of five attractive sisters. Anna's parents were Leonard SPRINGER (1855-1901) and Katharina KOVACS (1857-1915). The eventual married names of the other SPRINGER girls were Elisabeth BINDER (1891-1937), Katharina MARTIN (1893-199?), Marianne POTWEN (1896-198?), and Rosalia ROSSMANN (1900-1994).

By March 18, 1906, my maternal grandmother Anna (1878-1920) had given birth to at least three (3) daughters including my mother Elisabeth MARTIN (1906-1944), their youngest girl. In 1920, my mother's oldest sister Anna MARTIN (1900-1934) married my subsequent Uncle Michael STEIGERWALD (1896-1944). Theresa ZIMMERMANN, Lisa ARB, and Peter STEIGERWALD are their direct descendants. My mother's sister Theresa (1904-1971) married Josef HUHN (1896-1968) in 1922 with whom she emigrated to Buenos Aires, Argentina in 1924. The family intended to immigrate to the U. S. with their infant Elisabeth, but was denied entry because of quota limitations. The married names of the couple's three daughters were Elisabeth ZOBAJI (1922-1996) and Catharina HÄUSZLER (*1924-2000); that of the youngest is Susana

17

LEDERER (*1931). - Additional information about the Argentine branch of the MARTIN/HUHN family is provided in chapter 15.

In 1907, when my mother Elisabeth (1906-1944) was just over one year of age, her parents Johann and Anna MARTIN sailed to America. They left their three daughters with the girls' grandparents Anton (*1829) and Susanna MARTIN née MICHEL (*1851) at Banat-Topola. Their goal was to earn a "grub stake" for a fresh start back home. According to the "List or Manifest of Alien Passengers for the U. S. Immigration Officer at Port of Arrival" (No. 43) at the National Archives in Washington DC, they sailed from the Adriatic port of Fiume on April 6, 1907 aboard the British steamship *Pannonia*. The couple arrived in New York on April 24, 1907.

Johann and Anna MARTIN'S destination was Reading, Pennsylvania where an unverified cousin named Josef MERKLER was allegedly living at 1426 N. 6th Street. Nothing further is known about this individual. Grandfather Johann MARTIN (1875-1919) worked (across the street) at the now defunct Reading Railroad yard as a laborer and Grandmother Anna née SPRINGER (1878-1920) may have worked for a dry cleaner in town who also did alterations.

According to further entries in the "List or Manifest..." mentioned, the couple had $4.55 in cash at the time of their arrival. Grandfather's height was 5 feet, 8 inches; his complexion is listed as "dark," his hair as "fair," and his eyes, though described as "yellow," were probably hazel. Grandmother's height was 5 feet 4 inches; her complexion was "reddish" from wind and sunburn no doubt. Her hair was "fair" and her eyes were "blue." Both were born at "Topolya," as their village was called for short in Hungarian back then.

Documentation of the couple's return home has yet to be located; however, their next child Jacob MARTIN (1909-1988), who became my godfather, was born on September 21, 1909, at Banat-Topola. Consequently, it can safely be deduced that my maternal grandparents stayed in America for over two years before returning to their loved ones in Europe. According to family lore, Johann and Anna were urgently summoned back by Susanna SCHWARZ née MICHEL (1863-1945), the 'hefty,' kind-hearted half-sister of the three daughters of Johann and Anna MARTIN who had been left in her mother's care. Susanna was genuinely worried that the girls' grandmother Susanna might maim them. At age 58, the grandmother undoubtedly was kept quite busy parenting three lively little girls whose ages were 8, 5, and 3! Rumor had it that the old lady used to discipline the girls by hitting the knuckles of their fingers with the back of a kitchen knife. The torturous chastisement was apt to cause painful swellings, which may have turned out to be a reason why my mother Elisabeth could not fully extend all of her fingers, as she grew older.

The money my grandparents earned and saved in America was invested at Banat-Topola in a thatched-roof inn at the village center. Within the next half dozen years, my grandmother Anna MARTIN (1878-1920) gave birth to three (3) more boys: Johann (1911-1989), Josef (1912-1977), and Anton (1915-1980); however, when WW I started in 1914, things began to go downhill for the MARTIN family. Although my grandfather had six children to take care of, he was drafted to serve in an Austro-Hungarian army unit before his seventh child Anton (1915-1980) was even born! At Przemysl, Poland, which fell to the Russians in 1915, he became a prisoner of war and nearly died of starvation by the time the historic armistice was reached in November 1918. Totally run down health-wise and utterly exhausted physically, he barely made it home from Russia only to contract double pneumonia, which led to his untimely death on February 20, 1919.

Nineteen months after grandfather Johann MARTIN (1875-1919) had suddenly passed away, grandmother Anna née SPRINGER (1878-1920) died of dropsy, leaving seven (7) orphans behind, whose ages ranged from 20 to only 5. Meanwhile, the oldest daughter Anna (1900-1934) had gotten married to my eventual Uncle Michael STEIGERWALD (1896-1944), as mentioned earlier. The couple was already planning to tie the knot when my grandfather came home from Russia but his illness and unexpected death resulted in an unforeseen postponement of the wedding.

In the midst of all the tragic happenings around them, there was also an occurrence that some thought of as humorous. When Michael went to pick up the rings at the jeweler in the district capital of Kikinda (about 12 miles each way), he happened to wear the suit in which grandfather was abruptly buried. It was not discovered until after the interment that no one had retrieved the bands of gold from the coat in which the deceased now reposed six feet under! When the customary year of mourning had passed, the young couple got married with a new set of rings.

The MARTINS' inn was sold on contract to a Hungarian named KARDOS János. My mother's cousin Mathias MARTIN (1891-1944) - see the schematic above - was appointed executor of the estate and guardian of the underage children including Theresa (1904-1971), Elisabeth (1906-1944), Jacob (1909-

1988), Johann (1911-1989), Josef (1912-1977), and Anton (1915-1980).

Anna (1900-1934), the oldest of the siblings, received her inheritance right after her parents' inn was sold. Not quite two years later in 1922 when Theresa (1904-1971) got married at age 18, she laid claim to her inheritance also; however, she could not collect her share because there were no funds in the orphaned children's account!

According to one explanation, KARDOS János who purchased her parents' estate on contract had failed to make the periodic payments agreed upon. Another interpretation was that the children's guardian Mathias MARTIN (1891-1944) invested the money received in his own farming operation instead of depositing it to the orphans' account. Before the matter could be rectified, Theresa (1904-1971), her husband Josef HUHN (1896-1968), and their infant Elisabeth (1922-1996) had emigrated to distant Buenos Aires, Argentina. Since no one kept pursuing the matter for them at Banat-Topola, Aunt Theresa ended up bilked out of her inheritance forever!

Years later, the topic still brought tears to my mother's eyes when she used to receive letters in which her sister Theresa continued to bemoan her unfair treatment and concomitant monetary loss. My mother felt bad for not having intervened in behalf of her sister, but she herself never came into possession of her own share of the inheritance either; however, that was not due to anyone's scheming or deceit. In true appreciation of the good care she and her brother Jacob (1909-1988) had received by Mathias MARTIN and his wife Katharina, née SPRINGER, my mother bequeathed her share to her guardian.

Upon having completed elementary school at Banat-Topola, my subsequent mother's oldest brother Jacob (1909-1988) was placed with a blacksmith/locksmith at Kikinda as an apprentice. My eventual mother, who was three years older than Jacob, worked in the same city as a maid in a Jewish household. It turned out to be an excellent environment for her where she was able to gain valuable insights into the lifestyle of wealthier folks who adhered to higher cultural standards. She wound up learning useful practical matters too, with regard to family life and homemaking for which other young women had to attend finishing schools. Her direct observations also prompted her to dismiss Hitler's eventual anti-Semitic propaganda as grossly biased and quite unfair.

My mother was an avid reader and she enjoyed retelling what she had read, to others. Her brown eyes were endowed

20

with excellent vision and she would often sit with a book until late at night, reading by a kerosene lamp or a lit candle since there was no electricity at Topola until the 1960's. A paperback suspense story that I bought her once, while at boarding school in Kikinda, had the title *Inges Flucht* (Inga's Escape). In addition to her command of German, my mother was also fluent in Hungarian since that was the language of instruction at regional schools prior to the end of WW I. Throughout her life, she would always carry out mathematical calculations in Hungarian. Her teacher Ferenc Sárik continued to have a hold on her mind even after she was a parent! Among the things that continued to occupy her were geographic directions. Often, she would practice the hand motions the teacher had the students use as they repeated "észak, kelet, dél, nyugat" (north, east, south, and west) in Hungarian. - My mother's height was about 5 feet 4 inches and her hair was brown like her eyes. Varicose veins made prolonged standing uncomfortable for her. She also lost quite a few of her teeth early in life. Ready access to a dentist was not among the options in our rural environment. Fluoridated drinking water was unheard of and the idea of dental floss evidently had not yet entered an entrepreneur's mind anywhere.

Shortly after Jacob MARTIN (1909-1988) had completed his apprenticeship to become a journeyman locksmith, he did his stint in the Yugoslav army and subsequently married Susanna WALTER (*1909) of Bocsár, Banat, whom he had met at Kikinda where she was employed as a household maid. On weekends and holidays, they used to see each other at dances that were held at an inn called "Gasthaus zum grünen Baum" (green tree inn). Upon his release from the military, he got a job working for a locksmith named Pressler at Bocsár, the birthplace of his wife and their son Hans MARTIN (1934-1999). Hans was eight months old when the young family emigrated to Sâo Paulo, Brazil in September 1934 where they joined Susanna's older sister Katharina (1905-1972) and her husband Peter Muschong (1901-1961).

Aboard the steamship on which they crossed the Atlantic, Jacob and Susanna MARTIN and a Jewish couple became friends for life. The Jewish woman, who had a baby also, became so seasick that she was unable to care for her child; thus, Susanna wound up breastfeeding Hans and the Jewish infant alternately. The MARTIN'S second child Peter was born at Sâo Paulo in 1940. - After many years of diligent persistence at hard work, Jacob, Susanna, their two sons, and a half dozen grandchildren became the owners of several plants with punch press and metal laminating operations. The first factory was called Indústria Metalúrgica "JotaeMe" Ltda. and the next one, Indústria de Aços Laminados Ltda. (INDAL). Two others were named StampTech and FITAFER. In 1999, operations at "JotaeMe" were terminated and plans were made for the establishment of another manufacturing location named NITRAM (Martin spelled backward).

When Jacob MARTIN (1909-1988) was about three years old, he got hold of some matches while his mother was racking off wine in the basement of the family inn at Banat-Topola. Playing by the crib of his baby brother Johann MARTIN (1911-1989), the bedding caught fire and little Jacob ran to fetch his mother. By the time she came and got things under control, Johann had suffered burns all over his back and the capillaries in his lungs were permanently damaged. In spite of that, Johann outlived all of his siblings! All his life, he exhibited symptoms of a person plagued by asthma but with continuing medical care including a portable oxygen tank in his later years, he was able to reach a ripe old age. The brothers Jacob and Johann "Hans" MARTIN both had brown eyes and brown hair. My godfather Jacob MARTIN had a height of about 5 feet, 8 inches. "Hansi-Onkel," as we called Johann, was the tallest of the siblings. His height was about 5 feet 11 inches. Jacob's final resting-place is in São Paulo, Brazil, and Johann's in the Los Angeles area, California, U.S.A.

My mother's brother Josef MARTIN (1912-1977) was already mentioned in conjunction with his adoption by the SCHWARZ family. He had blue eyes and blond hair. His height was about 5 feet 7 inches. At Banat-Topola, he earned his living as a farmer. As a hobby, he played a b-clarinet in the local brass band. While retreating across the Tisza River under Russian gunfire during WW II, he had to self-amputate part of a middle finger that got pinched in between bridge girders. After that, his clarinet was equipped with a special lever to enable him to play again. He also happened to have a good singing voice. Tragically, just before he retired as a floor layer from the Deutsche Asphalt AG at Munich, he found out that he had colon cancer, which led to his death. His wife Elisabeth, née SCHWARZ (1912-1990) is included in the schematic above. The couple had a very happy marriage but remained childless. Their final resting-place is at Munich, Germany.

Anton MARTIN (1915-1980), my mother's youngest brother worked as a coal miner in Austria during WW II. He was blond and blue-eyed, had a stocky build and a height of about 5 feet 6 inches. He enjoyed lifting weights. After an incomplete apprenticeship in cabinetmaking, he worked in farming. While making deliveries of finished pieces of furniture, it made him feel "grown-up" to be offered gratuities in the form of cigarettes; thus, he started to smoke at an early age and could not quit until it nearly killed him. In 1948, he and his (third) wife Justina née FESTINI had a son Anton (*1948) who bears great physical resemblance to his father. For several years, the elder Anton worked in a flourmill at Bad Ischl. In time, the ravages associated with smoking combined with the effects of flour particle and coal dust inhalation overtaxed his lungs and he experienced difficulty breathing with prolonged coughing spells. Eventually, his heart could no longer take it and he died. His final resting-place is at Haiden near Bad Ischl, Upper Austria.

To sum up, several of my mother's ancestors migrated from Lorraine to the Banat, which was a Christian frontier in the Eighteenth Century, facing territories controlled by Islamic Ottomans. After about seven generations, the outcome of WW II forced the groundbreakers' descendants to re-adopt a pioneer spirit for new beginnings in widely scattered locations on three different continents. My mother Elisabeth and her oldest sister Anna died in the part of Europe to which their ancestors were attracted. Three of the four descendants of Elisabeth (Rose, Jacob, and Tony) and two (Theresa ZIMMERMANN and Lisa ARB) of Anna's three wound up in the United States of America. Aunt Theresa HUHN, my mother's other sister, transplanted her family bough to Argentina. The descendants of my mother's oldest brother Jacob MARTIN thrive in Brazil. Uncle Anton MARTIN'S son Anton Jr. lives in Austria, and the surviving members of Johann MARTIN'S family reside in California. Only my Uncle Josef MARTIN had no offspring at all. Still, if replenishing the earth is a higher calling of mankind, then the contributions of the former MARTINS of Lorraine and their relevant respective spouses was rather impressive, n'est-ce pas? (Don't you concur?).

3. Franconian Paternal Ancestry: Via Vértesacsa to the Banat

During the Eighteenth Century, my paternal ancestor Johann Heinrich STEIGERWALD (+1788) was among thousands of colonists who settled in Hungary after the country's liberation from Ottoman domination. A host of factors prompted residents of various regions of the Holy Roman Empire of the German Nation to relocate to other parts of Europe or to venture overseas. Among inducements for such momentous decisions, there were restrictive economic conditions, population growth, persecutions on religious grounds, feudalistic social factors, political strife, etc. In the Spessart forest area, privation was a notoriously familiar phenomenon so that the epithet "Spessartnot" had become symbolic for woeful indigence in certain areas throughout the realm.

Demographic considerations prompted many communities to impose burdensome fees on outsiders moving in. Until the beginning of the Nineteenth Century when general tax laws made fiscal obligations of the citizenry less confusing, there was an astonishing array of levies, tolls, duties, imposts, tariffs, salvage dues, etc. to be paid. Specific types included:

1. *Schatzungen, to* support armed forces.
2. *Kopfgeld,* newcomers fee.
3. *Beisaßgeld,* non-native residents tax.
4. *Ungeld,* a surcharge on beverages in taverns for local defense provisions.
5. *Niederlagegeld* was paid by outside traders for doing business locally.
6. *Zoll,* an import duty on goods brought in from outside a given locality.
7. *Einzugsgeld* was due when an outsider married into a particular locality.
8. *Wachgelder,* a valuation for night watchmen's pay.
9. *Altfeldergeld,* a land uses levy.
10. *Kaufhafergeld,* tax on oats not grown on land allotted to individuals.
11. *Feuergeld,* for purchasing fire-fighting equipment.
12. *Vogteigeld,* regional administration fees.
13. *Allgemeines Unkostengeld,* local administration fees.
14. *Forstgelder,* a forest services fee.
15. *Wolfsgelder,* wolf-population control-fees.
16. *Forsthafergeld,* a timber/grain exchange levy paid to the overlord.

17. *Waidhafergeld*, grain levy for grazing rights in timber-
   land.
18. *Mahdhafergeld*, levy for hay from forest clearings.
19. *Dehem*, levy for letting hogs forage in the woods.
20. *Weidegeld*, a grazing land fee paid to a community.
21. Etc., etc.

Many Eighteenth Century immigrants to Hungary generally encountered debilitating hardships in their new environment as well. According to a popular contemporary German
saying, the initial settlers met with death from illnesses attributable to an unaccustomed climate, inadequate housing, malnu-
trition, infestations, etc. The next generation still had to endure
inestimable personal hardships while engaged in backbreaking
work and still having to cope with shortages of food and supplies. Only subsequent descendants eventually came to enjoy
the blessings of a better life including plenty of food to share
with multi-national co-inhabitants as well.

Therein lies part of the historic legacy of the colonists
whose progeny came to be known as "Danube Swabians" although only some happened to be of actual Swabian origin.
Generally, the colonists hailed from various Habsburg domains
encompassing what was known as the Holy Roman Empire of
the German Nation, which was said to be neither holy nor entirely German. The settlers and their descendants tenaciously
converted widely scattered wastelands in old Hungary into a
cohesive breadbasket whose proceeds benefited the ethnically
diverse indigenous population altogether. Nevertheless, roughly two centuries later, the heirs of the original German-speaking
settlers were literally booted out of their habitats in Yugoslavia
by Tito's cohorts at the end of WW II. Unfortunately, many
communists were even less concerned about human rights and
moral integrity than rightfully ousted Nazis had been.

It has yet to be ascertained, whether the person named
Heinrich STEIGERWALD who was christened at Frammersbach in the Spessart on January 15, 1710 was an ancestor of
mine. Adam and Margaretha STEIGERWALD were this individual's parents. In some records, my actual forefather named
Heinrich is often listed as Johann Heinrich. Since a younger
brother of his was actually named Johann (1722-1784), the
older sibling was generally called Heinrich. According to other
entries in the church ledgers at Frammersbach, Heinrich's father Adam STEIGERWALD was born in 1681. Adam's father
was named Albert. He was born in 1632 and died about 1711.
Albert's father Jacob was born in 1608 and died around 1683.
These people are listed as witnesses at weddings and as god-

parents at christenings, but their respective place of birth is not given. They may have moved to the Spessart forest area from the wooded "Steigerwald" region that is located between Würzburg and Bamberg in Franconia. Since other folks adopted that geographic appellation as their surname also, not all persons named STEIGERWALD ever were blood related. The earliest documentation of this family name is found among the *magistra* for the year 1363 at the praemonstrator convent Schäftersheim in Germany.

The exact date of the relevant J. Heinrich STEIGER-WALD'S migration to Hungary has not been determined; however, church records show that he married a woman named Margaretha (1716-1759) at Vértesacsa, Hungary in 1737. Their first child Maria Elisabeth was born there on April 7, 1738. His wife Margaretha (maiden name unknown) gave birth to at least eight additional children at Vértesacsa before her death on November 30, 1759 at the age of 43. Their youngest child, Johann, was born on February 3, 1754 at Vértesacsa, which was also called Acsa for short in Hungarian and Otschau or Atschau in German. – Applicable additional information can be found in Stefan Stader's monograph on this town in the Bakony forest: *Familienbuch der katholischen Pfarrgemeinde Atschau = Vértesacsa im Schildgebirge. Mit einer siedlungsgeschichtlichen Einleitung von Anton Tafferner* (Sindelfingen: Arbeitskreis donauschwäbischer Familienforscher, 1993).

J. Heinrich STEIGERWALD'S second wife Barbara, née HORN was born in 1713 (location unknown); she was the widow of Karl Greifinsfeld. Barbara and Heinrich got married on November 26, 1760. Their son Michael was born at Vértesacsa on October 11, 1761.

According to the list of settlers at Heufeld, Banat (now part of Novi Kozarci, Vojvodina), Heinrich STEIGERWALD arrived there with his wife Barbara and two unnamed sons plus an unidentified daughter on June 10, 1770. They were assigned to house number 65, which remained a family residence for several generations of STEIGERWALD heirs. Along with the house, the family was also allotted about 62 acres of farmland. - Cf. Hans Gerhardt, *Heimatbuch der Heidegemeinden Heufeld, Mastort, Ruskodorf* (München, 1987).

The unidentified daughter mentioned in Hans Gerhardt's book might have been an offspring of Heinrich's second wife Barbara (the former widow Greifinsfeld). The girl also could have been Heinrich's youngest daughter Barbara from his first marriage who was born at Vértesacsa on March 5, 1751. The two unnamed sons were Johann (1754-1822) from Heinrich's first wife Margaretha and Michael (1761-1836) from his second wife Barbara. My paternal grandmother Marianne STEIGER-WALD (1863-1943) used to explain why her last name was the same as that of her husband. She would also point out that under prevailing marriage laws, she and my grandfather Anton STEIGERWALD (1855-1930) could not have gotten married if their kinship had been closer than it turned out to be, namely a total of seven steps removed. Upon sorting things out as follows, it becomes apparent that J. Heinrich happened to be the couple's common ancestor:

Johann Heinrich STEIGERWALD (?1710-1788)

& his 1st wife Margaretha	& his 2nd wife Barbara
I (half step)	I (half step)
Johann (*1754) & A. Maria	Michael (*1761) & Rosina.
I (full step)	I (full step)
Nikolaus (*1788) & wife Cath.	Josef (*1816) & wife Marg
I (full step)	I (full step)
Johann (*1820) & wife Magd.	Anton (*1840) & wife Sus.
I (full step)	I (full step)

Anton (*1855)=my grandpa & Marianne (*1863)= my grandma

Elucidation of left column entries: Anna Maria LEHNHARD of Marienfeld (Teremia Mare) Banat, became the wife of Johann STEIGERWALD (1754-1822). They got married on February 9, 1779 at St. Hubert, Banat and were blessed with twelve (12) children at Heufeld 65, Banat. Their son Nikolaus STEIGER-WALD (1788-1836) got married on February 5, 1810 at Mastort, Banat, to Catharina HESS. She was born at Heufeld 16, on August 4, 1789. They had seven (7) children. Their son Johann STEIGERWALD (*1820) got married on November 8, 1842 to Magdalena BUCHNER who was born in 1824 at Mastort, Banat. They had five (5) children. Their son Anton STEIGER-WALD (1855-1930) was my paternal grandfather.

Elucidation of right column entries: Michael STEIGERWALD (1761-1836) was the son of J. Heinrich and Barbara, née HORN (1713-1802). Michael's second wife was Rosina ROSS (1780-1852). She was born at Canach, Luxembourg and died at Heufeld, Banat. They got married at Heufeld 62 on January 11, 1803 and were blessed with eleven (11) children. Their son Josef STEIGERWALD (1816-1890) married Margaretha Magdalena LEUTNER of Heufeld, Banat. Of their eight (8) children, at least three (3) reached adulthood. Their son Anton STEI-GERWALD (1840-1919) married Susanna DECOL (1849-1922) of Klek, Banat. This couple had twelve (12) children, but only four (4) of them survived childhood. Their oldest daughter was my paternal grandmother Marianne STEIGERWALD (1863-1943).

LDS microfilms 1190302 and 1190385 in Salt Lake City, Utah, contain some church and civic records of Heufeld. In the latter, it can be seen that Heinrich STEIGERWALD transferred title to house number 65 to his son Johann (*1754) and Johann's wife Anna Maria, née LEHNHARD on November 8, 1779. Thirty-one years later, Johann signed the title over to their son Nikolaus (*1788) and his wife Catharina, née HESS (also spelled Hahs and Hass) on January 29, 1810. Nikolaus (1788-1836) eventually attained the honor of a local civic leader called "Richter" in German.

Upon Johann Heinrich's death on December 6, 1788 his wife Barbara relocated to house number 62 where their son Michael (*1761) was living with his first wife Maria Anna, née Bernard (1757-1802) whom Michael had married upon the early death of her first husband Matthias Hartmann. Michael and Maria Anna took possession of house number 62 on June 28, 1787 as shown at the end of microfilm I 08673 1190385, available at a Family History Center of the Church of Jesus Christ of Latter-day Saints. Maria Anna and Michael had three girls and three boys by the time she died at the age of 45; however, their descendants were not part of our continuing bloodline. Josef (1816-1890), one of Michael's eleven children with his second wife Rosina ROSS (also spelled Rohs and Russ) was destined to be the perpetual link.

In his book on Novi Kozarci, Hans Gerhardt also provided glimpses of village life involving descendants of the colonists. At Heufeld and Mastort, most of the inhabitants were Roman-Catholics. At Ruskodorf, members of other faiths were present also. Among generous donors whose contributions were direly needed for rebuilding the fire-ravaged church of Heufeld during the 1840's, the heirs of Michael and Rosina STEIGERWALD received honorable mention and so did Anna Maria, née LEHNHARD, the widow of Johann STEIGERWALD (1754-1822).

On May 1, 1840, a major catastrophe had occurred at Heufeld, Banat. A fire that started in a corn stalk pile at the home of Michael STEIGERWALD Jr. (*1807) claimed 28 houses along with the village church! Strong prevailing winds made the fire spread quickly to thatched roofs of other dwellings. When flames had consumed essential timber supports of the steeple, the church bells tumbled down onto the vaulted ceiling over the choir area. The heat was so intense that the top end of the smaller bell melted partially, which made it unusable.

28

The staircase to the steeple consisted of 100 wooden steps. It was a total loss, but the new church organ escaped damage due to the bravery of some residents who managed to shield it. The interior of the church was browned on one end and blackened on the other. Candelabras and the crystal chandelier shattered when they fell to the ground. Some among the populace thought that the entire village was doomed! At the house where the fire had started, Michael STEIGERWALD'S 3-year old daughter Katharina died of smoke inhalation.

By about 1840, opportunities for young couples to establish themselves at Heufeld and Mastort (Novi Kozarci) were scarce since there was no uncommitted land available locally; thus, many looked for options elsewhere. Quite a few people relocated to other places in the Banat, including Lasarfeld (YU-23214 Lazarevo), Ernsthausen (YU-23242 Banatski Despotovac), and Kathreinfeld (YU-23212 Ravni Topolovac). My great great-grandparents Josef STEIGERWALD (1816-1890) and his wife Margaretha Magdalena (1818-1882), née LEUTNER (also spelled Läutner and Leitner), relocated to Torontáltopolya, as Banat-Topola was called back then. They worked on the extended agricultural estate of the Counts of Karátsonyi whose main residence was at Bocsár, Banat.

At least three (3) of the eight (8) children of Josef STEIGERWALD (1816-1890) and his wife Margaretha Magdalena (1818-1882) reached adulthood. Their daughter Eva (*1838) eventually married a man named FUCHS. Another daughter, Rosalia (1847-1896) became a cook at a priest's residence with whom she had an illegitimate child, Eduard Konstantin STEIGERWALD (1878-1931), who established himself as a successful milliner at Kikinda, Banat. His son, Eduard STEIGERWALD (1904-1988) studied medicine at Graz, Austria, and opened his first practice at Kikinda, Banat, and his final one at Schwenningen am Neckar in Germany. Dr. Hermann STEIGERWALD (*1938), Eduard's son and Dr. Gerlinde (*1940), Eduard's daughter, took over their father's practice. Dr Eduard STEIGERWALD and his wife Käthe, née Klein, also had a son named Dietrich (1941-1942) who died as an infant. Anton STEIGERWALD (1840-1919), a son of Josef (1816-1890) and Margaretha Magdalena (1818-1882) was one of my paternal great-grandfathers.

Around 1862, my great-grandfather Anton STEIGERWALD (1840-1919) married Susanna DECOL (1849-1922). Spellings of her last name include Dekol, Dekoll, Dekolt, Dekold, Dekoldt, Tekoll, and Thekoll. She was born at Klek (YU-23211) in the Banat. Since her ancestors came to the

Banat from Luxembourg, it is reasonable to assume that the family name was derived from the French form D'École. She and Anton, i. e., my great-grandparents had twelve children including a feeble-minded offspring. Only four of their progeny reached adulthood: My grandmother Marianne (1863-1943) was the oldest. Her younger sister Elisabeth (1865-1939) eventually married Hans PRINZ of Ecska, Banat, with whom she had six children: Michael, Lorenz, Katharina, Maria, Eva, and Hans. All had children of their own.

The oldest son of my great-grandparents Anton and Susanna was Michael STEIGERWALD (+1917). He was killed in WW I as an Austro-Hungarian soldier. His wife's maiden name was DEKORSI. Their only daughter Margaretha STEIGERWALD (1907-1997) married Michael Schmid (*1901) with whom she had three children. When Michael STEIGERWALD was killed in 1917, his wife sold their house at Sigmundfeld (YU-23261 Lukicevo), Banat, but my great-grandparents Anton (1840-1919) and Susanna, née DECOL (1849-1922) were able to continue to live there as retirees. This was quite advantageous for my great-grandfather Anton because cataracts had robbed him of his vision. When Anton died around 1919, his wife Susanna relocated to Banat-Topola where she stayed with my grandmother Marianne (1863-1943), i. e., her first-born daughter, for the remainder of her life.

My grandmother Marianne's youngest brother Lorenz STEIGERWALD (1885-1963) was still living at Sigmundfeld (YU-23261 Lukicevo), when advancing Red Army units were approaching his hometown area in autumn 1944 whereupon he and his family fled to Austria with other ethnic-Germans from the Banat and elsewhere. Had he not done so, Tito's partisans would have most likely killed him along with other hapless members of Yugoslavia's German minority on whom pent-up anger was vented in those days. As it turned out, Lorenz met with accidental death about nineteen years later at Haid, Austria upon being hit by a car as he made a left turn on a bicycle.

Lorenz STEIGERWALD (1885-1963) and his wife Maria, née WELTER (*1886) had four children: 1) Katharina (1905-1990), whose husband from Elemir (YU-23208) fell victim to partisans at Ecska (YU-23203). The couple's son (*1926) died in 1945 on the way to the Soviet Union where he was being taken as a forced laborer. 2) Andreas celebrated his 93rd birthday at Sigmaringen on January 15, 2001. His deceased wife's name was Anna SCHULZ (1914-1967). 3) Juliana (1910-1996) married Nikolaus SPRINGER (1903-1995). 4) Theresia (*1914) was married to Nikolaus BRAUN (*1908); their son

(*1933) has two daughters. In 2000, he resided at Spaichingen, Germany with his mother.

On March 27, 1942, my great-uncle Lorenz' son, Andreas STEIGERWALD (*1908), was inducted into a German military unit; he was confined to a Yugoslav POW camp as of May 1945. Upon his release on October 18, 1948, Tito's partisans sent him to work in a copper mine at Bor (YU-19210), Yugoslavia. In 1950, he managed to obtain a passport for a trip to Trieste, Italy. From there, some Americans enabled him and others to go to Germany. Until his retirement, Andreas worked for the City of Sigmaringen. His only daughter Katharina (*1928) MÜLLER is living at Pasching, Austria.

It is not known what prompted my father's paternal grandparents Johann STEIGERWALD (*1820) and his wife Magdalena, née BUCHNER (*1824) to sell their property at Heufeld and to buy some acreage at Giera(?), Banat. It turned out to be a bad move because their newly acquired land became flooded which prompted them to sell it at a loss. Upon considering possible relocation to Ruskodorf (YU-23314 Rusko Selo), Banat, where a relative of Magdalena (*1824) had come to reside, the family elected to take up residence at Banat-Topola instead. My great-grandfather Johann (*1820) was a tailor by trade. His oldest son Adam (*1845) also became a tailor. Another son, Johann Jr. (*1847), had a daughter who was known as "Parazer Kristine" at Banat-Topola. Margaretha (*1848), the only daughter of my great-grandparents Johann and Magdalena STEIGERWALD married a man named NICOLET. My great-grandparents' third son Anton (1850-1851) died as an infant and their fourth son who was also named Anton (1855-1930) became my paternal grandfather. He was supposed to take up tailoring as well, but his sour stomach made a sedentary occupation quite unbearable; thus, he chose to make his living in farming.

When my grandfather Anton STEIGERWALD (1855-1930) decided to get married in 1883 at the age of 28, he had saved enough of his earnings to buy a house of his own plus a horse, a cow, some land, and essential implements to begin farming independently. By the time his children listed below reached adulthood, he had acquired over eighty (80) acres of arable land through long hours of steady hard work and thrift. During the latter part of his life, Anton suffered from asthma-like symptoms. A feeling of constriction across his chest made breathing difficult for him at times; nevertheless, he had reached the ripe old age of 75 when he died.

The descendants of my paternal grandparents Anton STEIGERWALD (1855-1930) and Marianne (1863-1943), née STEIGERWALD are featured next. As infants, the children were all blond and blue-eyed but after puberty, my father's hair was dark brown. The hair of Johann (1888-1969), Michael (1896-1944) and Katharina (1897-1978) remained blond until it began to gray as they grew older. Since I never met my Uncle Adam, I cannot say what he looked like.

1) Magdalena (*1884) died of diphtheria at the age of 7 or 8.

2) Uncle Adam STEIGERWALD (1885-1966) became a shoemaker. Having learned his trade at Budapest, he was up to date as far as fashions and the latest work techniques were concerned. He owned his own store at Hatzfeld/Jimbolia, Banat (RO-1913) where he employed around sixteen (16) journeymen and up to five (5) apprentices. After WW I, Hatzfeld/Jiimbolia was temporarily occupied by armed forces of the Kingdom of Serbs, Croats and Slovenes, later known as Yugoslavia. Uncle Adam could wait on customers in German, Hungarian, Romanian, and Serbian; thus, he was not anxious to pay homage to Alexander I (*1888, king: 1921-1934) by displaying his portrait in the store. He declined to purchase one, saying that he had no use for it, unless it was to be placed in the outhouse. A disgruntled Serb worker who had been fired took offense and threatened to take Uncle Adam to court on charges of lesemajesty. Before it came to that though, his geographic area was ceded to Romania in exchange for some territory around Modos/Jasa Tomic, which became part of Yugoslavia. Eventually, Uncle Adam's family took up permanent residence at Arad (RO-2900) in the Northern Banat. He and his wife had two daughters and two sons. The second married name of the oldest daughter was Eva GUTUI (1909-1985); her son from her first marriage moved to Böblingen, Germany, where Eva spent the final years of her life also. She had three (3) grandchildren, including twins named Anneliese and Edmund who were born in 1957. Brigitte, Eva's third grandchild, was born in 1969.

3) As a young adult, Uncle Johann STEIGERWALD (1888-1969) worked in the United States of America for a short while. In response to a summons by Emperor Francis Joseph I of Austria when WW I started in 1914, he returned home. After his release from active duty in the Austro-Hungarian army, Johann married Anna GUTHRE of Beodra(?), Banat. They had one daughter Anna (1921-1980) who married Julius KNESEVIC (+1940) with whom she had a daughter named Mimi. Uncle Johann, whom we called Hansi-bácsi, and his wife Anna, called Néni, owned a small condiment store; however, due to a very

low volume of sales and frequent defaults by customers who made purchases on credit without being charged interest, the couple could not make a living at it.

Hansi-bácsi's inadequate farming skills also made him a loser in that area. He was particularly prone to having horses die on him. Time and again, he purchased ailing critters from Sinti or Roma with questionable reputations. Within a matter of a day or two after bringing home an undernourished horse with a big belly time and again, the creature was unable to get back up on its feet once it had laid down to rest. In efforts to help, the good uncle attached a pulley to the overhead beam in the stable to hoist it up to no avail. Each time, he had to borrow a healthy team to haul the corpses to the village burial grounds for dead animals. One thing our kindhearted uncle had a knack for though, was bee keeping. His caring wife used to treat us children to delicious honey whenever we paid them visits.

By the time Uncle Johann learned his lessons about horses on their last leg – no pun intended, he no longer had any land to sell either for a fresh start; thus, he took a job at an area hemp factory where he worked until his retirement. A couple of years later, he and his wife sold their house at Banat-Topola and moved to Zrenjanin (YU-23000), formerly known as Becskerek, Banat, where the couple lived with their widowed daughter Anna (1921-1980) until the elders passed away in 1969. Néni was dark-complected, short, and stocky, with black eyes and black hair. Uncle Johann was always skinny and had a height of only about 5 feet 4 inches. His eyes were a clear blue and his blond hair turned gray in old age. Because of his friendly deportment, he was nicknamed "Lacher Hans" (smiling John). He and his wife as well as their daughter Anna were fluent in German, Hungarian, and Serbian.

Mimi was the only grandchild of Johann and Anna STEIGERWALD. She and her descendants are living in former Yugoslavia.

4) In his youth, Josef STEIGERWALD (1894-1940), my father, was an apprentice in a general store at Ruskodorf (YU-23314 Rusko Selo), Banat. The storeowner Anton BUCHNER (*1856) was a relative of Josef's BUCHNER-grandmother. While working at Ruskodorf, Josef also learned to play a b-clarinet. Mr. BÜCHNER and his wife Elisabeth, née CASTORI (*1857) had a daughter named Louise (*1894). When it became apparent that Josef and Louise had amorous feelings for each other, the boy was told to leave at once, because her folks envisioned her marrying a wealthier man when the time came. On October 24,

33

1915, while my father-to-be was serving in the Hungarian army, Louise got married to Josef Ballauer of Ruskodorf/Rusko Selo.

Unlike many recruits who did not make the grade for induction, Josef STEIGERWALD (1894-1940) was assigned to the Hungarian elite troops known as "Honvéd." Upon returning home when WW I ended, he followed his entrepreneurial impulses and became the very first person to acquire a machine for producing flavored and unflavored club soda at Banat-Topola. He also delivered bottled soft drinks to neighboring villages with a horse and buggy. Soon he added a sideline by importing and selling white hogs from Bavaria to supplement the prevalent local species called "Mongolica."

In 1922, Josef married Victoria KARDOS (+1924); she was a daughter of KARDOS János, the Hungarian who had acquired the inn of my eventual mother's deceased parents. Less than a year after giving birth to their child Michael STEIGERWALD (1923-1956), Victoria died of a lung ailment whereupon Josef's mother Marianne (1863-1943) had to care for the baby until my father-to-be married my subsequent mother Elisabeth, née MARTIN (1906-1944) in 1925.

As mentioned in the preceding chapter, my father Josef's brother Michael (1896-1944) was married to my mother's oldest sister Anna, née MARTIN (1900-1934). Anna assumed the role of matchmaker in an effort to get Elisabeth, who had her eyes on a fellow with the surname KONRAD, to marry my father instead. Aunt Anna felt that by doing so, her sister would come into possession of an already established household without having to slave and save for years to get there on her own. The fact that my father was rather handsome may have turned out to be a deciding factor as well. In any case, they got married even though there was a 12-year age difference between them. Including myself, my parents had four children: Josef (1926-1977), Rose, Jacob, and Anton.

Grandchildren and *great-grandchildren* of Josef and Elisabeth STEIGERWALD are located in Austria (at), Germany (de) and the U.S.A. (us): Hildegard Steigerwald+ (de), Jakob Michael Steigerwald (de), Maria Spacil, née Steigerwald (de), *Claus Spacil* (de), Josef Steigerwald (at), Adelheid Krolokh, née Steigerwald (at), *Karl Josef Krolokh* (at), *Heidi Krolokh* (at), Hans-Peter Steigerwald (at), *Vicki Steigerwald* (at), *Peter Steigerwald* (at), Alfred Steigerwald (at), Brigitte Day, née Kapitaen (us), Marianne Kapitaen (us), Erich Kapitaen+ (us), Carl Jacob Steigerwald (us), Ellen Susanne Steigerwald+ (us),

Richard Peter Steigerwald (us), *Nicholas Richard Steigerwald* (us), *Matthew Joseph Steigerwald* (us), Kristine Marie Steigerwald (us), and Lisa Emilie Kuenn, née Steigerwald (us).

5) Uncle Michael (1896-1944) was a successful farmer. As a hobby, he played the base drum in a local band. He and his wife Anna, née MARTIN (1900-1934) had three children: Theresa, Lisa, and Peter. When Anna died young of an abdominal infection, her widowed Aunt Elisabeth BINDER, née SPRINGER (1891-1937) took care of the children; however, in 1937 the aunt also died of an abdominal infection. About a year later, Uncle Michael married a childless widow named Margaret from St. Hubert, Banat. Margaret was rather fond of Peter but she vied with Lisa for her father's affection. Toward Theresa, who was married and out of the house pretty soon, she was nice and civil. The next person to leave home was Peter. He was placed with a saddler and harness maker at Kikinda (YU-23300) as an apprentice. Lisa stayed at home where she worked very hard doing farm work in addition to household chores.

Just before Christmas 1944, Theresa and Lisa were among the ethnic-Germans from East Central Europe who were sent to the Soviet Union as forced laborers. My cousins wound up in the Donets Basin working in coal mines for 3 and 5 years respectively. By May 1945, Tito's partisans had placed all remaining indigenous ethnic-Germans in Yugoslavia in domestic forced labor and starvation camps. My Uncle Michael STEIGERWALD (1896-1944) wound up among older men who were tortured and executed by Tito's partisans at the infamous dairy in Kikinda (YU-23300), Banat, where Nazis had mistreated and executed some Serb patriots earlier. Communist functionaries wanted the public to believe that all indigenous Germans fled the country towards the end of WW II in anticipation of expectable retributions for crimes committed by Hitler's followers during the German occupation of Yugoslavia (1941-1944). This partially valid rationalization overlooks the fact that nearly 200,000 local Germans were unable or unwilling to flee, since they were unaware of any wrongdoing on their part. Still, they wound up having to suffer for real culprits who were beyond the reach of partisan retaliation now.

Grandchildren and *great-grandchildren* of Michael and Anna STEIGERWALD reside in Germany (de) and in the United States (us): Terri Lawler, née Zimmermann (us), *Kate Lawler* (us), *Michael Lawler* (us), Liz Zimmermann (us), Erica Ozols, née Zimmermann (us),

Stephen Ozols (us), *Evan Ozols* (us), Hilda Julitz, née Tkacz-Weber (us), Linda Tkacz-Weber (us), Georg Steigerwald (de), *Michael Steigerwald* (de), *Robert Steigerwald* (de), *Andy Peter Steigerwald* (de), Angelika Waiser, née Steigerwald (de), *Katrin Nitzl, née Waiser* (de), *Doris Waiser* (de), *Angela Waiser* (de), Michael Steigerwald (de), Christine Elsner, née Steigerwald (de).

Thomas Nitzl (*2001) is a great-great-grandson of Michael (1896-1944) and Anna (1900-1934) STEIGERWALD.

6) Aunt Katharina (1897-1978) got married to Nikolaus BARBA (1893-1987) in 1919. Uncle Nick's ancestors hailed from Otange, Lorraine, but he was born at Nakodorf (YU-23311 Nakovo), Banat. The couple took up residence at Kikinda (YU-23300), Banat, where brothers of Nikolaus were living also. Katharina and Nikolaus made their living as farmers. They had two children: Magdalena (1920-1996) and Andreas. Magdalena married Joe WEISZMANN, an established farmer at St. Hubert, Banat. By the end of WW II, the BARBA and WEISZMANN families wound up in Austria as refugees. In 1950, they immigrated to the United States and took up residence at Chicago, Illinois. Andreas BARBA, his wife Käthe (+1998), and their respective children Ingrid and Reimar joined them there in 1952/53.

The grandchildren and *great-grandchildren* of Nick and Katharina BARBA, née STEIGERWALD are living in the U.S.A. Their names are Andrew Weiszmann, *Johnny Weiszmann, Ron Weiszmann*, Hildegard Ann Draper, née Weiszmann, *Eric Lloyd Draper, Bryant Kevin Draper*, Joe Weiszmann Jr., *Kristina Ann Hansen, née Weiszmann, Laura Jean Minor, née Weiszmann*, Ingrid Osinski, née Barba, *Jamie Osinski, and her brother*. Erica WEISZMANN and Jason Kent MINOR are Katharina and Nick's great-great grandchildren.

It is readily apparent that the descendants of one of the former STEIGERWALD clans at Banat-Topola are quite scattered geographically. Like innumerable other WW II-era upheavals, their conclusive dispersal was a consequence of ethnic rancor that is still causing much grief in former Yugoslavia.

A Distressing Childhood

My earliest recollections include vague images related to our relocation from a roomy and comfortable one-family home to a smelly village inn called "Gasthaus" in German and "vendéglö" in Hungarian. At our new residence, four of the seven rooms were committed to business functions, which drastically limited space for privacy. Furthermore, the freshly remodeled tenement in the village center of Banat-Topola came with a grumpy lifetime resident in one room! He was my half brother Michael's maternal grandfather named KARDOS János (*about 1882). While János seemed to care about his grandson Michael, he certainly did not emit favorable vibrations toward me. Subsequent impressions also suggest that my other siblings never developed a feeling of closeness to the old man either.

The idea of moving literally made me sick. Before our actual relocation, my mother had a family picture taken in the hallway of our erstwhile residence even though my father was away at the time. The photograph conveyed a rather somber mood and rendered an image of me sitting on my paternal grandmother Marianne STEIGERWALD'S (1863-1943) lap. My mother Elisabeth, née MARTIN (1906-1944) and my siblings, i. e., my half-brother Michael (1923-1956), my brother Josef (1926-1977), and my sister Rose were shown standing. My pale appearance was indicative of my unidentified malady that manifested itself through poor appetite and light sleep, with concomitant fatigue and overall physical weakness.

My tentative state of health caused my mother to mull over my chances of survival with grandmother. Mother said that she had the "Totenhemd" (shroud) ready in the event that I would expire. Looking back now, her demur remarks may have subconsciously awakened my will to live. Having been brought into this world, it was now up to me to achieve growth! In those days, people were not inclined to see a doctor right away when someone felt out of sorts. There was no resident physician in our village of Banat-Topola anyway to serve the population of about 1400 men, women, and children.

The nice, roomy home we vacated on Soujanc Street was sold to Uncle Johann STEIGERWALD (1888-1969) and his wife Anna, née GUTHRE (+1969). Their previous residence was located toward the village end of the same street. During subsequent visits at the residence that used to be my first home, I was able to get a good impression of the layout, even though the parlor had been converted into a condiment store:

< S o u j a n c   S t r e e t >

```
┌──────────┬──────┬──────────┬────────────────────────┐
│          │      │          │ Entry Gate             │
│  Parlor  │ Den  │ Bedroom  │                        │
├──────────┴──┬───┴──────────┤                        │
│             │   Hallway   ║║║                        │
│  Kitchen    │              ║║║      Kettle           │
├─────────────┤──────────────┘       Oven             │
│ Club Soda   │   Ivy and                              │
│ Bottling    │   water                                │
│ Room        │   well                                 │
│          ≡≡≡┘                                        │
├─────────────┤                                        │
│  Stable     │                                        │
├─────────────┘                                        │
│ Corn            Open Courtyard                       │
│ Crib,                                                │
│ Hog                                                  │
│ Bins,                                                │
│ Chic.                                                │
│ Coop,                                                │
│ Out-        Cornstalk and straw                      │
│ hse.        piles, hay stack, chaff,                 │
│ Shed        etc.                                     │
```

F r u i t & V e g e t a b l e G a r d e n

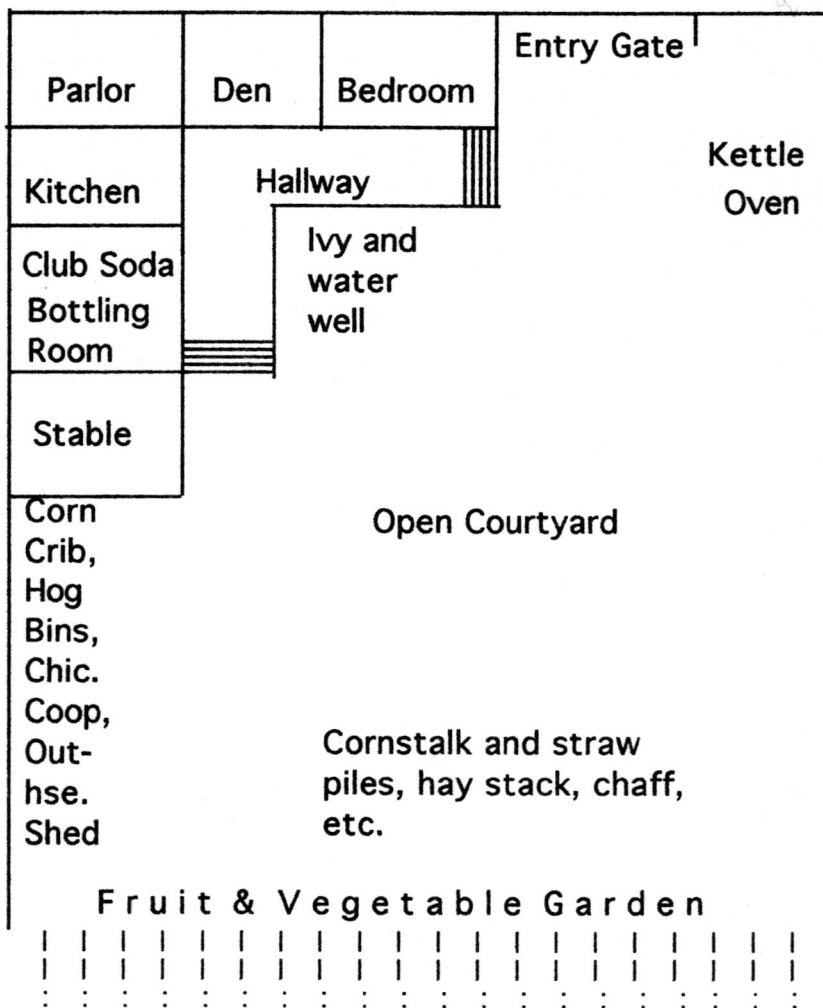

What prompted our family's relocation was a fire that destroyed the inn KARDOS János had acquired in 1920 when the estate of my mother's deceased parents Johann MARTIN (1875-1919) and his wife Anna, née SPRINGER (1878-1920) was liquidated. Thus, by a twist of fate, mother inadvertently wound up moving into her rebuilt childhood home again; however, there were strings attached which made it a highly questionable venture. Before the place even became inhabitable

38

again, major renovation had to be carried out, which rendered the following layout:

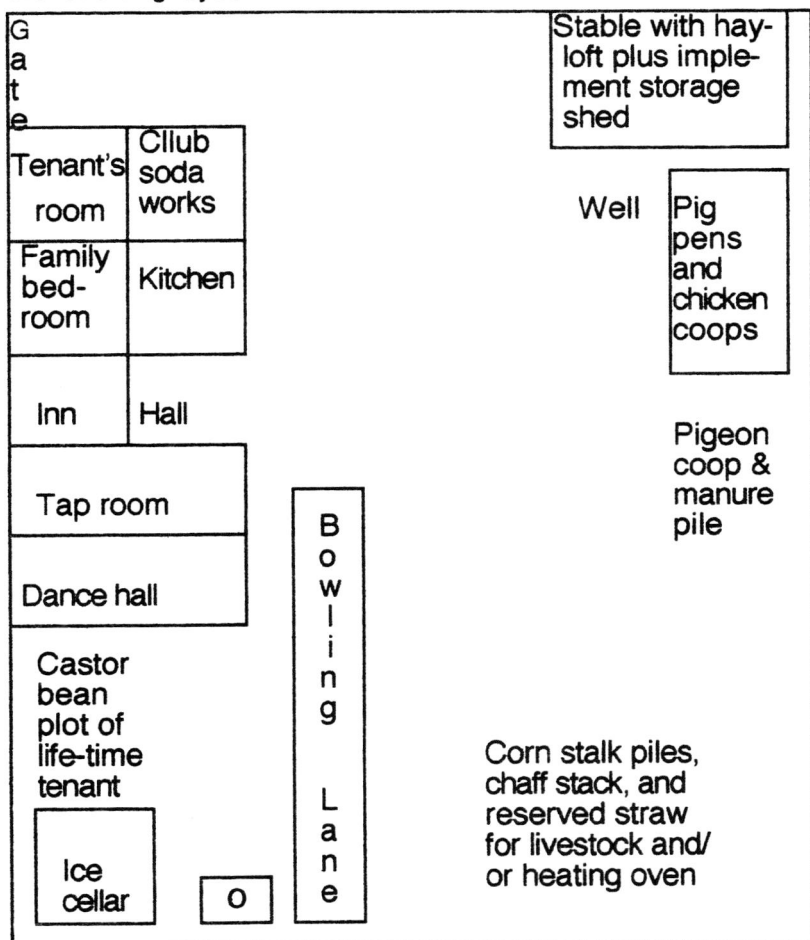

Gate			Stable with hay-loft plus implement storage shed
Tenant's room	Cllub soda works		
Family bedroom	Kitchen	Well	Pig pens and chicken coops
Inn	Hall		Pigeon coop & manure pile
Tap room			
Dance hall		Bowling Lane	
Castor bean plot of life-time tenant			Corn stalk piles, chaff stack, and reserved straw for livestock and/or heating oven
Ice cellar	O		

The STEIGERWALD Inn Adjacent to the "Agraria" Co-op

Since János had no liquid assets for reconstruction and because he was unwilling to sell even part of his eighteen acres of land, he persuaded my father, his former son-in-law, to pay for everything. In return, title to the property was transferred to my half brother Michael STEIGERWALD (1923-1956), a grandson of János.

Although it looked like János was sacrificing a lot, he had actually struck an excellent bargain: He was now rid of his business headaches and enjoyed all the comforts and security of an established retiree who could count on the proceeds from his farmland. As part of the agreement with my father, he retained rent-free perpetual tenancy rights and my mother had to cook for the clever man, too. Some years before, the first wife of János had fallen victim to a fatal stabbing committed by his own intoxicated brother Gergö who mistook her for someone else one night in an unlit hallway. Pevy was the second wife of János with whom he fathered a daughter named Maris. His second spouse left him, because he was apt to become quite mean under the influence of alcohol. For this reason, he was refused service at our inn, too.

At what was now the STEIGERWALD inn, János enjoyed his own private chamber while the living space available for our entire family consisted of only one slightly larger room plus the kitchen that János had to pass through when entering or leaving his quarters. Of the other four rooms in the house, one was being used for bottling club soda, another one was the dance hall, and the other two were taprooms with tables and chairs for customers. Besides beer, wine, cognac, brandy, rum, and flavored liquors, our inn offered club soda with or without raspberry syrup, and two carbonated fruit-flavored soft drinks called "Kracherl" in Austria. Customers used to smoke tobacco products while engaging in loud conversation. After consuming a couple of alcoholic drinks, the aim of some men was visibly impaired when they tried to use a spittoon. I still get nauseous at the thought of mother having had to clean these germ-laden floor vessels upon emptying their contents including malodorous, soggy cigarette butts!

In the larger taproom, there was a coin operated billiard table. Suspended lamps called "Petromax" provided illumination. They required methylated alcohol or kerosene for fuel. Periodically, the portable lamp had to be pumped to effect steady vaporization of fuel through a jet into a miniature silk pouch whose bright glow emitted more lumens than contemporary kerosene lamps could. - Electrification of Banat-Topola was still decades away! My enterprising father purchased a Telefunken radio for use at the inn. It was powered by a so-called "accumulator" that had to be taken to a neighboring town with electricity for periodic recharging.

The furniture in our one-room living quarters at the family inn consisted of three single beds, a wardrobe, a credenza, plus a table and chairs. As kids, brother Josef and sister Rose normally slept with our parents while I generally joined Grand-mother Marianne (1863-1943) in her bed. Michael, the oldest, either slept on a large sheepskin placed on the floor or on a bunk bed in the stable. When our youngest sibling Anton was born, he slept in a cradle next to our mom's bed. Having children share beds with their parents was not at all uncommon in that part of the world. It also helped to keep everybody warm during winters when the masonry ovens fueled mostly by corn-stalks or wheat straw had cooled down at night. Most people had down duvets and pillows but only wealthy folks owned mattresses. So-called "straw sacks" were prevalent in most households. They were made of coarse linen and had two slits in them through which they were stuffed annually with carefully selected soft cornhusks or oat straw. Every morning when the beds were made, the husks or straw had to be fluffed up to avoid sleeping in ruts formed during the previous night.

What made life at the inn uncomfortable in addition to cramped quarters and having to put up with KARDOS János included the following particular circumstances:

1) Loud music on weekends when dances were held or wed-dings were celebrated.
2) As much as we tried to keep the door to our bedroom closed, some biting smoke and alcohol fumes found their way in anyway.
3) Sometimes inebriated customers would be disoriented and stagger right into our bedroom on their way outside to go potty.
4) When we needed to go to the outhouse, we had to walk through a taproom since the other exit led to the "tenant's" quarters.
5) At times, customers would wake us up by knocking on a window after closing time for a so-called "nightcap."
6) Since we had no adjacent garden now to grow our own vegetables, many of our meals were less nutritionally bal-anced than before.
7) Having to serve customers at the inn left our mother less time for childcare now.
8) With the outsider János present at mealtimes, family dis-cussions were limited in scope and subject matter.
9) Periodically, János would go out of town and return intoxi-cated whereupon he often behaved in threatening obnox-ious ways.
10) The low tolerance János had towards children greatly di-minished our chances for inviting friends to play in our own yard.

From a broader perspective, some of the advantages of living in the village center rather than near the periphery should be pointed out also:

* The church was nearby.
* The village hall was even closer.
* School was not far away either.
* Right by the school, there was one of the two local artesian wells.
* The Schödl locksmith/blacksmith shop was across the street from the well.
* The general store of Matthias Bogner was located next to the school.
* Around the corner from our inn, there was Huhn's butcher shop.
* The seamstress Anna Huhn had her shop in the same corner building.
* The midwife Ilona Huhn also lived in the corner house.
* The agricultural co-op "Agrária" was next door in the other direction.
* A few doors down, there was the blacksmith shop of Ács Jóska.
* A shoemaker named Franz was a couple of houses farther down.
* Across the street, there were the general stores of Michael Martin and Franz Haberland.
* Panna Néni, who sold homemade bread, was opposite the agricultural co-op.
* Next to her was Hans Simon, an egg and chicken dealer.
* Last, but not least, frequent exposure to customers who spoke other languages stimulated my linguistic curiosity.

Stories that my older siblings and their classmates related from school were among things that drove fear into me as a child. Just as it happens among people in general, school children rarely talked about normal functions and positive things that transpired on a day-to-day basis. Instead, they preferred to relate "sensational" happenings like news of kids who got in trouble for misbehaving or for failing to complete their homework. Consequently, I became increasingly terrified as the time approached when I was to enter school myself. I just could not understand why I should have to go to a place where punishment was meted out so regularly! Why would anybody even want to be at such a place? My early image of school was akin to a frightening nightmare in the offing. It prompted me to reject the very idea of entering school.

Expectable consequences of my refusal to go to school, as explained by adult jokers around me, were even more horrifying. I was told that unless I went on my own, I would be picked up and taken there in a wheelbarrow that had a bed of pointy spikes sticking up. It made me visualize being punctured and bleeding all over my back! What were my pals going to think when they would hear me screaming in pain? Ultimately, kind words from mom got me to go there reluctantly. To my surprise, it did not take long for me to recognize potential benefits of attending school! I began to see it as a cornucopia replete with useful knowledge and information from which everyone can benefit in accordance with efforts invested. As of that time, I never wanted to miss a single day!

In the first grade, my class was taught the so-called "Gothic" alphabet that was still used in German-speaking areas back then. In second grade, we learned the Roman alphabet and in third grade the Cyrillic alphabet was introduced along with formal lessons in Serbo-Croatian, my second foreign language next to casual daily exposure to spoken Hungarian. When I entered fourth grade, I fully expected to become acquainted with yet another alphabet. Since no new one was in the offing, I concentrated on learning about other things. Luckily, my own studious inclinations kept me from being among students who were punished for one reason or another. The fact that the teacher, Mr. Johann PECKL (+1947) occasionally visited our inn and maintained good rapport with my parents also contributed toward allaying my fear of school.

Before I had completed fourth grade, my ailing father passed away at the age of 46. Evidently, having become an innkeeper was not good for his health. While trying to be a congenial host, he would let customers persuade him to imbibe alcoholic beverage with them, which gradually overtaxed his liver. He died on April 21, 1940. I was not quite nine years of age then and very stunned by the event. The water table at the village cemetery was so high that the grave that had been dug for him kept filling with clay-colored liquid into which his black coffin was lowered with ropes. As the water seeped into the pine box, it suddenly shifted as if even the lifeless body was revolting in the last minute! The bizarre vision recurred to me for some time to come.

While my dad could still run the business, he tended to be busy in the inn with customers or with procurement of beverages from other towns. Many of the farming tasks had to be delegated since he could not attend to everything himself. He enjoyed entertaining guests and he laughed a lot with them. He also liked to tease my mom who was known to dislike tobacco fumes. Sometimes, he would quietly walk up to the kitchen window and blow smoke through it in child-like anticipation of her vigorous reaction. Although he was not a smoker, he kept cigarettes on hand for customers who ran out. Among brands available then, "Drava" cigarettes were low in price, "Ibar" medium, and "Zeta" high.

Dad's fashionable corpulence was suggestive of stamina before he began to lose weight in connection with failing health. He also had a rosy complexion with a stylish trim moustache on his upper lip area. During winters, he loved to stand with his back firmly against the masonry oven, which gave some of his skin a brownish hue as if it had been roasted. After one bout with serious illness, he literally had to learn how to walk again.

Being too weak to do much frustrated him and made him cynical. Sometimes he would tell me to ask my grandmother, i. e., his mother, who prayed a lot with a rosary, whether she was about done counting change. She would have gladly traded places with him so that he could take care of his family. It must have been heartbreaking for her to watch him become skinnier with each passing day. At times, he would send me to a general store for a can of sardines, which he usually shared with me including the tasty olive oil that I still enjoy. People in our area were not apt to know about proper diets; they generally ate what was available. Nobody spoke of vitamins or calories.

Since none of us children were of age yet when my father died, Uncle Michael STEIGERWALD (1895-1944), our half-brother Michael's godfather, was appointed as his guardian and our mother found herself having to take over as a fulltime innkeeper. It certainly proved to be a heavy burden despite periodic assistance from her brothers Josef (1912-1977) and Johann (1911-1989) MARTIN. Thankfully, she also received strong moral support from her sister-in-law Anna STEIGERWALD, née GUTHRE (+1969) who paid us frequent evening visits.

Our Hungarian waiter Kanász István was laid off because of speculation that he had been diverting funds. That did not prove to be the case, so he was rehired. Since "Pista bácsi," as we called him, had lost a leg atop a threshing machine at age 13, he hobbled around with a strapped-on wooden limb while serving customers rather efficiently. He was a cartwright by trade but his volume of business was quite low so that he had time for a side job. His younger brother András became mayor of Banat-Topola after WW II. Unfortunately, a hotheaded partisan shot him fatally.

One year after my father had died in 1940, Yugoslavia, the country where we happened to reside was drawn into WW II due to political machinations. When the federated kingdom was invaded and occupied by German, Hungarian, Italian, and Bulgarian troops in April/May 1941, its cohesion was further weakened as various nationality groups within the multi-ethnic state pulled in different directions. The Banat, where we were living, came under the jurisdiction of German occupation forces; thus, pro-German indigenous factions were able to gain increasing influence in public affairs including matters concerning education. Children of ethnic-German families were now expected to attend schools where coverage of contemporary German national affairs was generally given priority over broader, traditional curricular content.

John F. Kennedy aptly said, "a child miseducated is a child lost." Viewed in that light, much of what I was taught about history in school during the German occupation of Yugoslavia (1941-1944) turned out to be rather useless later. Some of the "heroes" that were discussed like Joachim Nettelbeck, Horst Wessel, or Lettow Vorbek had not distinguished themselves in ways that merited universal acclaim, while personalities who did, remained untreated! Similarly, scores of song texts we were taught in place of worthwhile poetry proved to be rubbish also, because they propagated biased thoughts, wishful thinking, and foregone conclusions. They served to brainwash us toward becoming unquestioning tools of a misguided regime. Instead of being subsequently scorned for my German background, I should have received free compensatory instruction! - Just how much leeway should state authorities have in wasting the mental capacities of its youth? A segmental review of some of the questionable songs from memory illustrates what I mean. For reference, the identifying line of the German original is given followed by my translated excerpts in English:

a) "Siehst du im Osten das Morgenrot?"
Do you see the rosy dawn in the East? It stands for freedom and bliss. We will stand by each other in life and death, come what may!

b) "Nur der Freiheit gehört unser Leben."
Our lives are dedicated but to freedom. Raise the flag into the wind. Let us form ranks in compliance with our destiny! Freedom is a fire - a bright beacon; as long as it shines, the world is not confining.

c) "Auf, auf zum Kampf!" (2nd stanza).
A man who weathered many a storm stands firmly as an oak tree but by tomorrow, he may be cut down like our comrade Horst Wessel.

d) "Ob's stürmt, oder schneit."
Whether we are up against storms, snow, or bright sunshine - scorched by day or freezing at night, what do our lives add up to? In battle, we rely on ourselves; thus, we thrust deeply into enemy lines.

e) "Eines Abends in der Dämmerstunde."
One evening at dusk, I saw two Panzer (tank) crewmembers standing guard. Their beautiful song stopped my girlfriend in her tracks: 'Panzer you alone shall be my joy!' Afterwards, she took me to her room, which had but a bed and no window. What transpired there, remained a private affair: 'Sweetheart, you alone shall be my joy!'

f) "Deutsche Panzer im Wüstensand!"
German tanks are fighting against England in the desert sand. The clatter of chains and howling motors pace the Panzers' advance. In the glowing sun over African soil, our tanks are humming their tune: (Da capo).

g) "Wir lagen vor Madagaskar."[1]
We were waiting off Madagascar with the plague on board. Our water supply was rotting in holding tanks [of U-boats] and some crewmember died daily: Farewell, comrades, farewell.

h) "Vorwärts, vorwärts!"
Forward, forward, the fanfares are blaring. Forward, forward, young people are fearlessly daring. No matter how lofty the goal, youth will attain it! Our flag is leading us jointly into the future. German glory is assured even if we should perish. The flag signifies eternity; it ranks above death.

i) "An der Front im Osten."

---

[1]This song has been associated with German efforts during WW II to gain access to Madagascar, the island where some Nazis wanted to establish a Jewish colony as an alternative to confinement in the notorious concentration camps. Cf. Gerald Reitlinger, *The Final Solution: The attempt to Exterminate the Jews of Europe, 1939-1945*. Second revised and augmented edition (New York: Yoseleff, 1968).

At the Eastern front, there stands a soldier on guard faithfully at his post day and night. Propellers are humming and there is thunder of cannons; yet, from among all the raucous turmoil a song emerges: 'Sweetheart of mine, I wish you were with me. I send you a thousand greetings from out in the fields. You are on my mind day and night. May heaven grant that I'll be with you again soon.'

j) "Mann an Mann marschieren wir."
Shoulder to shoulder we march without concern about our destination - somewhere into a bivouac area. With spirits high, we sing of our sweethearts. What a joy it is to be a soldier!

k) "Soldaten sind immer Soldaten."
Soldiers are always true to their calling. Duty is all they know. Their vows are borne out by action and they do not betray a trust nor can they be bribed. Duty is all they know.

l) "Aufhebt unsre Fahnen."
Raise our flags into the crisp morning breezes! Let it admonish those who are still uncommitted.

m) "Türme und Mauern bau'n sich andre vor uns auf."
Others erect walls and towers to interdict our advance but none keep us from achieving victory.

n) "Und keiner ist da."
No one is there - but cowards despair! Only the weary question the direction in which our flag is taking us.

o) "Vorwärts den Blick."
Look ahead and march for there is no going back! May our flag wave proudly where we gather as comrades!

p) "Infanterie."
Infantry, you enjoy primacy among all armed services. Victory never eludes you! With you, the fame of a great epoch in German history marches into eternity.

q) "Weit ist der Weg zurück ins Heimatland."
The way back to the homeland is rather distant. There, among the stars over the edge of the woods a new era is beckoning.

Like modern commercials, these tools of propaganda played a considerable role in attitudinal conditioning. Further studies in this area would lead to a better understanding of Hitler's deadly grip on the German nation. However, such studies require effort and time, which are notoriously in short supply. Therefore, most people will probably continue to base their concepts on media reports and popular interpretations. Since controversy sustains the media, they must not really be expected to promote better understanding that could lead to actual forgiveness and lasting peace. Media audiences would conceivably not know what to do with themselves out of sheer boredom either if the sensational were not capitalized upon. Although controversial reporting usually occurs at somebody's expense, invectives tend to be seen as justifiable if they appear to confirm perceptions on which the culpability of scorned parties is based. False accusations and perpetuation of misconceptions are part of this ongoing process unfortunately.

One glaring example of wrongful collective group defamation occurred through the propaganda media in the Third Reich regarding Jewish people. A blanket indictment of all Germans for Hitler's atrocious crimes was and is similarly unfair; however, that has not kept politicians, journalists, and even educators from leveling charges of guilt against all persons of German nationality even if they had to suffer unduly for the deranged dictator's madness themselves! How could my family be presumed culpable for instance when my parents and five generations of their forefathers never even set foot into Germany? When my father was born as a member of the German minority at Banat-Topola in 1894, the village was part of Austria-Hungary. At the time of his natural death in 1940, he was a citizen of Yugoslavia who never had voting rights in Germany where Hitler became the duly elected chancellor in 1933. I was less than two years of age at that time! Such differentiating details evidently are of no concern to people who wish to denigrate others by invoking the unfounded "collective guilt" notion.

Since learning is largely an outgrowth of activities and experiences in daily life and not only of time spent in school, it is essential to look at environmental factors that may have influenced a person's formative years also. By listening to some customers at our inn who were trying to drown out their sorrows with alcohol, it seems that their most coveted concern was to be regarded as a decent and honest person (in Hungarian: Tiszteséges, becsületes ember vagyok). Among virtues inculcated and esteemed in my hometown setting were honor, truthfulness, modesty, diligence, faithfulness, neighborly civility, compassion, thrift, sense of duty, trustworthiness, and self-

48

reliance. Little did I know then that in many parts of the rest of the world, rules of conduct did not always include these or similar values; in fact, some of the listed concepts like modesty for instance are regarded as self-denying foolishness in many places.

When I was in elementary school, sex education was not yet offered to children; but in our rural environment, acts of copulation could be seen routinely among all kinds of domestic animals. Very few adults were willing to discuss the subject of procreation with us children but among ourselves, we would snicker and comment about what we saw or thought we had seen. Some older boys tried to impress us with their knowledge about the matter, which was not always accurate either. Male adults would sometimes deliberately make us boys blush by asking embarrassing questions like "do you have a girlfriend" or "were you treated to a poke yet?"

Parents were visibly uncomfortable or even embarrassed to discuss the subject with any offspring. It was something one did not talk about since it was sinful for people to have sex out of wedlock in the first place. Mothers seemed to view the matter as distasteful, denigrating, and lowly. If a boy inadvertently forgot to close the fly on his pants when getting dressed or after urinating, he would be admonished to close his "pigsty." As I recall, I learned a few things about the birds from roosters, hens, and other creatures at Banat-Topola, but my knowledge about the bees remained quite sketchy until I was in a position to take some college courses in Biology, Botany, and Zoology years later.

What kept me from gaining sexual experience as a teenager, certainly was not a total lack of opportunities. There were occasions now and then when a presumably complaisant female of appropriate age could have been approached; but I failed to act accordingly because of a variety of considerations. For one thing, personal pride made me very selective. Then there was my idealism, which caused me to envision love making as a natural complement of romance. I imagined my partner to be a beautiful decent girl. In real life, such girls were not exactly running around unguarded and loose for me to grab and seduce!

Another set of considerations that mattered in connection with my amorous teenage urges and desires had to do with fear. Uppermost was the fear of contracting a venereal disease, which might not only have ruined me for life but also would have posed a threat to the health of possible progeny in years to come. The fear of accidentally having an illegitimate child also served as a powerful deterrent against having sex with just any consenting female. The likelihood of having to pay alimony or the idea of having to marry someone with whom I would not have wanted to spend the rest of my life had the effect of ice cold showers upon my impressionable psyche.

The notion of visiting a prostitute did not sit right with me either, especially when I visualized the scores of other guys she probably had been with including individuals whose negligence concerning their own health also made them a threat to others. As I look back now, it appears that providence played a role in keeping me out of potential harm's way whenever I might have caved in to temptation despite my trenchant apprehensions and profound rational behavioral criteria.

My mother firmly believed that providing us kids with a formal education would go a long way toward enabling us to enjoy a decent standard of living. Michael, our half-brother was going to take possession of the inn in addition to our father's thirty acres of farmland. The only material inheritance that was in the offing for the rest of us siblings encompassed about seven acres of land our grandmother Marianne (1863-1943) still owned plus some of the inn's furniture including the billiard table.

When my oldest brother Josef (1926-1977) was old enough to enter upper primary school, he was sent to Becskerek (now called Zrenjanin) in 1938. He was provided with room and board at the rather tiny apartment of our cousin Anna KNESEVIC, née STEIGERWALD (1920-1980) and her husband Julius (+1940) who was a teacher. The couple had a daughter named Mimi. She eventually majored in Music and Mathematics at Belgrade University and subsequently got married to a Yugoslav government official who was anxious to keep her German ancestral background a secret lest it might interfere with his chances for career advancement under communism. He even denied visiting rights to Mimi's mother Anna who hardly got to see her grandchildren. When Cousin Anna died in 1980, contact with Mimi and her family was lost entirely.

Our brother Josef was treated like some sort of maid in the household of Julius and Anna KNESEVIC, but he was very good-natured and not at all inclined to complain. After Julius died in 1940, Josef transferred to the upper primary school at our District Capital of Kikinda. Upon completing his coursework there in 1942, he entered the teacher training institute (Lehrer-bildungsanstalt = LBA) at Vrsac, Banat. His formal studies were interrupted in September 1944 when advancing Red Army units caused him and his classmates to be hastily inducted into a military unit. Upon retreating to Austria, Josef and other boys his age were enabled to resume their teacher training at St. Pölten. After a while, he had to quit teacher training and look for a job to support himself. It took many years before he got back on track again, eventually attaining a rank of school principal, just before he died at the age of 51.

My sister Rose completed middle school at Kikinda where she was awarded the school leaving certificate signifying the "kleine Matura." At first, she enjoyed room and board at the home of our Aunt Katharina BARBA, née STEIGERWALD (1897-1978) but later Rose availed herself of a boarding school arrangement that gave her more study time and a better chance to make friends. - Our youngest sibling Anton, better known as Tony, was the first in the family who had the opportunity to attend a regular kindergarten at Banat-Topola where he also completed a couple of years of primary school before our formal education was interrupted in 1944 by wartime developments.

Upon having completed four years of primary school at Banat-Topola, I passed the test for admission to the so-called "Hauptschule" (upper primary) at Kikinda. While staying at a boarding school there, I managed to complete two years by summer 1944. Classes did not reconvene in fall because the front happened to pass through our area as of early October whereupon Tito's communist partisans became the new rulers. In accordance with declarations by AVNOJ in November 1944 at Jajce, Bosnia, Yugoslavia's ethnic Germans were to be disfranchised and eliminated as an unwanted indigenous minority. As a result, my formal education was interrupted for years to come! This radical turn of events has left me with feelings of deprivation to this very day.

Like Anne Frank, I had become an object of immense hatred because of my ethnicity. At a stage in life when young people in civilized countries are normally provided with curricular opportunities to discover their career potentials, I was deprived of all human rights. Could I as a child have somehow averted the evils committed by misguided followers of Hitler? Obviously not, but that did not keep Tito and his partisans from exacting emotional, psychological, and physical "payments in kind" from me through subsequent subjection to hardships as a detainee in starvation and forced labor camps. Tito's riff-raff followers were too eager for vengeance to take into account that the unlawful treatment that the members of the hapless residual ethnic group were going to be put through was as criminal and as contemptible as nazi atrocities.

Within six or seven months, all members of Yugoslavia's German minority who had not left the country before the arrival of the Red Army wound up in concentration camps that existed until April 1948. A large percentage of those confined died of maltreatment, starvation and various other illnesses in dozens of large and small attrition and forced labor compounds. - Is it not rather confounding that by the time the world becomes aware of acts of impending or ongoing genocide and long before a readiness to intervene materializes among nations, entire populations get wiped out? All too often, like in the case of Tito's partisans, the perpetrators get away with heinous crimes against humanity entirely unpunished!

A little over a month after the front swept through our area in October 1944, my mother Elisabeth died of dropsy on November 10. Dr. Vlajnich, our Serbian doctor from Basaid, who had treated my parents along with other villagers for years, was under strict communist orders not to attend to ethnic-German patients any longer, because none of the country's scarce medical resources were to be "wasted" on disfranchised group members! With a medicine called "Digitalis" my mother's life could have been prolonged beyond the age of 39!

During those fearful days, ragtag groups of Tito's partisans repeatedly appeared at the homes of members of the indigenous German minority where they purported to be looking for "military contraband." They were using that as an excuse in lieu of legal search warrants. Things like cameras, watches, jewelry, or other valuables were subsequently often missing, but there was no one to whom Swabians could have turned for judicial recourse. Since the partisans had jurisdiction over life and death, very few people had the courage to protest. One could never be certain whether objections raised might be taken as provocations to which the response might be dealt from the throat of a pistol or by means of a rifle butt. It was truly hard to distinguish between the behavior of these so-called "liberators" and that of reckless nazi aggressors.

Tito's expulsion of Germans from their homes began in late fall 1944. Members of the minority who lived in villages and towns that also had Slavic residents were rounded up first and taken to communities whose inhabitants were non-Slavs. Some expellees from other places were brought to Banat-Topola where the population consisted of ethnic-Germans and Hungarians. The ousted ethnic group members were assigned to the homes of local Swabians who were expected to provide them with free room and board. Locally housed expellees included former inhabitants of Basaid, Bikac, Bocar, and other places. The five expellee-boarders who were assigned to the home of my Aunt Margaret STEIGERWALD, where my sister and I also resided since we became orphaned, ranged in age from 63 to 80. They often just sat there weeping and shaking their heads wondering why fate was so cruel to them now in their old age since they had never deliberately wronged anyone at all.

Around Christmas 1944, ethnic-German men and women between the ages of about seventeen and forty-five were rounded up in East Central Europe and sent to the Soviet Union as forced laborers. Nobody knew if any of them would ever be able to return home. As it turned out, about fifteen percent succumbed to the harsh conditions under which they toiled mostly at reconstruction sites and in coalmines. As mentioned earlier, my cousins Theresa TÖRÖK, née STEIGERWALD and her unmarried sister Lisa wound up in the Donets Basin whence they were released to Austria after three and five years respectively.

Remaining able-bodied members of the German minority were regularly summoned for forced labor assignments around our area and farther away. My sister Rose was among them. They had to go out in freezing conditions during the middle of winter to pick the corn that was left in the fields because the area had been a war zone at harvest time.

On April 18, 1945, as the war was winding down in Europe, Tito's partisans evicted all remaining ethnic-Germans at Banat-Topola and herded us into a makeshift local concentration camp. Broad Street, now called "Oslobodilacka ulica," which had the largest concentration of German-speaking inhabitants, was designated as the local compound. While we expellees were gathering at the churchyard in the wee hours as ordered by armed guards, partisans had the houses of German residents along Broad Street completely emptied of all furnishings. In the meantime, we were required to file through the vacant clergy residence. Hoping to find hidden valuables, a male or female partisan frisked some of us respectively. Then, they assigned us to the evacuated houses according to age and gender groups. We were issued some confiscated horse blankets and bedded down on straw-covered floors throughout the emptied former ethnic-German residences.

At concomitantly established soup kitchens each of the confined ethnic-Germans received one ladle of paltry soup three times a day. Every detainee was also issued about 350 grams of bread once a day. Some people got mouth sores from the coarse, hard corn bread. Most often, pea soup was dis-

53

pensed. Typically, cooked beetles that tend to grow inside some varieties of this legume floated on the surface in kettles and bowls. Since we detainees were not issued any spoons or other eating utensils, there was no easy way to skim off the dead beetles that wound up in one's dish. Rather than simultaneously throwing out some of the scant nutrients afloat in the soup, it was best to close one's eyes and to swallow the unsightly slops.

Sanitary facilities were non-existent. Privacy for taking sponge baths with rags was also hard to come by. The detainees went potty in stables, on manure piles, and in outhouses where available. At some locations, open-pit arrangements were built with a horizontal wooden beam for support. Medicine was withheld from us captives since we were regarded as personae non grata. - Individual accounts of life in Yugoslav starvation and attrition camps for ethnic-Germans are included in the Bibliography at the end of this volume. Katharina Elisabeth Flassak, Konrad Gerescher, Wendelin Gruber, Magdalena Heilman-Märzweiler, Maria Horwath, Maria Schnur, and Elisabeth B. Walter are among the authors of relevant books.

Shortly after the initial confinement of the ethnic-Germans at Banat-Topola, one repeatedly heard about old men who hanged themselves in despair. Adjusting to an existence in confinement proved to be difficult for the Swabian detainees because according to their standards of conduct such denigration was normally only visited upon real criminals! Every day including Sundays, younger women and teenagers of both genders were divided into work groups and escorted out into surrounding fields by armed partisan guards to perform involuntary agricultural labor. No compensation was ever provided for any of it. I happened to be assigned to a group that was taken to vineyards. My function entailed hammering wooden stakes into the ground. Others secured vines to them so that ripening grapes would not come to rest on the ground where insects and decay could spoil them. Helping to enhance the country's food supply on an empty stomach in farmland seized from our kinsmen whose forefathers had tamed it, felt rather weird and accentuated the circumstance that, as a member of Yugoslavia's contemptuously banished German minority, I was professed to be some sort of villain.

Visiting relatives or friends in the detention areas was strictly forbidden; thus, I could not look in on my brother Tony at all. He was only nine years of age then, and I was not quite fourteen. Within a couple of weeks after we were placed in confinement at Banat-Topola on April 18, 1945, I wound up among approximately forty-six (46) detainees that were marched to the internment camp at Banatsko Veliko Selo (YU-23312), i. e., Charleville, Banat, on a balmy spring day.

Surprisingly, being escorted by armed Yugoslav partisans from my birthplace forever in my early teens evoked little emotional or psychological anguish. Banat-Topola had already ceased to feel like home, because of its radical demographic transformation due to the influx of unfamiliar Slavic colonizers from other parts of the country. They now occupied the houses of forcibly ousted ethnic-German residents.

What preoccupied me for some time to come was the bleak outlook for the future, since I found myself summarily stripped of basic "inalienable" rights regarding life, liberty, and the pursuit of happiness. On top of having been rendered homeless, I was now subjected to dictates of rag-tag gun-toting partisans, within whose incoherent ranks of men and women a frightful number bandied about with blood in their eyes. It gave us captive ethnic-Germans pause to wonder, whether one of their demonstrably expended bullets might have the name of one of us on it. In those days, partisans were at liberty to "liquidate" members of the unwanted German minority without adverse repercussions.

II. THE RUGS PULLED OUT FROM UNDER

5. Orphaned and Uprooted by Tito's Partisans: As a Refugee in Romania, Hungary, and Austria

As a forced laborer at the Banatsko Veliko Selo/Charleville internment camp for ethnic-Germans, I initially toiled in the fields of nearby St. Hubert. Under the watchful eyes of armed partisans, some of us detainees were belatedly planting communal corn in the middle of May 1945. The freshly established dictatorship of Josip Broz(ovic) Tito (1892-1980) was receiving various kinds of aid from the United States of America including bright orange/yellow tractors and other farm equipment. In the process of carrying out communist aims, extensive land areas were now being tilled by recently trained young Slavic workers who expeditiously removed all telltale wooden and metal markers that designated boundaries of former private acreage including tracts of forcibly evicted ethnic-Germans. The expropriated farmland was indisputably regarded as state property. With a taunting gleam in their eyes, individual partisans delighted in saying "sve nas," meaning 'it's all ours.'

Due to bigger plowshares involved in power tilling, there were many sizable clumps of compacted soil in the fields that prevented some seed corn from being immersed into the ground by the mechanical planting boots of machines. The boulder-like clods also proved to be a problem for us teenage boys, because they interfered with our efforts to guide the horse-drawn planter along straight lines. I wound up being tossed back and forth like a rag doll whenever a big lump in the path of a wheel made the steering rod jerk forcefully. My weakened stamina was not up to the task at hand. The situation in which I found myself was further aggravated by our meager internment camp rations that lacked essential nutrients. I felt truly drained and perspired a lot. Under given circumstances, I dreaded the onset of each successive day and fervently wished for a less strenuous forced labor allotment.

Help came from former classmates with whom I had attended boarding school at Kikinda (YU-23300). Having been born and raised in the local area, their ability to seek out better work options exceeded mine. My new duties entailed gathering hay atop a horse-drawn mechanical rake in small fields interspersed between vineyards dotted with fruit trees including some whose products were just beginning to ripen; thus, I was able to supplement the skimpy camp food with important vitamins. My friends and I did not regard this as stealing since the partisans had seized all of our property except the set of clothes we wore. On top of that, they were now exacting slave labor without providing appropriate nourishment in sufficient quantities for us growing teenagers. As Greg Steinmetz pointed out in an article, communist Yugoslav leaders wanted to keep this crime against humanity hushed up: "Northern Yugoslavia, 1946: According to Official History, this Ethnic Purge Never Happened," *Chicago Tribune* (November 12, 1992), sec. 1, p. 11. Consequently, no government in Belgrade has of yet gotten around to offering compensation similar to what has been tendered by Germany and Austria for slave labor extolled from captives there during WW II.

Since sanitary provisions in the Yugoslav camps for ethnic-Germans were less than minimal, fleas and lice soon plagued the detainees, too. My buddies and I were less susceptible to hosting such human pests because we slept in a stable under horse blankets whose common odor seems to serve as a natural repellent. Having no respect for religion either, Tito's communist cadre also had us working on Sundays. As of autumn 1945, some of my fellow detainees and I were required to haul sacks of grain from Charleville to the train station at Kikinda. The distance was about 12 km. At a railroad crossing near Kikinda, there would often be mischievous Slavic boys with slingshots waiting for us as we approached atop our wagons. Repeatedly, they pelted us without reprimand from our armed partisan escorts. Condoning such roguish behavior was also indicative of our general degradation as an ethnic minority in Yugoslavia. One of my friends named Ludwig could have lost an eye when a sharp pebble pierced the skin on one of his cheeks one day before our wagons had gotten out of the slingshot-rascals' range.

On the first Sunday in November 1945, I was again scheduled to haul wheat to the railroad station at Kikinda. After lunch, I gave my homemade slippers to a fellow detainee in exchange for having him take charge of my team the rest of the day. I did not dare tell him or anyone else in the camp that I was planning to flee to Romania with three other boys ranging in age from 14 to 15. Around 6:00 p. m., upon early seasonal nightfall and before our teams had returned, we quietly moseyed from the stable through the backyard to open fields. Then we headed east stumbling across various kinds of terrain in the dark. Now and then we paused, squatted down, and listened for suspicious sounds but all we could hear were audibly feasting partisans and dogs barking at a safe distance. The former were continually celebrating their ascension to unchecked power over people who had been part of the law-abiding mainstream of society right up to the communist take-over that ironically could not have been achieved without the help of widely scorned capitalist Western allies. Reinstatement of the monarchy in Yugoslavia would have represented a more humane way out of the country's dilemma after WW II and decades later.

The four of us running away reached the outskirts of Comlosu Mic/Ostern in Romania (RO-1967) without incident by about 9:00 p. m. Luckily, the first people we encountered at the outskirts of the town happened to be a local German-speaking couple on its way home. Upon a brief conversational exchange, we were directed to the residence of Ludwig Lenner, a tractor mechanic with whom a member of our group was acquainted. Mr. Lenner put us up for the night after some delay attributable to a raid conducted by local gendarmes. While hiding behind a cornstalk pile in Mr. Lenner's yard, we wondered whether the authorities had been alerted to look for us or whether the "razzia" (raid) merely constituted a periodic border town event.

Mr. Lenner advised us not to stay at Comlosu Mic/Ostern because we might be asked for identification at any time and we had no papers whatsoever. He gave us the name and address of a friend of his who was living at Tomnatic/ Triebswetter, Banat (postal code RO-1974). It took all morning and half of the afternoon for us to get there on foot but we were warmly welcomed and enjoyed our first substantial meal in a long time. Before the man took us to prospective local employers, we shared information about our respective personal background and apprised him of current conditions in the area we had just come from.

A lad named Franz was the tallest member in our group. The seemingly irrevocable sadness in his eyes mirrored a great deal of the ongoing suffering to which our fellow compatriots were concurrently subjected. Franz hailed from Charleville, Banat, was 15 years of age and very good-natured. To our great dismay, he had the misfortune to be taken into custody by a Romanian gendarme a short time later and we never heard from him again! The ethnic-German father of Karl Stein, a group member of my age (14), could not return home from Bavaria for fear of being imprisoned or executed in Yugoslavia for having served in the German military. Karl's Hungarian mother was still living at home in Charleville. Besides German, "Karcsi," as he was affectionately called, also spoke Hungarian and Serbian. By virtue of my bilingual Austro-Hungarian birthplace, I had also acquired a passable knowledge of Hungarian along with some Serbian in school and from customers at my parents' inn.

The fourth member of our group was Peter Schenk, age 15. He was the oldest son of an ethnic-German shoemaker at Charleville, Banat. Peter's absent younger brother Franz had been a classmate of mine at upper primary school (Hauptschule) in Kikinda. Peter was the driving force behind our risky extrication from one of Tito's internment camps for Yugoslavia's ethnic-Germans. Regrettably, his ability to size up situations diagnostically caused him to be regarded as a know-it-all by snobbish employers even when his ideas had the makings of laborsaving shortcuts. Since they expected compliant obedience rather than enlightened suggestions from workers, he wound up changing jobs seven times at Tomnatic/Triebswetter (RO-1974) before trying his luck in neighboring Nerau (RO-1969) with identical results.

The farmer Nikolaus Frecot of Tomnatic/Triebswetter, my subsequent employer for sixteen (16) months, was a descendant of French settlers who were among the founders of the town in 1770 under the auspices of Empress Maria Theresa. A man in his early forties, Mr. Frecot owned a couple of houses, about 140 acres of land, and a small tractor that had to be hidden in a barn under a lot of chaff to keep it from being requisitioned. His livestock included three horses, one cow, eight sheep, a half dozen or more hogs as well as some chickens and ducks. A dachshund and two larger mongrel dogs contributed toward the estate's security. Mrs. Maria Frecot was of ethnic-German ancestry. Most local inhabitants happened to speak German since the descendants of the original settlers from Lorraine had become assimilated during the Nineteenth Century. Many residents also spoke Hungarian and/or Romanian as a second or third language. The couple's only daughter Anna was born in 1932. She attended the Catholic finishing school at Periam/Perjamosch Banat (RO-1963). Their son Ewald was enrolled in public school locally. Deplorably, the entire family wound up among area residents who were sent to the Baragan steppe in 1951 where Romanian State agencies conducted an ill-conceived experiment to determine whether the arid terrain in the lower Danube delta could be transformed into an agriculturally productive resource.

My duties at the Frecot estate involved farm work of all kinds. Room and board constituted my primary compensation, which was supplemented by periodic gifts of clothes and some pocket money. What proved to be especially difficult was for me to get up at wee hours day after day during the planting, growing, and harvesting seasons. By sun-up, we had already been around the field twice with our team of horses pulling a plow or some other farm implement. Prior to trekking to a particular field, we had to get up and feed the horses, eat breakfast, load provisions and equipment onto a wagon, hitch up the team, and travel for about fifty minutes on unpaved often muddy roads. I am still wondering how I survived those untoward conditions for a total of sixteen months in a crucial growing stage as a teenager! I probably consoled myself with the realization that I was still better off than I would have been in one of Tito's officially eclipsed attrition camps for ethnic-Germans.

During evenings and on Sundays, I did not dare to go and congregate with young people at public places in Tomnatic/Triebswetter, because I was afraid that I might be asked for identification papers, of which I had none. Under given circumstances, I was compelled to live in seclusion without being able to go out and freely participate in activities teenagers like and normally engage in. I also did not dare to correspond with anyone lest I be discerned, apprehended, and deported back to Tito's Yugoslavia where Germans were about as welcome then as Jews had been in nazi-Germany. The scattered members of my clueless family could merely hope that no serious harm had come to me. My younger brother Tony was the only one whom I had apprised of my intended escape to Romania. However, Tony was even less likely to get a chance to communicate with relatives than I, since he was later successively placed into various Yugoslav homes for children along with other Danube Swabian orphans as described by Karl Springenschmid for instance (see bibliography). Thus, no other family member had any idea where I was. Conversely, I was also oblivious of everyone else's whereabouts.

By word of mouth, I learned of other refugees who were at Tomnatic/Triebswetter incognito. Periodically, we got together on a Sunday afternoon in some stable and exchanged stories concerning our respective background and experiences. On one particular occasion, we bought some wine for our gathering. It was then that I discovered my limits regarding this intoxicating beverage. Without being consciously aware of it, I drank more than I should have. It made me so confused that I began to do my morning chores at nightfall: No manure-laden wheelbarrow ever performed more geometrically inimitable serpentines than the one I was pushing onto a pile that evening! To my incomprehension, even my best efforts toward normal conduct made everyone in the household walk around me at a wide berth with wondrous facial expressions.

I often marveled about the ways in which providence protects us when our rational faculties are in disarray for some reason. In 1946, Mr. and Mrs. Frecot hired a Romanian household maid whose name was Vetta. She was eighteen years of age, had natural red cheeks, brown eyes, brown hair, appealing body proportions and good posture. Despite her impressive appearance, she was not arrogant toward me but rather playfully coquettish at times. One night, after she had completed her kitchen chores, she peeked into the stable where my bunk was, just as I was getting ready to go to sleep. Her ominous chuckle made me follow her as she hastily entered the garden to help herself to some cherries off a tree. Her silhouette among the bizarre shapes of the branches seen against the night sky evoked the biblical image of a serpent in my mind's eye, which hit me like a cold shower and effectively canceled any thoughts of pursuing her then and there.

On another occasion, Vetta and I were out in the fields cultivating corn. When it suddenly seemed like it was going to rain any minute, we took refuge under a tarp draped over the wagon shaft. An auspicious look in Vetta's eyes indicated that she was in a mood for love, which also had pervaded my thoughts many times before. However, before we even had a chance to progress to a petting stage, I happened to notice that our employer was approaching on foot to see how work was progressing. His arrival at that point in time cooled me down quite abruptly. As I later reflected on this foiled romantic interlude with attractive Vetta, I wondered how things would have turned out if we had unintentionally created a baby. At age fifteen, I certainly would not have been able to support one; thus, my fleeting moment of self-indulgence could have resulted in compounded hardships for at least three people including a child! As anxious as I was to make out with a pretty girl, I had to admit that the timely interference that prevented our having sex even just once was tantamount to protective divine intervention.

In due course of time, our existence in Romania as illegal aliens prompted my fellow refugees and me to reassess our situation. We wondered whether we might not be better off in Austria or Germany. It would have been quite helpful if we could have learned about conditions in these countries through the media, but in the communist country where we found ourselves temporarily stranded, this was not an option. Hans Wasza, a fellow refugee from my hometown who left for Austria with Karl Stein in autumn 1946 had not written to me either as he promised he would. During the following year, after my own arrival in Austria, I was shocked to learn why I never heard from

61

Hans again: He had suffered fatal head injuries upon jumping off a moving train in the darkness of night.

Hungarian authorities had apprehended Hans and Karl along with other refugees and they were transporting them back to Yugoslavia against their will. When the armed escort dozed off, the desperate captives tried to countermand their ordered deportation through quick action that proved to be disastrous. Evidently, jumping off a moving train at night in unfamiliar terrain appeared less terrifying to them than a confrontation with Tito's dreaded partisans! Karl survived the unfortunate event with a broken leg. After he had recovered at a hospital in Hungary, he was able to join his father in Bavaria. I found out about the debacle of Hans and Karl when I ran into Peter Schenk unexpectedly near Bruck on the Leitha River, Lower Austria, in 1947/48. Upon learning of their cruel fate, I realized why an ominous premonition had kept Peter and me from accompanying them on their perilous journey.

My own trek to Austria commenced on March 18, 1947 at Tomnatic/Triebswetter with three fellow refugees. Georg, age 24, was the oldest among us. Each of the other two members of our group was seventeen years old. Their respective names were Hans Elmer and Tony Lafleur. They hailed from Banatski Despotovac/Ernsthausen, Banat (YU-23242). Their intention was to join relatives at Moosburg, Bavaria. Compared to these big boys, I was quite naive and immature at sixteen. They would not have agreed to have me tag along with them if my knowledge of Hungarian had not exceeded theirs. I was to prove useful to them as a translator on our way through Hungary.

A surprising thing happened to me just before we left Tomnatic/Triebswetter. I had casually spoken with Kati on previous occasions. She was a household maid where my compatriot Tony Lafleur was working. Yet, I never thought that the eighteen-year-old, blue-eyed Hungarian girl with ash blond hair had a soft spot for me. As I was waiting for my buddies on the street in front of her employer's house the night of our planned departure, she unexpectedly pulled me into a dark area and hugged me closely wearing only a shift. It was the first time I felt a woman's well-shaped caressing body excitedly pulsating against mine. It endowed me with instant warmth all over! However, the timing of Kati's amorous volley could not have been worse since my pals were about to leave without me. Much to my regret, I had to tell amiable Kati the Hungarian equivalent of "mañana" as I extricated myself from her exultant embrace to join my impatient travel companions forthwith.

Our migration did not pan out as planned although we had hired two guides to take us to the frontier separating Romania and Hungary near Cheglevichi/Keglewitsch, Banat (RO-1978). Having increased the size of our group to six proved to be our first mistake: According to some contemporary local ordinances more than three people together constituted a crowd and crowds were only allowed to congregate with special permission from the police. Consequently, our group attracted more than casual attention. Soon, two uniformed Romanians came out of a house by the roadside and stopped us nonchalantly for questioning before we had even reached the border area.

First, they asked us where we were going. Since we had not jointly discussed what to say in case we ran into a patrol, the responses given to them were not identical. Our dissimilar answers raised suspicions and prompted them to examine what we were carrying in our rucksacks. Our provisions consisted of some bread, half-slabs of smoked bacon, four liter bottles of brandy, a hefty bunch of leaf-tobacco, and about 2.5 kg of homemade soap. Upon seeing what we had, they thought we were black marketers or smugglers.

How might we have countered the interrogators' erroneous assumptions without revealing right off the bat that we were transients without papers? In the fluster of the unexpected confrontation, it was hard to decide which applicable legal condition might be regarded as a lesser offense. We had opted to carry goods rather than money to avoid difficulties with currency exchange involving identification papers we did not have. Upon selling our provisions in Hungary, we were hoping to have travel-money for at least part of the way.

Without even attempting to arrive at a fair assessment of our situation on the basis of our explanatory chat, the two constables proceeded to help themselves to everything we had while intimidating us with unprintable cuss words. As they were intermittently guzzling our brandy, the afternoon sun highlighted the rising air bubbles inside the inverted bottles. Then, they ordered the two guides and me to take our shoes off, which were kept as contraband, too. Mine, like those of each of the guides were worth about 300 000 Lei per pair, for which an adult farm laborer had to work a whole month! Soon the two officials who sported only one unloaded rifle between them were beginning to stammer and sway. Brusquely, they commanded us to scram lest we wanted to be taken to their station.

Valuing our freedom above all, we lost no time in making ourselves scarce. With tears in their eyes, the now shoeless guides went their own way empty-handed since the guards had also taken the money we were going to pay them. Until nightfall, the four of us refugees hid in a vineyard hut that stood well off the main road. As we peered out through some crevices later in the day, we could see gendarmes with dogs riding by in a jeep. Luckily, they did not stop near our location where the dogs could have picked up our scent from my confiscated shoes, for example. Fortunately for me, a fellow group member had an extra pair of well-worn, oversized, Oxford-style shoes left in his rucksack which kept me from having to go barefoot in the month of March when some days still tend to be wintry. In addition to my shoes, the Romanian representatives of law and order also kept the two pairs of pants and my personal food supply that I had in my rucksack. They even reached into my inside coat pocket where two neatly folded 100 000 Lei bank notes were placed. Luckily, the money had slipped through a hole in the pocket so that I was able to retrieve it later from inside the lining.

Under cover of darkness, we made it to the border where we came upon a stone marker that had a tactilely discernible M for "Magyarország" (Hungary) chiseled on one side and an R (for Romania) on the other. As we continued to advance northward cautiously, we had to stop and lie still repeatedly, because some dogs at farm houses in the vicinity kept on barking in a manner that could have given away the direction in which we might have been pursued. While we tried to forge ahead as quietly as possible, it kept getting darker and darker, which was good in a way, but it also hampered our orientation. We literally had to hang on to each other's coat tails to avoid wandering off in different directions. After a while, we began to fear that we might be going around in circles so we decided to stop for the night in a field storage shed we had come upon. Multiple layers of vineyard stakes covered the ground inside, but that did not keep us from falling fast asleep as soon as we took the load off our feet.

At daybreak, two of us woke up while the others were still snoring. To our great disappointment, we could see a border guard through the morning fog on a nearby watchtower. There was no chance of continuing our journey now without being seen for sure! We had no choice but to remain in the shed all day until nightfall. It occurred to us that the owner might decide to come out to do some work, but luckily neither he nor anyone else did. By chewing on a strip of salty rind from a piece of bacon that one fellow had in a coat pocket, we tried to still our hunger somewhat. Naturally, it made us quite thirsty. With nothing to drink, the day turned out to be even more of a drag. While reconnoitering the area through small crevices in the walls, we could see that at a short distance toward the tower there was a ditch with a footpath alongside of it leading toward a paved road that seemed to go in the direction of the nearest Hungarian town.

After nightfall, we first headed for the ditch and quenched our thirst not caring about possible pollutants or parasites that might have been in the water from early spring runoffs. We nervously took turns with our flask that only held about eight ounces. That night I learned how to drink out of a bottle without siphon interference. Afterward, we walked to the nearest town, which turned out to be Kiszombor, Hungary (H-6775). At the Market Square, the four of us approached a man by the artesian well and asked for information. When he failed to respond to my second question posed in Hungarian, I remembered the definition that three persons were regarded as a crowd. Thus, we relented and quietly quenched our thirst whereupon we entered one of the side streets in search of shelter for the night. Since most occupants of houses chose to ignore our knocks on their doors, we were about to give up and move on when we met a man who seemed to be waiting for us in front of his small residence.

He kindly invited us to come inside where we met the members of his family including a set of grandparents. Upon introducing ourselves, we sat down and told them about our intended trek to Austria. In turn, we were told about the recent conversion of the Hungarian currency from Pengös to Forints in early March 1947. They also showed us some of the tremendously inflated old banknotes which had a very high face value printed on them. Pointing to a basket containing worthless Pengös, they indicated that the pouch for carrying money often had to be larger than the bag holding the goods one got in return. Store clerks were no longer even able to tally amounts with endless digits whose totals ran into trillions and more; thus, shopping transactions resembled a form of bartering where individual banknotes were simply exchanged for certain items.

It was quite obvious that the two-generation family living in the small house did not have any room to spare, but they offered to let us bed down on some straw in the open hallway for which we were very grateful. In the morning, they purchased my empty rucksack that actually was a doubled-up grain sack. The two Forints I received amounted to more than we needed to cover the toll that was payable upon crossing the footbridge spanning the Tisza River at Szeged. None of the regular bridges had been rebuilt yet. Another way of crossing would have been by ferry upon payment of a fee as well.

Our attempts at Szeged to sell some of our clothes for travel money remained futile. Hungarians we talked to turned out to be very kindhearted. Rather than trying to take advantage of us by offering a mere pittance for our coats for example, they advised us not to part with our clothes since nights could still be quite chilly. A Good Samaritan persuaded us to report to authorities that would provide transportation to Austria. In essence, the kind man was right, but his prediction did not materialize without a hitch. Just as we were about to enter a law enforcement facility, an overly zealous official or plainclothes detective happened to come out the door. Upon hearing the Good Samaritan's summary of the situation, the person said that he would take care of things. To our great dismay, he presented us to the desk sergeant as vagrants he claimed to have apprehended wandering on the street! Since the scoundrel purporting to represent law and order entered corresponding formal charges, we were now subject to due process.

Initially, we were placed in a clean unfurnished room along with other refugees present; then, the four of us were locked into a regular cell where we had to spend six days for having crossed the border illegally - "határátlépés-véget," as it was officially called. Since no charges had been leveled against the other refugees who had entered the country the same way, they were fortunate enough to be spared the composite humiliation of incarceration and louse infestation through filthy jail cell mattresses! After a total time delay of about twelve days at Szeged, all of us refugees were put on a train headed for Budapest. We arrived there in early April 1947. Like thousands of other post-war refugees, we were cleared through the processing center known as the "tolonc-ház" (abode for transients).

The fortified compound in which the "tolonc-ház" was located had high walls all around from which armed guards were watching all the time. The largest massive brick building within the walls served as the refugee-housing center. A somewhat smaller brick building within the complex was called "kis fogház" (small prison). Its occupants included convicted black marketers, pickpockets, petty larcenists, and women who were practicing the world's oldest profession without an officially issued license.

Off to one side was a smaller building that had one large room and an anteroom with about three toilette stalls and only one lavatory. This building was called "egeres" (mouse

66

bin). It served as a holding area for newly arrived adult males. Families were placed in the large building upon going through a delousing procedure. The "mouse bin" was so crowded when we got there that it was difficult to get to a toilette without stepping on someone in the darkness of night. People were lying all over the tiled floor since there were not enough bare wire berths available to accommodate everyone.

The toilettes turned out to be quite a mess also and it became apparent that some detainees suffered from bleeding hemorrhoids. Tissue paper was in very short supply. Other materials used as napery like notebook paper, pages torn out of books, newsprint, cloth, etc. caused clogged pipes and overflowing bowls. Fortunately, we were not kept in this "facility" for long. At the delousing station, we had to bundle our clothes; they were processed through heated malodorous fumigation drums while we took a shower and had our pubic hair shorn. Upon donning our treated clothes again, we were placed in collective dorm rooms at the "tolonc-ház."

Three times a day a ladle of warm soup was dispensed in individual bowls that were handed out, but there were no spoons provided. Once a day, we were issued about 350 grams of good-tasting wheat bread. Rather than eating it themselves, some internees used theirs for barter or to "pay" for things like haircuts or cigarettes. Seeing grown men who seemed sensible in other respects eager to trade their scanty bread rations even for recycled tobacco demonstrated how utterly demeaning it was for a person to become addicted to something. Many languishing smokers stooped to beg for a single puff out of someone else's slobbered-up cigarette butt. It certainly looked pitiful and disgusting to me! Another thing that surprised me under given realities was that selfish exploitative capitalist behavior flourished even under communism where solidarity was supposed to prevail. Trading and bartering was going on unimpeded so that several entrepreneurial individuals wound up with a pile of mildewing bread stashed among their clothes, while the masses around them had to contend with perpetual hunger! Human foibles become more visible among people confined in close quarters.

My companions Georg, Hans, and Tony wound up in the dorm room across the hall from where I was placed. The rooms had no furniture other than wire berths on which most detainees slept fully clothed. Knee-high walls about six inches wide lined the walking area in the center. They were meant for detainees to sit on. Smooth linoleum on the floors facilitated cleaning. Sizable undraped windows on two sides made the rooms rather bright especially when the sun was shining; however, we were admonished to keep away from them because the guards had orders to shoot at people seen there.

Most detainees were quite tense, sullen, and sort of detached. It was as if they feared revealing too much of themselves by talking in the presence of a medley of unfamiliar faces. There also seemed to be considerable indecision regarding proper conduct under newly adopted communist ways of doing things. Everyone was focused on getting out of there as soon as possible in order to continue the intended journey. Mealtimes constituted highlights of each boring day. There was momentary excitement when starving men dashed to retrieve food particles off the floor that had accidentally fallen from a ladle as chow was dispensed from a portable kettle.

One day as I was sitting on the knee-high wall trying to tell time by the incidence of sunlight as it traversed the floor in the course of a day, a young Hungarian in-house worker came to the dorm room and asked loudly, "ki akar dolgozni?" (Who wants to work?). Without hesitation, I told him that I did. He looked me up and down and said he was hoping to find somewhat older workers; but since no one else volunteered, he asked me to follow him. I was given an oval metal identification tag about 3X5 inches in size to hang around my neck with a string. The inscription in black letters on a white background read: "Házi Munkás 55" (in-house worker #55). The tag had to be worn visibly on my chest whenever I left the dorm so that the guards would not regard me as someone who was not entitled to move about freely within the compound. I was assigned to clean-up duties at the "kis fogház" (small prison). My tasks included a) washing the stone floor in the main lobby, b) handing out metal bowls to inmates at mealtimes, c) washing the bowls afterwards, d) helping to pick up bread rations for distribution once a day, and e) cleaning vacated jail cells.

Although I received no pay for any of this work, there were compensatory benefits involved like reduced boredom and opportunities to meet local staff including a guard called "Tasi tizedes-ur" (corporal Tashi). Furthermore, there was usually extra food left over for us in-house workers. Often I even managed to supplement the rations of my confined companions whose hungry tummies were discernible right through their languid eyes! Occasionally, some harlots behind bars jokingly sported samples of their seductive verbal utterances and thereby inadvertently provided spontaneous entertainment. Last, but not least, I was able to hear contemporary songs by inmates who sang like birds in a cage. One song that I heard from a cell for the very first time was the Hungarian version of the Spanish song "Besame mucho" (kiss me passionately). As I recollect, it went like this: "Szeretlek-én, jö vissza hozám. Szeretnék lázassan csokolni ujra a szád. Ejnye ugy sir a nota! Nélküled keled-be tél van és nem lesz nyár." (I love you. Come back to me. I would love to passionately kiss your lips again. Oh hear the plaintive song! Without you, there is winter in the East and summer never arrives).

After having spent about four weeks at the "tolonc-ház" in Budapest, my compatriots Hans Elmer and Tony Lafleur were among those who were expedited toward Austria near the end of April 1947, which ended my contact with them. A day or two later, it was Georg's and my turn, but our departure was delayed because of the observance of May 1st as one of the communists' most important holidays. Although this was the only day when meat was on the menu even for us detainees, I would have preferred to get out of there right away. Upon being separated from those who remained behind, Georg and I wound up in heavily bedbug-infested quarters. As soon as it got dark, the pests crawled out from behind the trim and from crevices in the wood floor of the crowded room where those of us scheduled for departure had to spend two nights. Normally, people who were shipped out spent only one night there, but we had to provide the blood-sucking critters with an encore during a second night! I was chewed up so badly that it looked like I had some sort of rash on the sides of my neck. I felt quite drawn too for lack of sleep. I often wondered what kind of communicative diseases the bedbugs could have transmitted.

A train took us from Budapest to Hegyeshalom where approximately sixty of us transient males were crowded into a room until nightfall. Females were kept in another room until it was time to leave. For supper, each of us received some bread with a delicious marmalade spread. Subsequently, we were given pointers on how to reduce chances of being caught while crossing the border into Austria stealthily. It struck me as quite ironic: At Szeged, my companions and I had to serve time for a boundary violation of the type that Hungarian authorities were now actually prompting us to carry out by crossing into Austria under cover of night! They instructed us to a) move very quietly in small groups, b) not to follow any roads but to walk across fields instead, and c) to go further inland rather than stopping at the nearest town on the other side of the border.

A Danube Swabian woman with her 3-year old boy approached us about tagging along with Georg and me. We consented to having them join us. Since the Hungarians only released small groups of refugees every so often, it got to be around 10:30 p. m. before the four of us were set free to venture across uneven terrain toward Austria. Fortunately, we encountered no Austrian guards along the way. We only happened to see another small group of people trying to get their bearings in the dark. After having walked for quite a while, the four of us arrived at a road junction that sported signs with German writing! It was profoundly exhilarating to be in a country at last where our native idiom was NOT a foreign language. One of the signs pointed to the border town of Nickelsdorf and another one to Zurndorf, which we thought was still too close to the border; therefore, we decided to keep on walking further inland. Around 3:00 a. m. we stumbled into a barn and hit the hay for some overdue sleep.

When I woke up at daybreak, a man was talking to Georg in an Austrian dialect with which I was quite unfamiliar yet. It turned out to be the owner of the barn who had come to fetch some feed for his livestock. The farmer did not seem surprised about our presence. He probably had encountered other refugees there before. The kind fellow said it was OK for us to rest there as long as we will leave afterwards; however, if we decided to stay, he would have to report us to the authorities in accordance with local ordinances. When Georg asked the owner for a cigarette, the man's face turned pale and he hastened to point out that smoking was not permitted on the premises, because it could start a fire! To me, the tense moment served as a reminder of another hazard associated with this contemptible habit! At that time, the U. S. Surgeon General had yet to determine that it was also seriously detrimental to people's health.

As we prepared to get moving again, it became evident that the little boy could not wear his shoes, because of large ruptured blisters on both of his heels. The broken skin revealed some pink subcutaneous tissue and made me shiver at the thought of how painful it must have been! I could not help but admire the little guy who made no fuss about it. When we were trotting along, his mother had asked him to keep quiet so that we could get across the border undetected. She explained to him that they would get to see his father sooner if there were no further delays to contend with. The little fellow obviously understood the situation perfectly.

We continued our journey by following the road to the next town, which was Gattendorf. The boy's mother and Georg alternately carried the little one. At Gattendorf, we were invited into the apartment of a woman whose husband was killed in

Russia where he was sent to fight as a German soldier. She shared her bedroom with the boy and his mother while permitting Georg and me to bed down on the kitchen floor for which we were truly grateful. The next morning, Georg and I took to the road again, but the boy and his mother were planning to take a bus with money that was to be wire-transferred to them by the boy's father from Linz, Upper Austria.

As Georg and I were walking along on the road leading from Gattendorf toward Bruck on the Leitha River, we encountered our first Austrian gendarme who happened to accompany an attractive young woman. They were headed in the opposite direction. The officer asked us questions about our destination and where we came from. Then he told us to be sure to report to the authorities in the next town, which was Neudorf. By the time Georg and I reached its outskirts however, we had decided not to submit to rigmarole of bureaucratic processing again that had cost us valuable time at Szeged and Budapest. Instead of continuing on the same road where the gendarme had threatened to pursue us all the way to Bruck, we followed a side road to a village named Parndorf. Upon talking to a local woman, we learned that her husband was a prisoner of war in Yugoslavia, of whom she was anxiously awaiting news. Although we had no relevant information to offer, she treated us to some welcome libation before we moved on.

From Parndorf, we followed the road to Pachfurt. We got there at high noon on the first Sunday in May 1947. There was no one to be seen anywhere until a man happened to come out of a house across the street. As we approached him, he began to smile and when we told him that we were refugees from Yugoslavia, he surprised us by saying, "so am I." He invited us to a most welcome hot meal and we talked about various things. Soon, other locally residing refugees joined us for more conversation. An elderly woman who sat on a chair next to mine kept looking at me from the corner of her eye, because of my chewed-up neck and my weird-looking attire.

My oversized shoes had to be tied around my insteps so that they would stay on my feet. The color of the originally white socks I wore had changed to an uneven light gray. They were rather visible because I had to pull them up over the lower part of my charcoal-gray corduroy riding pants. On my torso, I wore a hand-me-down, snug, red cardigan sweater with puckered upper sleeves, which used to belong to Anna Frecot, the daughter of my former employer at Tomnatic/Triebswetter, Romania. My appearance obviously made the good woman in the next chair wonder about me! While the weather had been on the cool side, my overcoat pretty well concealed my ill-fitting array of clothes.

Our compatriots at Pachfurt felt that the chances of finding satisfactory employment were greater at nearby Höflein, because it had a larger number of wealthier farmers. We were referred to a fellow refugee who happened to live and work in that town. Upon visiting with this man and his family for a while and telling them about ourselves, he introduced us to prospective employers. Georg wound up working for two women who needed a man for farming. I was lucky enough to be hired for 50 Austrian Schillings ($2.00) per month plus room and board by Michael and Katharina Artner whose only child Richard was six years old. Their residence at Höflein 20, Lower Austria, also became my address for the next eighteen months from May 5, 1947 until October 12, 1948. After having had to endure various kinds of privation by age sixteen, it was great to have arrived among compassionate people who accepted me on good faith as a hired hand.

6. Emergent Teenager in a Ruined Country

The Lower Austrian town of Höflein is located 5 km from Bruck on the Leitha River and about thirty-five km SE of Vienna. The steeple of Höflein's Catholic Church atop a hill constitutes a prominent area landmark. Notwithstanding its religious purpose, retreating German troops used the sanctified structure as a military observation post while being pursued by advancing Red Army units in 1945. A Soviet artillery shell quickly demolished the structure. Another local manifestation of wartime cataclysm could still be seen in 1947 right in front of the house of the Michael Artner family where a Russian tank was blown up by a German land mine. Propelled by the powerful blast, the turret landed on the roof of the family residence causing considerable slate and structural damage. One of the tank's crewmembers was thrown about forty feet across a small pond against the house façade. He expired of internal injuries in the very room that I moved into about two years later.

My employer Michael Artner was fifty-six years old when I was hired in May 1947, at age sixteen, and his wife Katharina, née Sailer was forty-four. Right after the war, Mr. Artner had been imprisoned for a year because of his membership in the National Socialist German Workers Party (NSDAP). He seemed to have actually enjoyed his confinement in a correctional institution that was shared with political inmates he had long admired! Mr. Artner was an avid reader of *Das kleine Volksblatt,* a conservative Christian newspaper that toed the line of the "Österreichische Volkspartei" (ÖVP - Austrian people's party). He apparently knew a lot about politics but I was far too uninformed and naive to be a competent conversation partner when he felt like talking. Upon realizing that his views and levels of thought transcended my half-baked adolescent ones, he would simply acquiesce. Obviously, the generation gap between us was just too great and our respective outlook on things quite dissimilar.

Mr. Artner dearly loved his wife and their son Richard whose ailing paternal grandmother also lived on the premises. The entire family was very civil and urbanely tolerant toward omnipresent post-war refugees. Mrs. Artner's father, Mr. Sailer, a retired blacksmith living in his house nearby, was seventy-four years old and hard of hearing. Part of his house was rented to a German expellee couple named Groiss, from Engerau, Czechoslovakia. Mr. Sailer's oldest son lost his life at the Russian front and his youngest son Hans had studied to become a priest, but later got married instead and raised a family. Mr. Sailer's other daughter, Mrs. Barbara Grießler, was living in Vienna with her two sons Adolf and Richard.

Mr. Artner not only worked his own farmland but also that of his father-in-law Mr. Sailer. Their joint holdings of about seventy acres included some vineyards and two cellars equipped with ancient winepresses. Each of these dinosaurs sported a wooden beam about 18 inches square and sixteen to eighteen feet long. A big stone block the size of a cubic yard had a spindle attached to it by means of an iron ball joint. The other end of the spindle was threaded through the beam. It served to lift the stone so that it would exert pressure upon grape husks stashed within a square space formed by small braced boards. Grooves directed the grape juice to a container that was emptied into barrels.

The Artners owned two horses, four cows, five hogs, and a flock of chickens. They also had a couple of gardens with some fruit trees. Mr. Artner took care of the horses and I attended to the cows except for milking, which was done by Mrs. Artner. She also fed the hogs and the chickens. In addition to the well in the garden for watering plants and livestock, the Artners had one faucet on the premises that dispensed municipal water. Their well by the kitchen door was no longer in use because of contamination through seepage and debris. The concrete manure-bin nearby had cracks in it, but the outhouse seemed to be at a safe distance across the yard by the barn.

The work tempo in the Artner household was much more temperate than what it used to be among Danube Swabian farmers, who were hard to keep up with. At Höflein, we got up at daybreak and quit working by nightfall. After lunch, Mr. Artner routinely sat down to read the newspaper and normally fell asleep in the process. During his siesta time, I usually kept busy cleaning the barn or tending to the garden. While working in the fields, frequent breaks were the norm to rest the horses, too. Invariably, we also had a snack between meals in adherence to local customs. The morning snack is formally called "Gabelfrühstück" and the one in the afternoon is known as the "Jause." Most often, we enjoyed some smoked bacon with Mrs. Artner's own blend of homemade whole wheat and rye bread that tasted delicious and was quite nutritious all by itself. Frequently, heavy syrup made from sugar beets was used as a spread. Having wine at break times was also customary and in no way frowned upon, as it happens to be in more demure societies.

For many of our meals, Mrs. Artner was uniquely adept in preparing a variety of dishes called "Sterz." One kind was made with farina, another with white flour, and yet another with potatoes. These hot dishes tasted particularly good to me with cold milk poured over them; however, my debt of gratitude to Mrs. Artner was not exclusively based on her culinary skills but also upon other obliging acts of kindness. Her first comforting demonstration of benevolence toward me occurred when she tactfully inquired about my chewed-up neck, which still bore visible traces of my irksome exposure to bedbugs at the "tolonc-ház" in Budapest. As a wise precaution, she offered to boil all of my clothes to make sure that I would be free of unwanted pests. It felt wonderful to wear clean clothes again and to be able to bathe regularly!

In due course of time, Mrs. Artner also managed to acquire items of used clothing for me by bartering food for them. On weekends, individuals called "Hamsterer" in allusion to hoarding, generally came from Vienna to trade all sorts of goods for food, which continued to be partially rationed until the early 1950's. Mrs. Artner was also instrumental in getting me "legitimized" with the authorities at the district capital of Bruck on the Leitha by obtaining identification papers and ration cards for me. Another example of the Artners' kindness was provided in conjunction with the country's currency devaluation in 1948. Rather than diminishing my scant accumulated earnings by two-thirds in accordance with the official three-for-one exchange rate, they agreed to pay me retroactively in new currency for the entire period of my employment with them. Even after I had quit my job there, the couple favored me with a package of fresh sausage, which was mailed to my subsequent place of residence at Bad Ischl, Upper Austria!

In post-war Austria, personal identification booklets were printed in four languages: English, French, German, and Russian. They also included a photograph. Upon the country's severance from the Third Reich in 1945, Austria was divided into separate British, French, Soviet, and U. S. zones of occupation. It took another ten years before the new republic was granted independence in 1955 with the proviso that it would pursue a policy of strict neutrality. While the country was under four-power occupation, Austrian citizens could freely cross demarcation lines from one zone to another but non-citizens were not allowed to do so under prevailing regulations. To permit speedier identification at checkpoints, the ID dockets of natives had light brown covers and the ones for non-citizens were olive-colored. By some stroke of luck, mine turned out to be brown also. Consequently, a casual glance at my papers did not reveal that I was a "stateless" person since Yugoslavia had rescinded my rights of citizenship in November 1944 (AVNOJ decree) along with those of that country's entire German minority.

In possession of valid identification papers at last, I was now able to reach out unafraid in efforts to locate the members of my widely scattered family. Since I had no notebook or old letters for reference, I had to rely on memory for addresses. I sent one letter to Gloggnitz, Lower Austria, where my mother's youngest brother, Uncle Anton MARTIN (1915-1980) had been working in coal mining. His former landlady Mrs. Antonia Streicher was good enough to reply but she was unable to provide a forwarding address. The best she could do was to let me know that he was transferred to mining operations near Ebensee, Upper Austria. In contrast to this partially useful response, my letter to our former waiter Kanász István at Banat-Topola yielded much better results. He happened to be in touch with my half brother Michael STEIGERWALD (1923-1956) who was languishing in a Yugoslav POW camp until 1948 as a former Wehrmacht (regular German army) soldier.

Upon getting in touch with Michael, I received the addresses of other relatives including that of my sister Rose. She was in touch with additional family members so that I was soon able to correspond with them also. The only close relative whom we were unable to locate for over five more years was our youngest brother Tony! In response to inquiries at the Red Cross, we were informed that he had joined "his" mother at Philadelphia, Pennsylvania. Since my sister and I had attended our mother's funeral with Tony at Banat-Topola, we were truly puzzled by this inaccurate reply. In January 1954 we were finally able to clarify the mystery surrounding the matter that served as the basis for the Armstrong Circle Theater TV episode shown on June 12, 1956. In partial reference to special legislation that was introduced to avert Tony's deportation, the program had the title "H. R. 8438 - The Story of a Lost Boy."

It turned out that Yugoslav orphanage personnel had mistaken our brother Tony for someone else so that he was indeed sent to America in lieu of a boy whose mother's name happened to be the same as that of ours. On December 28, 1944, this woman had been taken to the Soviet Union as one of many ethnic-German forced laborers from East Central Europe. Her small children Maria (*1937) and Johann (*1939) stayed with their grandmother until all ethnic-Germans remaining in Yugoslavia were confined to local forced labor and attrition camps in April 1945 as part of a knowingly disavowed "ethnic cleansing" policy carried out by Tito's partisans (cf. Greg Steinmetz in the Bibliography). When the Russians released the mother of Maria and Johann to East Germany in June 1947 because of illness, she was permitted to come to the U.S. where she was born. Efforts to have her children brought to her from Yugoslavia took almost three years because of complications attributable to Yugoslav bureaucratic entanglements that unduly prolonged anxiety, privation, and heartaches notwithstanding the eventual favorable outcome.

Many experiences of other relatives were also depressing, enervating, and dramatic in some ways. Fragmentary accounts of what all of us had been through respectively were included in our correspondence during the post-war era. When I was not writing letters in my spare time, I often enjoyed reading books, like my mother used to do. One of the titles I remember was *Der hohe Schein* (Tall Beacons) by Ludwig Ganghofer (1855-1920) whose novels romanticize Alpine beauty and down-to-earth folk life. *Das Gewissen der Welt* (Worldly Averment), an opus by a different author, was another book I remember reading. It had an American setting and included a family named McCormick. Since some protagonists in the novel were involved in manufacturing farm machinery, I could not help but wonder whether there might have been a connection between them and the makers of the McCormick-brand harvester my family used to own back at Banat-Topola.

On weekends, I would join other locally employed refugees for conversation and relaxation. Sometimes, we attended area dances or visited a movie theater at Bruck on the Leitha, which was about three miles from Höflein. One black-and-white Russian film I saw there had the title "Die steinerne Blume" (The stone flower). The plot dealt with a soldier and his girl whose mutual devotion and youthful idealism had to overcome quite a few harsh twists of fate. My own contact with girls remained rather superficial at Höflein and never culminated in having even casual sex with anyone; however, there was one local girl around my age that appealed to me. The sparkle in her blue eyes suggested an innate potential for happiness that I could have seen myself nurturing far longer than my uncertain existence permitted me to even try to project. Her lucid blond hair seemed to reflect sunlight even under overcast skies! She was slender and about five feet and two inches tall. Her name was Mitzi (Mary) and her family lacked wealth so that even a pauper like me might not have faced prompt rejection upon trying to approach her. One of her two older sisters had a child out of wedlock. The idea of me getting Mitzi into a similar situation made me resist thoughts of actually pursuing her.

Attending cultural events in neighboring towns was both time-consuming and physically tiring because of distances involved in getting to and from nearby places on foot. Consequently, I dreamt of owning a bicycle, but I did not have enough money to buy even a good used one. Upon foraging in area scrap heaps, I was lucky enough to find an old rusty but intact frame with some usable parts still on it. Digging around in junk was fraught with danger at the time because some of the piles contained live grenades, discarded shells, and unexploded duds. In due course of time, I managed to assemble a working unit but getting tires and inner tubes proved to be quite impossible since rubber products continued to be rationed and in short supply until the early 1950's. Thanks to the skills of Grandpa Sailer's tenant Mr. Groiss, we were able to splice pieces of inner tubes together so that they were inflatable. By overlapping sections of tires on the rim, it eventually became possible for me to ride my own bicycle; however, grains of sand invariably found their way to the inner tubes and punctured them. They required patching after almost every trip out of town. The situation did not improve until I was finally able to get a brand new set of Semperit tires some time after I began to earn more money as a painter's helper at Bad Ischl, Upper Austria.

By mutual agreement with the Artners, I planned to join my sister at Bad Ischl in October 1948 after harvest-time. Rose was employed as a maid in the household of the city mayor Mr. Fridolin Schröpfer. Before I could go from Lower Austria in the Soviet zone to Upper Austria in the U. S. zone, I had to cross a boundary called "demarcation line." While the Western allies already allowed unchecked travel between zones by then, the Soviets were still screening passengers entering and leaving their areas of jurisdiction. My attempt to cross as a refugee could have been thwarted by them since only Austrian citizens were granted free passage. That is where I lucked out with my identity booklet, which happened to be of the same color as those of indigenous residents.

Before crossing the demarcation line in October 1948, I visited my Aunt Katharina BARBA, née STEIGERWALD (1897-1978) and her husband Nick (1893-1987). They and their daughter Magdalena's family were living at another location in the Soviet zone of Austria near Waidhofen on the Ybbs River. While spending a few days with them and discussing our future, they spoke of their intention to emigrate. Uncle Nick's cousin Peter BARBA was living in Chicago, Illinois, and he agreed to be their sponsor. Aunt Kathi also offered to find a sponsor for me if I decided to join them in America. Due to lengthy screening procedures and backed-up quota allotments it got to be 1950 before they were finally admitted to the U. S. In my own case, three years went by from my initial thoughts of emigration until my actual immigration in October 1951. Considerable soul searching was conducted in the meantime.

When the day arrived for my impending crossing of the demarcation line, I boarded a train headed toward my Upper Austrian destination. My apprehensions about being caught and detained by Soviet inspectors were somehow counterbalanced by optimism. It was a bright sunny day and I did my best to act self-assured when the train stopped for Russian personnel to come aboard. While I looked out a window seemingly unconcerned, a rifle-toting soldier tapped me on the shoulder and asked for my "Ausweis" (identity papers). I calmly took it out of my inside coat pocket and handed it to him with a smile. Upon briefly looking at the photograph inside the front cover and glancing at the last page which was in Russian, he gave it back to me saying "gut" (OK). I thanked him curtly and continued to look out the window, albeit with a lump in my throat. As soon as the train began to move again, I was finally able to relax. The next stop was in the U. S. zone as I could see by some lettering on railroad stock. I felt like shouting for joy but I had to restrain myself out of concern for the other passengers present. Up to that point in my seventeen years of life, I had spent the first ten in the Kingdom of Yugoslavia (1931-1941) under Alexander I (1888-1934) and his brother Regent Paul Karageorgevich (1893-1976). During the next seven years, I was under the jurisdiction of three dictators: Hitler (1889-1945), Tito (1892-1980), and Stalin (1879-1953). Now I could finally look forward to enjoying conditions of freedom in realms where democracy reigns.

At Bad Ischl, my Uncle Anton MARTIN (1915-1980) and his wife Justina, née FESTINI consented to having me stay at their small apartment with them and their infant son Anton Jr. (*1948). I agreed to pay for room and board at the going rate. Housing was truly scarce in post-war Austria and Germany because of the influx of many millions of refugees and as a result of the extensive devastation of many cities that were heavily bombed by the allies right up to Germany's surrender on May 8, 1945. While the challenging task of finding affordable housing was quickly taken care of, my job searches at Bad Ischl seemed to lead nowhere. Officials at the state employment agency wanted to place me with an area farmer since I had applicable experience and because there was a shortage of labor in agriculture. Due to notoriously long working hours and low pay in farming, most of us seeking employment wanted to find jobs in business or industry. I was unable to find work as a construction helper because the season was just ending and my lean built caused potential employers to wonder whether I was strong enough for the heavy manual labor involved.

Indications were that I would have to be separated from family members again while trying to earn a living elsewhere. Meanwhile, Mrs. Schröpfer, the mayor's considerate wife decided to speak with the painting contractor who happened to be working at her house. Being a devout Christian, Mr. Josef Neureiter agreed to employ me on a trial basis as a house painter's helper; thus, I started a job that might have developed into a career if I ever could have taken a liking to it. Exposure to intoxicating paint fumes, contact with lead as well as other chemical substances that were not entirely harmless, and getting paint spattered all over me on a daily basis made me dislike the work from the very beginning! About four years later after I had advanced to the status of a journeyman painter in America, there also were increased pressures to deal with in efforts to satisfy fastidious customers on one hand and profit-conscious employers on the other.

On a personal basis, it should be noted that Mr. Neureiter evidently thought enough of my performance to defend my right to work for his company while native Austrians were unable to find a comparable position. Officials at the local state employment agency were trying to deny me a work permit but Mr. Neureiter told them unequivocally: It's him I want or no one! Reluctantly, a work permit was issued but it had to be renewed every six months and was only valid for the duration of my employment at the Neureiter Company.

Bad Ischl had a population of about 15 000 at the time; however, in spite of its small size it was a renowned saline and sulfur-bath spa and the historic summer residence of Francis Joseph I (1830-1916), Emperor of Austria (1848-1916). The composer Franz Lehár (1879-1948) was one of the city's famous contemporary residents when I moved to Bad Ischl in October 1948. Upon his death shortly thereafter, he was lying-in-state at the local Catholic Church; thus, I had a chance to pay my respects, too. It felt like I was saying good-bye to the proverbial good old days. In addition to having composed "The Merry Widow" and other memorable operettas, his musical creations also included rousing marches and beautiful waltzes of which the one entitled "Gold und Silber" is probably best known.

Since the number of journeymen painters employed by my master contractor at Bad Ischl was quite small, I wound up with countless opportunities to get involved in ceiling, wall, and trim area preparations and in actual applications of a variety of coatings to diverse surfaces. Working alongside professionally trained painters, I learned quite a bit during the next three years of employment there, from October 19, 1948, until September 21, 1951. My cumulative specialized knowledge and practical experience proved sufficient for me to be admitted to the Chicago painters' union a few months after my eventual arrival in the United States.

In addition to what I had learned about house painting at Bad Ischl, I also completed some evening courses in other subject areas at the local *Hauptschule* and privately. Areas covered included English, French, Typing, Shorthand, and Ballroom Dancing. I also had occasions to attend concerts and theatrical performances with my sister Rose who enjoyed going to dances with me as her chaperone. To improve my comprehension of English, I frequented local cinemas where Hollywood movies were shown "undubbed" with original sound tracks. Some films also provided realistic glimpses of life in America.

Certain aspects of life anywhere can seem rather implausible. An experience I had at Bad Ischl fell into such a category. Gretel was a single girl in her mid-twenties living on the upper floor in the same house with her widowed mother. One night, Gretel came down to my room in her pink nightgown as I was lying in bed reading. We conversed as we had on previous occasions in the hallway, for instance. Since it was a bit chilly in my room, I invited her to come into bed with me. She did and we continued our conversation. Gretel was a brunette of average intelligence, height, and features, but she did not appeal to me in an amorous or erotic way. In other words, I did not get excited or even slightly aroused having her next to me in the same bed! I did not feel an urge to kiss her either. After a while, she left and I continued reading as before. As I reminisced about this occurrence later, I could not help but wonder about celestial forces that may guide us or even predetermine the course of our existence.

Occasionally, I took a train on weekends to see relatives and fellow compatriots at other cities especially those living in or around Salzburg. Many commemorative snapshots were taken at such gatherings but their significance has faded with the passage of time. In contrast to that, the museums and architectural landmarks we visited continue to be of interest to travelers from near and far. Austria's beautiful landscapes also remain sources of enjoyment for natives and tourists alike, along with unforgettable culinary delights one can still enjoy in that country. Even simple things like salt sticks or Kaiser rolls tasted better to me there than anywhere in the world. Their excellent assortment of sausages and the famous Viennese pastries continue to speak for themselves.

Experiencing life in Austria even as a post-war refugee constituted a positive step forward for me despite the fact that the country itself was still quite out of kilter. However, integration into society there would have taken quite a bit longer than in the U. S., for example, where I had to learn a new language to boot! Unlike people in America who see themselves as part of a nation of immigrants, indigenous Austrians take pride in being moored in traditions. There is a feeling that newcomers have to pay protracted assimilation dues in kind before they can expect to be viewed as quasi-equals. As an adolescent who had been set adrift along with Yugoslavia's entire unwanted German minority, I yearned to gain a foothold somewhere in order to resume a normal life. My schooling had been interrupted and there was no apparent chance to continue my formal education any time soon. While having to make do with a job I did not like, my propitious formative years were slipping away irretrievably. It prompted the question, what kind of future I would be able to carve out for myself under given circumstances? My provisional work permit at Bad Ischl gave me a feeling of being suspended in some sort of limbo going nowhere.

According to predictions circulating at the time, young people's career opportunities were going to continue to be limited in Austria for a couple of decades to come, because it was going to take that long just to clear away all the war-time rubble! I could not see myself trudging along for years without reasonable career prospects. I had no way of foreseeing the approaching "Wirtschaftswunder" (economic miracle) that started in the mid-1950's and ushered in unheard-of opportunities for workers right in the heart of Europe. From my perspective, based on circumstances around me in the early 1950's, emigration to an overseas country seemed to offer a way to get somewhere vocationally. My endeavors to get in touch with Aunt Theresa HUHN, née MARTIN (1904-1971) in Buenos Aires, Argentina, and Uncle Jacob MARTIN (1909-1988) in São Paulo, Brazil, remained entirely fruitless. I could only conclude that conditions in their respective countries were not favorable enough for them to invite displaced European family members to come there for a new start in life. That realization clearly diminished my options and intensified my hopes of being able to qualify for immigration to the United States of America.

82

Aunt Katharina BARBA kept her promise to find a U. S. citizen who would sponsor me as an immigrant in accordance with contemporary laws. Sponsors had to give the U. S. government signed assurances that the person(s) in question would not become a public liability. In my case, a total stranger named Walter Ziegler was gracious enough to assume that responsibility vis-à-vis Uncle Sam. By autumn 1950, I received a letter from the American embassy, in which I was asked to appear at Linz, Upper Austria, for initial processing. There were forms to fill out and questions to be answered in verbal interviews. I also had to submit a *Leumundszeugnis* (certificate of good conduct) issued by police authorities. A complete physical examination also constituted part of the thorough screening. If I would have had a criminal record or taken illegal drugs, I would not have been able to pass muster.

Within a year, I had my U. S. immigration papers. Upon reporting to an office near the fire-damaged "Hotel Europa" at Salzburg in September 1951, I boarded a train for Bremerhaven along with other emigrants. Until then, I had never set foot into Germany proper. Housing was provided at two installations: *Lager Grohn* was primarily for families and *Lager Lesum* for adults traveling solo. I wound up at the latter. While waiting day by day until my name was among those posted on a bulletin board for impending embarkation, I went sightseeing with other young emigrants. Though I personally felt like I had been set adrift once again, meeting so many new people in a similar stage in life was suggestive of certain new beginnings. Single young adults like me also had opportunities to enjoy the company of unattached girls of comparable age and to swap a "good-night" kiss or two.

Among a handful of eligible bachelor girls in my circle of acquaintances there was a pretty blue-eyed blonde nineteen years of age. She appeared to be complaisant enough to cooperate in having me experience what I was dreaming of since the onset of puberty; however, at the decisive moment someone entered and turned the lights on in the dorm room where we happened to be. The abrupt intrusion not only shattered the singular mood then and there, but it also prompted deferral of evocative romantic pursuit to longed-for opportunities in the New World.

III. IMMIGRATION - ACCULTURATION - NATURALIZATION
7. Crossing the Atlantic and First Jobs in Chicago

Decommissioned U. S. troop ships were used for transporting emigrants from Europe to overseas countries during the late 1940's and in the early 1950's. The vessels *General Sturgis* and *General Taylor* were among those that made several voyages to the United States. The ship named *General J. H. McRae* aboard which I immigrated only served once as a carrier of newcomers to America. Having been built in 1944 for the U. S. Navy with a rating of 13,000 gross register tons (G.R.T.), it could achieve a maximum speed of 18 knots. Its length was 190 meters and its width 24 meters. The ship propeller was powered by a 9,000 horsepower steam turbine. Steam was generated in boilers that were heated with fuel oil. "Our" crew included 185 merchant marines and 20 navy men. Mr. Nils Gelin was the ship's captain. Transport commander was L.C.D.R. Harlow Hines. IRO Escort Officer Mr. J. Bjorn Vennorod and his Assistant Miss A. Svingjorn served as liaisons between passengers and ship personnel. Most of the vessels used by the International Refugee Organization (IRO) were rented from the U. S. government. IRO was working closely with about sixty volunteer relief agencies from various countries to facilitate the movement of refugees and displaced persons (DP's).

By means of forty ships, IRO resettled over one million persons between July 1947 and December 1951. Michael R. Marrus provided applicable information in his book *The Unwanted: European Refugees in the Twentieth Century* (New York: Oxford University Press, 1985), pp. 343-344. Destinations included ports of call in the Americas, Australia, and New Zealand. Otto Folberth provided further statistics in his article "Mensch und Materie in der Bilanz der IRO," *Berichte und Informationen des österreichischen Forschungsinstituts für Wirtschaft und Politik*, vol. 6, No. 279 of November 23, 1951 (Salzburg, 1951), p. 3. Destinations and respective numbers of people involved: USA 308,491, Australia 179,501, Israel 131,934, Canada 113,299, England 86,094, France 38,317, Argentina 32,162, Brazil 27,583, Belgium 22,447, Venezuela 17,091, Paraguay 5,834, Chile 4,867, and The Netherlands 4,315. - Data reprinted by Anton Hochgatterer, *Entre Rios: Donauschwäbische Siedlung in Südbrasilien* (Salzburg, 1986), p 18.

My transatlantic passage commenced at Bremerhaven, Germany on October 2, 1951. The duration of the voyage was supposed to be eight days; however, because of stormy weather it took us ten days to reach New York. Due to the customary observance of Columbus Day on October 12, we could not disembark until the following day. The crossing proved to be a trying time for most of the 829 or so immigrants, since many happened to get seasick.

My own tummy was squeamish for a day or two also until I learned two techniques for counteracting the effects of the ship's incessant teeter-totter up and down movements under prevailing conditions. One technique entailed eating only enough so that the stomach remained half-empty even though the food was tasty and plentiful. The other technique consisted in the adoption of what some refer to as a sailor's way of walking, i. e., with knees slightly angled so that one's legs can be somewhat distended whenever the floor seems to drop away from under one's feet. On the rebound, when the deck is forcefully heaved upward, bent knees tend to absorb some of the impact; thus, the sensation of one's stomach being surreptitiously subjected to movements of a yo-yo is quite a bit lessened.

At the outset of our journey, many of us passengers were enlisted to help perform certain housekeeping and maintenance tasks to help the crew and to avoid boredom or restlessness. Some men were instructed to scrape and paint portions of the upper deck. Others, including myself, were assigned as dishwashers. A number of people were given the important task of cleaning floors in dormitories, washrooms, and stairwells. Dorm room accommodations consisted of steel-framed canvass berths attached to walls in sets of four over one another. The space between berths was insufficient for sitting up; thus the dorms were not well suited as day rooms. Supervision was carried out by so-called "block leaders" who were also selected from among the ranks of the passengers. Good job performers received honorable mention and task dodgers risked having their landing papers withheld.

During the first couple of days when it did not rain and the sea was calm, many passengers chose to spend time on deck sitting in lounge chairs under blankets. A few people played shuffleboard. Another possible way to pass the time was by walking around between decks, since there were not enough ship lounges to accommodate everyone. During evening hours, crewmembers were watching movies in a lounge but they were not averse to having individual passengers join them. Some of us also attended informal sessions to learn American folk songs like "I've been workin' on the railroad,

"She'll be comin' around the mountain when she comes," "From this valley they say you are going," "Down in the valley," "You are my sunshine," "Home on the range," and others.

The onset of bad weather a few days into our journey put an end to practically all activities mentioned and an increasing number of passengers became sick so that most of the plentiful food remained uneaten and had to be dumped overboard routinely. Creatures of the sea eagerly devoured it. I had never seen so many golden fried whole chickens stacked on open shelves like firewood inside a walk-in refrigerator, ready to be consumed. To me, a refugee who had experienced periods of starvation, it was as though I were belatedly hallucinating! My precarious footing on the shifting vessel made me realize quickly though that relatively few passengers were physically in a position to eat much under the weather-related circumstances.

Groping along in what seemed like a time-lapse rocking motion, the bow of the ship sometimes poked right into the water so that simultaneously approaching heavy waves would actually roll onto the surface of the deck. The massive impact temporarily lifted the aft section out of the water whereupon one could hear the propeller spinning idly in the air. At such times the ship's speed was abruptly reduced so that stainless steel food trays slid off the anchored tables and scampered all over the floor. People had to sit down or hold on to secured structures to keep from suffering bumps or sustaining nasty falls. Some folks inadvertently spilled hot coffee on themselves or on others nearby. During rough sailing episodes like that, the mess hall became truly messy in a hurry with spilled food everywhere. In hallways, stairwells, on decks and in dormitories one was certain to encounter seasick people.

Persistent strong winds made it impossible for passengers to be on unsheltered decks where ropes had been strung to keep crew members from being tossed or swept overboard while they commuted between areas. For long hours on end, unrelenting winds held the ship in a tilted position. Individuals walking in hallways were actually positioned diagonally in the rectangular space as they attempted to maintain their equilibrium. To most of us landlubbers who never experienced anything like it, the scene appeared to be a complex ruse spawned by sinister forces that made everyone desperate for equanimity.

With limited daytime visibility outdoors and the sea churning, it was as if some monster were trying to stir it from the bottom up, rolling wave upon turbulent wave and making the ocean look like a contentious grayish mass at odds with itself. A steady mist sprayed the ship and wetted those who ventured on deck for a breath of fresh air or to satisfy their curiosity. Under given circumstances, it was not surprising that most people on board wished for a speedy termination of the highly uncomfortable voyage.

About a day before "our" ship reached New York, the sea had calmed down enough to permit more restful sleep. It enabled us passengers to overcome the effects of seasickness and helped toward regaining our composure. On Friday, October 12, 1951, we were instructed to take our luggage to Deck B, except for items individuals wished to hand carry ashore. Upon docking at 8:00 a. m. on Saturday October 13, our luggage was unloaded by local employees and taken to a customs inspection area. Among papers given to every passenger the day before, there was the coveted "green card" that identified us as legal U. S. immigrants. A white card that had been issued was the permit for going ashore where we met with a physician who collected and checked our medical records once more. Another form we had filled out aboard ship the day before had to be presented to U. S. customs officials when we picked up our baggage.

The morning of our actual landing, all passengers were scheduled to get up at 4:00 a. m. Breakfast was served as of 4:30 a. m. The linen on all berths had to be replaced with a fresh set that was provided the night before. Cleaning crews were instructed to get the ship into the same shape in which it was at the time of embarkation. Block leaders had to remain in their respective sections until final inspection was carried out by crew members around 6:30 a. m. All of these activities took place while the ship was being maneuvered to its docking place.

My partner in the dishwashing room and I took turns to go on deck in order to see the illuminated New York skyline and, most of all, the mighty Statue of Liberty. She looked awesome and mysterious against the predawn sky and appeared to be larger than I had imagined. Her lofty gaze seemed focused in the direction from which we had just arrived. The sight of the famous icon made me think of the many newcomers before me, including some who stayed in America only temporarily like my maternal grandparents Johann (1875-1919) MARTIN and Anna (1878-1920), née SPRINGER. They were in the U. S. from 1907 until 1909. My Uncle Johann STEIGERWALD (1888-1969) arrived in America a couple of years before WW I. Along with other newcomers from Austria-Hungary, he heeded the summons of Emperor Francis Joseph of Austria and returned to his homeland when fighting had started.

The first passengers to go ashore were families with small children. The next groups included handicapped and elderly folks. Single individuals like me were among the last to disembark. Ellis Island was no longer used as a processing center by then so we never set foot on it. Instead, we were ferried to another location where our luggage had also been taken. During processing, I was given an envelope by representatives of the Travelers Aid Society from my cousin Magdalena WEISZ-MANN, née BARBA (1921-1996). It contained some spending money and a one-way coach ticket to Chicago on a Baltimore & Ohio (B & O) train at the going rate of about $33. Altogether, I owed the Weiszmann family $45 upon my arrival at Chicago along with a debt of gratitude for helping me get off to a decent start in the New World.

The 26-hour train ride from New York to Chicago was by far the longest one I had ever experienced. It gave me a chance to make the acquaintance of other fellow immigrants who traveled in the same direction. I also met some friendly American passengers. One of them showed me an entry in the *Philadelphia Bulletin* that reported the arrival of the vessel *General McRae*. It augmented some of the above data that was gleaned from the mimeographed "General McRae" newsletter No. 4 of October 11, 1951, which was issued aboard ship in several languages. Alfred Liquornik, Joseph Funk, and A. Schaefler edited the German version.

Upon arriving at Chicago on the rainy afternoon of October 14, 1951, I was welcomed at the train station by my cousin Magdalena and her oldest son Andrew WEISZMANN. In my dazed mental and physical condition that was attributable to lack of sleep, nervousness, and fatigue, I had failed to remove my dangling identity tag from my overcoat. Some alert children who passed by in a car while I was getting into a taxi evidently knew what that signified. They promptly shouted: "DP, DP" (displaced person). A fine welcome, I thought, in the land renowned for its tolerance! On second thought, the incident served as a reminder of how similarly blunt children are everywhere. Having barely reached adulthood myself by age twenty, I realized that what was yet to come involved a lot of learning on my part as well.

The taxi made its way to 1317 North Larrabee Street where my Aunt Katharina and her husband Nick BARBA were living in the house they rented from Uncle Nick's cousin Peter BARBA. Along the way, I was able to catch some glimpses of

Chicago while conversing with my relatives in the cab. It looked like a jungle out there with rows of parked cars along curbsides lining the sullied streets. Houses were close together with some porches looking rather lopsided.

The run-down neighborhood where my aunt and uncle lived was in a state of transition as I was told. There used to be quite a few German-speaking immigrants among area residents but many had moved to suburbs along with other Caucasian families. People of Italian descent and black folks were living in the neighborhood now and local grocery stores carried corresponding ethnic foods. Local brands of Italian sausage and bread tasted good to me also for an occasional change. Fortunately, we did not have to travel too far for Hungarian-style sausage and other goodies to which we were more accustomed.

Aunt Katharina whom I called Bäsl-Kathi was famous for the fine pastries she loved to bake. The warm welcome I received upon arriving at her residence was underscored by a delicious meal to which I was treated. Bäsl-Kathi and "Vetter Niklos," as I called Uncle Nick, made me feel right at home and we agreed that I would stay with them and pay $20 weekly for room and board. After a couple of days of rest, cousin Andrew WEISZMANN accompanied me to a job interview by city bus since he already knew his way around parts of Chicago. After having had to face repeated rejections by potential employers in Austria, I was rather pleasantly surprised to be hired right away at Walker-Jimieson, Inc., 311 S. Western Avenue. I began to work in the electronic supplies store picking orders as a stock clerk at the starting rate of $1.00 an hour.

The company's want ad was printed in English but it appeared in the *Abendpost*, a German daily published on Franklin Street in Chicago. I preferred a job where I would have to speak English in order to attain proficiency more rapidly. The private English lessons I had taken in Austria merely enabled me to get by. My work entailed filling written orders for resistors, capacitors, cathode ray tubes, electronic tubes, antennae, etc. Salespersons took orders for parts by telephone or over the counter. To get to my job, I had to ride an Ogden Avenue bus for about 30-40 minutes. The return trip in the evening often took longer because of more sluggish traffic. I worked 44 to 46 hours weekly including half a day on Saturdays. My net weekly pay was between 36 to 38 dollars.

After three months, I received a five-cent hourly raise. Upon paying for room and board, I was left with 16 to 18 dollars weekly. Most of the clothes I had brought with me from Europe were out of style in my new environment. In addition to wanting a new wardrobe, I needed money for transportation, reading materials, accordion and violin lessons, snacks, postage, knickknacks, and leisure activities like going to see movies and attending dances at different German club events. Accordion lessons were offered at the Werk School of Music on 3039 Lincoln Avenue and violin lessons were given by Mr. Hoffmann, an elderly gent who repaired and sold string instruments at his store on Larrabee Street just north of North Avenue.

Some of the "German" dances were held at the Lincoln Turner Hall on Diversey Avenue. Others took place at the Social Turner Hall (now a city parking lot) on Belmont Avenue west of Lincoln and Western Avenues. Opportunities for dancing were also provided at the Roscoe Hall near Damen Avenue and at Paul Habetler's Tavern on North Avenue. The nearest cinema where German and Austrian films were regularly shown was located on North Avenue at Orchard Street. Before long, the Davis Theater located north of Wilson Street on Lincoln Avenue also began to cater to German-speaking audiences.

Right after I had gotten a job in Chicago as of October 19, 1951, I began to attend Americanization classes at the North Avenue YMCA on Larrabee Street during a couple of evenings weekly. The teacher's name was Stephen Mendak. He was of Hungarian ancestry but refused to speak to us in any language but English. Thanks to his efficient instruction, I was sufficiently advanced by the end of the school year to be among classmates who were awarded an eighth grade diploma from the Chicago Board of Education; thus, I was eligible to enroll in high school courses. One of the instructional materials used by Mr. Mendak was the *Federal Textbook on Citizenship: Our Constitution and Government.* It provided *Lessons on the Constitution and Government of the United States for Use in the Public Schools by Candidates for Citizenship.* Simplified Edition, by John G. Harvey. Original Edition, by Catheryn Seckler-Hudson (Washington, D. C.: U. S. Government Printing Office, 1951).

My confidence in Mr. Mendak was high enough that I turned to him for vocational counseling as well. I asked him what career he would pursue as a person in my position. His response was quite apropos but it did not point in a solid direction as I had hoped it would. He simply said, "anything is good, if you are good!" Although his response did not give me anything tangible to go by, it made me realize that I was neither linguistically, psychologically, socially, or economically in a position yet to take full advantage of the freedom of choice America provided. Insufficient self-confidence amounted to an additional handicap that I had to deal with. What had kept me from developing the kind of self-assured deportment that often characterizes young adults was attributable to denigrating personal experiences and other negative factors including the following:

a) Upon becoming orphaned at age thirteen, I felt utterly exposed and vulnerable with no haven of family security to turn to in times of distress.

b) Because of my German ancestry, I was even unwanted in the third-world country of Yugoslavia.

c) As an expellee and subsequent post-war refugee, I had no country to call my own.

d) For reasons of ethnicity, my formal education in Yugoslavia was blocked by partisan decree after I had completed grade six.

e) Germany, the country whose nationality my family and I shared even though none of us ever lived there, had lost an ill-conceived war in which crimes against humanity were committed.

f) My work experience in farming offered no prospects for a decent income.

g) Pursuit of a career in house painting did not warrant immigration to America since that line of work never appealed to me in the first place.

In a word, I felt like a fish that suddenly found itself in an ocean after having been raised within restrictive confines of some cracked basins!

A 32-page booklet that was designed to assist immigrants like me has the title *Guide for New Americans. An Introduction to Your New Homeland.* It was prepared under the sponsorship of the American Council of Voluntary Agencies for Foreign Service, Inc., 20 West 40th Street, New York 18, second Printing: February 1950, by Astoria Press, New York, NY. It made me aware of a number of things including the enormous size of the U. S., which extends over four different time zones and is almost as large as the entire European continent! Texas alone is larger than pre-war Germany used to be.

I also learned of the presence of many religious bodies in America that do not exist where I came from; however, the U. S. government maintains strict separation from all churches. Consequently, they are on their own in trying to support themselves. Upon worshipping at Roman-Catholic churches in America, I was taken aback during services when priests solicited donations for such mundane necessities as roof or gutter repairs, concrete work, etc. By contrast, masses I had attended in Austria seemed much more conducive to pious reflection because secular topics only came up in religious contexts. Money for maintaining the houses of worship in Austria is collected as a special tax by government agencies and proportionately distributed to the handful of church denominations that are recognized by the state. Religious freedom exists in Austria as well but the ways in which it can be exercised are much more numerous and varied in the U. S.

Little differences in the way of doing everyday things tend to catch the attention of newcomers in amusing or disconcerting ways. A couple of phenomena that caught my eye concerned school children that I saw at bus stops. Invariably, they would have their arms full of books as they tried to get on or off awkwardly under rain-or-shine conditions. Maybe there were no satchels large enough to fit their materials into. In Austria, books were deemed too precious to be exposed to the elements unprotected; therefore, children on their way to and from schools normally carried satchels even when materials for making such were scarce like during and after the war! It seemed odd that in America, the land of plenty, kids would not be provided with a means to carry their books more conveniently. Another thing that struck me as quite irrational was teenage girls' insistence on wearing only white bobby socks even though the exposed skin beyond areas covered looked unmistakably purple from the winter cold!

The desirability of community involvement and concerted efforts to contribute to society in positive ways is also stressed in the guide mentioned above. Adhering to such conduct even appears to be problematic for individuals who always lived in the U. S., as I found out one night while walking home after having attended an Americanization class at the North Avenue YMCA. As I passed the African-American "Evergreen Club" located on the SE corner of Clyborne Avenue and Larrabee Street, not far from where I lived, a black man wearing a dark green suit was standing outside near the entrance. Out of the blue, he mumbled, "want me to f_ your mother? Want me to f_ your mother?" I kept walking, because I knew from my exposure to intoxicated persons at my parents' inn that it was best to leave them alone. I also realized that having to make allowances for aberrant ideas concerning proper conduct was part of becoming Americanized.

The *Guide for New Americans*...also referred to newspapers as an important source for keeping informed concerning different aspects of given issues. In addition to the German *Abendpost* daily at Chicago, there was a Sunday edition entitled *Sonntagspost.* The papers also featured news from Wisconsin in a section called "Milwaukee Deutsche Zeitung." Another German weekly of the greater Chicago area, which is still in circulation at the time of this writing, has the title *Eintracht* (Harmony) and is published at Skokie, Illinois. It originally catered to Austro-Hungarian readers under the editorship of Jakob Himpelmann. There were also a couple of German language radio programs on the air at the time of my 1951 arrival in Chicago that have been replaced by others since then. One was called "Germania Broadcast." Franz Gerstenberg hosted it evenings for many years. The other program was aired at 7:30 a. m. It was called "Die Wiener Radiostunde" (The Viennese Radio Hour) and featured Hans-Leo Reich as the host.

It did not take me long to realize that postage was a bargain in the United States. Ordinary letters within the U. S. only required a 3-cent stamp. Domestic Airmail letters up to an ounce or 28.3 grams required a 6-cent stamp. Domestic post cards were delivered for a penny each and postage for air mail letters up to a half ounce or 14.15 grams going to foreign countries cost 15 cents or 25 cents depending on their destination. In contrast to that, letters I used to send to America from Austria required considerably more postage so that I often had to forego having a snack in order to buy a stamp for a letter going overseas.

Making telephone calls in America also was a lot easier than in post-war Austria because of lower U. S. rates (5 cents for local calls) as well as easier accesses to telephones, which were much more plentiful here. In America, one could drop in additional coins if a call exceeded the allotted time interval. In Austria, a person making a local call from a pay-telephone was automatically cut off after three minutes and the dialing process had to be re-initiated with another coin. To make a long distance call in Austria, one had to go to a post office. On a slip of paper, callers had to write their respective name along with the number to be dialed including the area code. The paper was handed to an employee whereupon a person was assigned to a booth, but often there was a waiting line to contend with. Clerks did the dialing and payment had to be made afterwards at a counter.

Dime stores and drugstores with lunch counters were unfamiliar American phenomena to me. In contrast to those types of establishments, a "Drogerie" in Austria offers no meals but one can buy non-prescription drugs as well as dime store items and things like wallpaper and paints there. Medicines are typically acquired at pharmacies called "Apotheke." Hot meals can be obtained at many a "Gasthaus" (inn) as well as at restaurants in Austria. Dinner, the main meal of the day used to be served at noon and supper was provided in the evening of course. The word "lunch" does not have a literal equivalent in German. It is understood to mean a short noon meal but there is no common term for it. Besides breakfast, dinner, and supper, a snack is customarily served around 9:30 a. m. and another one around 4:00 p. m. in Austria. Observance of these dietary customs contributes greatly toward the proverbial Austrian "Gemütlichkeit" for which there is no adequately descriptive single word in English.

Beverages that were new to me in America included root beer, ginger ale, 7UP, highballs, and other mixed alcoholic drinks. In the land of recognized freedoms, it surprised me that even experimental consumption of alcohol by underage individuals elicited shock among many people. In Austria, nobody thinks anything of it if parents let children taste such drinks in public for example. It has not broadened problems of alcoholism in the country either. Some puritanically inclined American co-workers of mine also thought that my enjoyment of poppy-seed strudel was akin to substance abuse. They seemed to believe that it would inescapably lead to opium addiction.

In Europe, I was used to metric weights and measures. The American system required getting used to; however, it proved to be no problem in the long run except where temperatures are concerned. To this day, I still cannot easily convert Celsius to Fahrenheit or vice versa. When it came to clothing, I simply tried to remember my sizes both ways rather than attempting to figure out corresponding equivalents. For conversions of miles to kilometers or vice versa, I usually get by with a 2:3 ratio calculation. I suspect that America has not generally adopted the metric system yet out of commercial self-interest. It costs foreign providers of goods extra in packaging, for example, to market their products readily in the U. S., too.

As a wage earner in Austria with no additional income, I never had to file an income tax return. My employers withheld the required amounts each time I was paid and forwarded them to the respective governmental agencies. Withholdings for social security including provisions for health care, disability, and retirement were the highest. Income tax withholdings were the next highest category. All deductions were clearly shown on the envelope containing one's net earnings in cash. Paychecks were not normally issued to workers. Having to file an income tax return annually in the U. S. is a good thing, because it makes a person aware of ways to manage one's personal assets more efficiently, which also tends to benefit the economy in general.

Since it was obvious that I needed more money, my cousin Magdalena's husband Joe WEISZMANN Sr., who worked as a bricklayer, urged me to increase my earnings by capitalizing on my Austrian experience in house painting. Upon seeing a painter's union representative at the so-called "German" local on 4219 North Lincoln Avenue, I was given a test by Mr. Joe Dumke. It included color identifications and questions regarding work procedures as well as common coatings and materials. I also had an interview with Mr. Art Lauschke, a Shop Steward. On the basis of my Austrian union membership, I was admitted to Local 275 upon payment of only ten percent of the regular initiation fee, which would have amounted to $150 at the time.

While attending regular union meetings, I met some painting contractors, too. One of them was Mr. Louis A. Wesserle, a German-speaking immigrant from Deutsch-Proben (Nitrianske Pravno, Slovakia) in former Austria-Hungary. He had just turned over business operations to his son Fritz. The number of their employees ranged from a handful to over a dozen depending on the season. Louis was a master when it came to wood graining and marbleizing. Some Jewish customers who truly appreciated above-average work performance rightfully called him an "artist." Following an interview with Louis and Fritz, I was hired in early March 1952 when permissive weather resulted in increased painting activities.

Mr. DeBones, my supervisor at the electronics supply store was surprised when I told him that I was terminating my employment at Walker-Jimieson. He was willing to give me another raise even though I had just received one; however, upon learning that I was going to start painting houses at the rate of $2.60 an hour, he simply said, "I can't match that!"

As I was adapting to the prevalent *modus operandi* among painters in Chicago, the meaning of Mr. Stephen Mendak's occupational remark, "anything is good, if you are good," became clearer. At Bad-Ischl, Upper Austria, I would have had to first serve a formal apprenticeship to become a journeyman painter. In America, all that mattered was my ability to do an acceptable job in that capacity. To my pleasant surprise, I had acquired more than minimal applicable expertise as a mere helper at the small Austrian painting company where I worked for three years. In due time, I found out that quite a few of my locally trained American co-workers never learned how to tint paints for example, let alone match colors! Due to insufficient training and an unwillingness to take on more responsibility, many served only as brush-hands while drawing wages according to union scales for journeymen. Some people are inclined to regard this practice as unfair equalization by labor unions, but it can also be seen as an economic leveling method based on humanitarian and social considerations.

8. Occupational Relapse and Induction into the U. S. Army

While providing quality house painting services as an employee of Louis A. Wesserle & Son, I occasionally had a chance to drive the company's meandering old panel truck on open road stretches with Fritz Wesserle at my side giving me useful pointers. Most customers happened to be living at scattered locations on Chicago's north side and in neighboring suburbs; therefore, it soon became evident that I needed a car of my own to get around, because public transportation did not extend to all locations. Around the middle of April 1952, I began to visit used auto dealers by bus on weekends to look at some of the vehicles on their lots. Since very few new passenger cars had been produced in Detroit for private civilian clientele from 1942 until 1945, I found that most used automobiles available in a low price range were old jalopies with high mileage.

The first vehicle I test drove happened to be a 1941 Buick. It looked well kept but its suspension was so soft that the car leaned over quite a bit during turns. I was unsure whether that was normal or a sign of excessive wear. Another car I tried was a 1941 Dodge with Fluid Drive, which meant that the motor did not die if a person started out in a wrong gear! In a way, it functioned like subsequent automatic shifting did in future models. Both of the cars mentioned had a 3-speed standard stick shift and each one was selling for $250. I had saved a little more than that already, but I did not wish to spend all of my money. When I decided to go ahead and buy the Dodge in early May, I was not quite twenty-one years of age yet. Uncle Nick BARBA agreed to cosign the purchase agreement; however, the title was made out in his name only, notwithstanding the fact that I alone had paid for the car. It made me wonder whom the law was actually designed to protect, but I was destined to find out real soon.

As fate would have it, on the second day as I was heading home from work with my own car, several circumstances culminated in a mishap. Pavement slicked by a drizzle, bald rear tires on the Dodge, and my inexperience as a driver thwarted my efforts to stop in time when a man in a 1946 Plymouth decided to cross Lincoln Avenue at Carmen (south of Foster) just as I was approaching the intersection. I wound up hitting his car broadside on the passenger side so that both doors were visibly dented. The front bumper of my Dodge was bent downward and the grill had also become cracked in a couple of places, but worst of all, the radiator got pushed back just enough to be ruptured by the fan so that the coolant leaked out. The man with the Plymouth was able to drive off after the police officer that appeared at the scene had given him a citation for failing to yield the right of way.

When I tried to start my car, it made quite a bit of noise as the fan blades scraped the radiator. Upon parking the Dodge by the nearest curbside, I was taken to a police station in the squad car, because my Austrian license turned out to be invalid in Illinois. I really could not blame the officer for not accepting the foreign permit since it actually only entitled me to operate a "Kleinkraftrad," i. e., a lightweight motorcycle; however, since neither he nor his superior understood German, that aspect did not become an issue.

While the desk sergeant was busy with different matters, one of the other two policemen present was having fun showing me a vacant jail cell and roguishly suggesting that I might be its next occupant. Back at the desk, the sergeant asked me about my occupation, address, arrival in the U. S., etc. I responded as well as I could in my broken English and told him that I was living with my aunt and uncle. One of the police officers wanted to know whether my uncle spoke English. When I explained that his command of it was even less than mine, he asked facetiously whether my uncle knew the meaning of the word "money." I assured him that he did whereupon it was suggested that I should give him a call. Since there was no telephone on the premises where we lived, I was unable to comply with that request.

From what I could gather, I was supposed to pay a fine of $25 for driving without a valid license. I pointed out that I only had nineteen dollars and some change on me. "That'll do" was their spontaneous reply. I promptly gave them the money and quickly left the station without further ado. The sergeant had been thoughtful enough to leave me with sufficient change to ride a CTA (Chicago Transit Authority) bus home but I decided to walk because my nerves were too agitated for me to sit and keep still.

As I walked along briskly, I wondered how I would handle my embarrassment when I had to explain to my aunt and uncle as well as to my employers and coworkers what had happened. It turned out that my relatives were glad that no one got injured. My employers, who hailed from an area in former Austria-Hungary, were amused by my description of the way I had slid into the Plymouth. I used the colloquial Austrian phrase, "i bin eam einig'rutscht," which struck them as humorous.

With the help of some borrowed tools, I managed to un-screw the bent bumper and to push back parts of the dented fenders so that the front tires were no longer rubbing against any metal. Upon getting the motor started, I was able to slowly drive the damaged car to my place of residence without over-heating the motor despite the fact that there was no fluid in the leaky radiator. As the days went by, I worked on the old buggy right on the street whenever I could. Luckily, a business called Standard Spring Works was located next door. The Italian se-curity guard employed there was kind enough to let me use a hydraulic jack and some tools after hours and on weekends. For necessary replacement parts, I scoured area junkyards on Saturdays. By the time I had the car in good enough shape so that I was not in violation of safety considerations, I had ac-quired quite a bit of mechanical savvy, too. Upon becoming twenty-one years old, I procured title to my car along with liabil-ity insurance and an Illinois operator's license.

Soon after the accident had occurred, I received a letter from the Illinois Safety Responsibility Division in Springfield. I was asked to send in $250 as an escrow deposit to cover dam-ages on the Plymouth in the event that I was going to be found negligent when our case came up in court. Since my Dodge had been registered in Uncle Nick's name, he was also sent such a letter with the proviso that my deposit could simultane-ously cover his potential liability as well. Uncle Nick was a per-son who never got into trouble with the law and since he had not been personally involved in my accident, it truly bothered him to be drawn into the affair at all. He readily accepted my sincere apology but it did not alleviate his worries entirely.

To help matters along, I hired an attorney named Schoenberger who also understood German. He represented me successfully before the judge. The driver of the Plymouth was found to be at fault because he had failed to yield the right of way as I was approaching from his right on a through-street; he also happened to be on a side street with a posted stop sign. My $250 deposit was refunded to me and I duly signed the check over to Mr. Schoenberger as payment in full for serv-ices rendered. The experience taught me that the convenience of owning a car does not come cheaply.

Meanwhile I was exposed to my very first summer in Chicago. It proved to be quite taxing both physically as well as mentally. I could not remember ever having had to work under similar climate conditions, especially as far as the sultry humid-ity was concerned. Often, I found myself drenched with perspi-ration while doing absolutely nothing. On so-called "muggy" days, the proverbial "windy city" of Chicago did not live up to its name at all for several days in a row! During such periods, even major portions of the nights were quite unbearable. Getting much sleep prior to the wee hours proved to be impossible. I tried sleeping on linoleum floors, in an empty cast iron bathtub, by open doors, etc. No matter how I sought to avoid the stickiness, it was all to no avail. The use of electric fans tended to impart stiff necks and sore muscles. Air conditioners in the type of housing that people like me could afford were not an option yet back in 1952. On countless occasions, I bitterly reproached the creator emphatically in several languages for subjecting humans to such physically ravaging conditions.

As I look back upon those dog days in earnest efforts to recollect why I did not move elsewhere in this great country, I am sometimes reminded of a sign I once saw in a movie on an old barn. It said: "We don't live here we just stay because we're too poor to move away." It seems that somehow a person wants to prevail at a given place once a foothold has been established for existence. Older immigrant coworkers with whom I discussed the prospects of relocation were convinced that Chicago was the best place for making a living. They were inclined to say, "if you can't make it here, you can't make it anywhere."

In view of the obvious fact that the millions of Americans living in the rest of the United States are doing just fine, I was skeptical about this line of thought. However, as a person who knew from own experiences how hard it is to get off to a new start at an unfamiliar location, I was also reluctant to leave behind what was sufficiently suitable or satisfactory in the greater Chicago environment. Favorable factors included proximity to relatives and friends, familiar hangouts, good prospects of employment, abundant ethnic foods, etc. Another deterrent to relocation was the requirement of non-US citizens to send a report on Form I-53 to the Immigration and Naturalization Service during the first ten days of January. In addition, young men 18 to 26 years of age had to register with the local draft board under the Selective Service Act of 1948. With the Korean War in full swing until July 1953, I reckoned that I would undoubtedly be among draftees before long.

Thanks to the outcome of collective bargaining between the painters' union and the contractors' association, my hourly wage was raised from $2.60 to $2.75 as of April 1952. Even while paying $25 weekly for room and board as of then, I still had more spending money than my first job had yielded. The pay raise also meant that employers expected amplified worker output; after all, increases in salary without commensurate growth in productivity tends to be inflationary! My junior boss Fritz Wesserle even got me to enroll in an evening course to be trained as a paperhanger. Mr. Placko conducted the course at Washburne Trade School in Chicago. Constant pressure to enhance one's output was much greater in the U. S. than what I had witnessed in Europe! In trying to meet expectations as a house painter at Chicago, I often felt totally drained of energy especially during periods of "muggy" weather when I was barely able to get a few hours worth of good sleep during many a night. In Austria, working conditions were much more bearable, but the buying power of earnings was also lower.

It occurred to me that observance of daylight saving time is detrimental to the wellbeing of humans. With an extra hour of sleep in the morning, people would be less accident-prone, too! Of course, from a business point of view, enabling people to sleep longer, would diminish their consumption needs and also reduce the time for activities after work, which promote tear and wear of everything from consumer goods to frail nerves. To hardly anyone's surprise, observance of daylight saving time will probably never be generally ruled out by government and business interests since it would be regarded as detrimental to the economy.

As of autumn 1952, I enrolled in classes at Wells Evening High School located on Ashland Avenue at Augusta Boulevard. The two courses I signed up for covered Radio Electronics and English, which was taught by Miss Harmon using a textbook entitled *English for Life.* The electronics course involved assembling an AM radio from a Heath kit. Mine ended up playing only intermittently, because some of my wire connections had too much solder that seemed to cause periodic overheating. When components involved cooled down sufficiently, the radio would play again in cycles. To this very day, my soldering skills have remained inadequate, but as "honest Abe" Lincoln (1809-1865) might have said, "it's better to try and fail than to fail to try."

Toward the end of October 1952, my friend Peter Kunst introduced me to a fellow immigrant named Adam Retzler while the three of us were swimming at the North Avenue YMCA pool. Before we parted company, Adam said, "by the way, I'm getting married next weekend. You're both invited." The wedding reception took place at what was known as the Social Turner Hall on Belmont Avenue a block or so west of the junction of Lincoln and Ashland Avenues. - Some years later the site was converted into a metered city parking lot.

My attendance of Adam and Betty Retzler's wedding turned out to be a fateful experience, because I was destined to meet my future spouse Marie HOLECSEK there. When I first set eyes on her, everything else around faded into the background as the thought registered in my mind like a *fait accompli* that this girl was going to be my wife. Since there were relatively few younger folks in attendance, I did not have to stand in line to ask beautiful Marie with wavy brown hair and sparkling hazel eyes for a dance. Both of us seemed anxious to learn about each other. While going downstairs for some libation, Marie was walking ahead of me and I caught alluring glimpses of her compelling trim fanny gracefully rebounding with each step she took in her supple mint green dress. The intermittent stroboscopic impressions sparked my imagination rather inadvertently.

We talked about our respective place of birth, the length of time we had been in the U. S., where we worked, etc. Marie's job in the stock transfer department at City National Bank on 208 South La Salle Street in downtown Chicago sounded quite impressive to me. I also met her parents Magda and Frank at that wedding. When I asked Marie for a date right in their presence, her father baffled me by saying, "why?" His apparent apprehensions about entrusting her to me were understandable and not at all unwarranted since she wound up leaving home to take her place by my side as things turned out four years down the road in 1956.

I was glad that I had traded in my battered Dodge for a 1948 Studebaker Commander before I met Marie. Now I was able to take her out on dates in a better sedan; however, since I was too persistent in trying to make love to her, Marie declined to go out with me again after a couple of dates. She was not ready to get serious with a fellow who was probably going to be drafted soon. Until that time actually arrived on April 21, 1953, we only caught glimpses of each other at dances we both happened to attend separately. Although we did not keep in touch at all, I listed Marie as the prospective beneficiary of my $10 000 GI life insurance upon commencing active duty in the U. S. Army.

Being drafted interrupted my second semester at Wells Evening High School, but it also may have saved my life. On the weekend after I was inducted, I was supposed to accompany a couple of friends to Cleveland, Ohio, by car. One of the two people was Jakob Wasza (1931-1953) who hailed from my hometown where we used to be both, playmates and rivals at various times. He and another fellow immigrant went on the trip as planned but never reached their destination: While trying to pass a truck on an uphill stretch of highway, they crashed head-on with another car and both of them died at the scene. Upon learning about their fatal accident, I could not help but be reminded of Ernest Hemingway's literary work, *For Whom the Bell Tolls* (1940). For the time being, I was obviously meant to remain among the living.

It was still dark outside at 6:00 a. m. on April 21, 1953 when I arrived at the designated location in Chicago where I was supposed to check in according to my draft notice. Since some of those who were scheduled to work there had not turned up yet, I was given a white frock and assigned to help with the fingerprinting procedure. In my eagerness to make a favorable impression, I kept at it all day until the people in charge began to examine their lists for individuals that had failed to report as ordered. My name was among those not checked off, because I obviously had not been processed yet!

Evidently, the workers from the earlier shift had failed to inform their relief persons that I was an inductee and not a fellow employee. Belatedly, I realized that keeping my nose faithfully to the proverbial grindstone was a mistake in an environment where job coordination was basically relegated to the realm of serendipity. I regretted not having spoken up earlier so that I would have been processed as scheduled. Upon becoming aware of their oversight at the last moment, one of the regular workers said that I should go home and come back the next morning. When I pointed out that I might be facing possible punishment if I followed this suggestion, the crew hastily completed the required paperwork and got me on an evening train.

By the time of my late arrival at Fort Sheridan, Illinois, I was exhausted and quite anxious for some rest. Upon receiving a set of linen, I bedded down on a vacant cot in some barracks where the lights had been turned off already and most occupants were soundly asleep. Having been warned about pickpockets before, I stuck my wallet into my pillowcase as I undressed in order to hit the sack without further delay. At one point during the night, I happened to open my eyes as someone in uniform was filching through my clothes! In a sleepy stupor, I asked what he was looking for. Keeping his voice down, he replied, "an ID card. Are you Private . . .?" Since he mumbled a name other than mine, I said "no" and he left whereupon I went back to sleep. The next morning, it came to light that the wallets of some recruits had been stolen.

During the next several days, I went through processing at Fort Sheridan. In one of the test sessions, some of us had green swatches placed on our desks. All other recruits were dismissed. Those of us with swatches were told that we had achieved high enough scores to be eligible for OCS (Officers Candidate School). Upon being told more about it, we were urged to consider signing up for the program. I decided against doing so, because I felt that I would have a hard time getting GIs born in America to carry out orders given by me, an immigrant with an accent who had not formally completed high school! It did not seem wise to get myself into that kind of situation.

While waiting for orders to be shipped out to some U. S. Army post for basic training, I was asked to tend to the coal furnaces of a couple of barracks. During break periods, I played familiar tunes on my harmonica. Sometimes, I even had an audience consisting of fellow recruits. On occasion, a GI would try to hold back tears when I played songs like "Home on the Range" for example. It may well have been the very first time that they were separated from their respective families or sweethearts. In early May 1953, I finally was sent to Camp Breckinridge, Kentucky for sixteen (16) weeks of basic infantry training under the "screaming eagle" emblem of the 101st Airborne Division, which had distinguished itself at the Battle of Bastogne; however, the constituents of my company were not trained as paratroopers.

We slept in wooden barracks and our theoretical training occurred in large, hangar-type structures. The physical training was conducted in desert-like terrain around the area where some GIs encountered rattlesnakes. Now and then, somebody killed one for its skin, which was allegedly used for making a belt. To counteract depletion of sodium levels in our bodies from profuse perspiration, we had to take salt tablets. Each of the barracks accommodated two platoons of about sixty (60) trainees each. One platoon occupied the first floor and the members of the other one including me, slept on the second floor in double stacked steel-frame bunk beds. There were fifteen of them on each side of the center aisle. The washrooms with showers, toilettes, and lavatories were on the first floor.

We were assigned to the bunks in alphabetical order. The names that appeared on the roster next to mine were Spanks and Stewart. Both recruits happened to be black fellows from Baltimore, Maryland. As a person who was exposed to a variety of languages and dialects in Europe, I noticed that their way of talking was different than that of George Schaefer for example, a Caucasian recruit from Philadelphia, Pennsylvania. When they pronounced the name of their hometown, it sounded like "bawl-da-mow." It made me pay closer attention to my own use of English as I was trying to improve it further.

The two fellow-GIs from Baltimore also struck me as rather unconventional in their deportment, which tended to inhibit spontaneous interaction with them. I had difficulty discerning their moral fabric, let alone relate to it. They did not even call each other by name; instead, they would cheerfully say, "hey, 'tyou do, mutherfock?" Stewart slept in the bunk above mine. One night, he returned to the barracks quite inebriated from excessive consumption of so-called "green beer," which only had an alcohol content of 3.2 percent. He fell asleep so soundly that he lost control over his bladder. When chilled urine dripped onto my thigh upon leaking through his mattress, I woke up in time to pull my bedding off the cot lest it be wetted, too. With the smell of beer permeating the air around Stewart, I knew he was not going to wake up any time soon, so I went to take a shower and flipped my mattress over on the floor before going back to sleep.

In the so-called "third world" country of Yugoslavia where I came from, it was considered a disgrace if a person got so drunk that he or she lost control over themselves. Individuals, who did overestimate their drinking capacities on occasion would subsequently seem embarrassed and show remorse. Stewart's reaction was quite devoid of any such feelings; he tried to laugh it off instead. His vague apology uttered between chuckles echoed by his pal Spanks sounded disingenuous to say the least! How was I, a person new to this country and as of yet largely unfamiliar with American mores, supposed to take that? Was the unethical behavior of these two individuals from Baltimore a characteristic outgrowth of the environment in which they grew up, or was it attributable to a personal lack of decency or respect for feelings of others? In any case, I figured that I was not the only one who had a lot to learn yet.

Another incident that occurred in our barracks was indicative of racial prejudice in America. One day, when a Caucasian GI from Kentucky could not find his fatigue-cap, he said, "I bet some nigger took it." He had barely spoken these words when a black recruit from Michigan punched him in the mouth. As the two guys began to wrestle, GIs of both races gathered around apparently just waiting for someone to come to the aid of one or the other, which would have undoubtedly resulted in a multiple brawl. It took someone who was perceived as nonaligned to end the scuffle. His name was Arkadji Rossol, a fellow immigrant from Russia who lived in Racine, Wisconsin. He stepped up and said that it was unworthy of Americans to behave this way. As members of the same army we should not let our frustrations out on each other but direct our anger against enemies of this country instead. The unexpected admonition by an outsider with a foreign accent had a sobering effect as it ended the fray and prompted a general reexamination of attitudes.

Sergeant Long, a well-liked member of the cadre, happened to be a black man. He taught us some marching songs including the following lyrics:

GI beans and GI gravy,
Gee I wish I'd joined the navy!
Honey o baby-mine.
I've got a girl in Evansville.
Honey, honey, honey.
I've got a girl in Evansville.
Babe, babe.
I've got a girl in Evansville.
If she won't do, her sister will.
Honey o baby-mine.

For a newcomer to America like me, being given a chance by Uncle Sam to rub elbows with guys my age from all over the United States constituted a terrific way to learn about the country's inhabitants and regional dialects. Until then, I had not been exposed much to Southerners for instance. I enjoyed hearing GIs say where they were from. Sometimes, I tried to imitate the speaker's particular inflection as someone said for example, "I'm from Alabama," or "I come from Dallas." One GI from Chattanooga, Tennessee with whom I enjoyed lengthy conversations was named James Bare. Another friendly fellow who offered me some of his chewing tobacco hailed from Kentucky. His name was Donald B. Robinson. Roland Robinson, a namesake of his, came from Michigan.

After giving lectures, some lieutenants liked to ask questions to see if the gist of their talk had come across. As they looked through the roster, they invariably selected names that were easy for them to pronounce. The name Robinson was often chosen whereupon a big silence would usually ensue, because each of the two persons so named waited for the other to respond. Some lieutenants then asked whether neither of the two Robinsons on the list was present. The one from Kentucky tended to be the first to get up and ask, "do you mean Donald B. or Roland, sir?" One frequent reply was, "which one are you?" or simply, "you will do," which elicited laughter among the soldiers. By the time we got back to business, even the person who posed it in the sweltering heat of the gathering place had often forgotten the exact question to which an answer was sought.

One day, a contest was held on the rifle range between different squads consisting of nine (9) GIs each. Every member of the group that had the highest cumulative score received a weekend pass and a paid hotel room in Evansville, Indiana, which was the nearest sizable town from Camp Breckinridge, Kentucky. Although I only achieved a "marksman" rating myself as compared to the higher "sharpshooter" or "expert" valuations, I wound up in the winning team due to our alphabetic grouping. Being back in civilization for a couple of days in a dust-free clean environment certainly felt good and made me look forward to the completion of our basic infantry training. Another event that brightened our outlook for the future greatly was the signing of the Korean truce agreement on July 27, 1953 at Panmunjom, which effectuated President Eisenhower's avowed aim to end the armed conflict.

Upon having successfully completed sixteen (16) weeks of basic infantry training at Camp Breckinridge around mid-August 1953, the members of my company were assigned to duty elsewhere. Most of us were sent to Fort Lewis, Washington, from where we probably would have been shipped to Korea if the armistice had not been achieved. Going through advanced infantry training stateside was preferable by far to the performance of duty in a combat zone! Only a handful of GIs from our company were sent to the European command (EU-COM). One of them who knew that I came from abroad indicated that he wanted to travel around while he was going to be stationed in Germany. To my surprise he asked, "how far is Germany away from Europe?" It made me realize that I was by no means the only one whose horizon was in the process of being appreciably expanded thanks to Uncle Sam.

On my very first furlough during the latter part of August 1953, I went to visit my sister Rose Kapitaen, her husband Joe, and their daughter Brigitte. The family had immigrated to Souderton, Pennsylvania since I had last seen them at Salzburg, Austria, in September 1951.

107

9. Naturalization, GI Attitudes, Study, Marriage, and Work

The train I boarded toward the end of August 1953 after visiting my sister's family in Pennsylvania arrived at Chicago around 8:30 p.m. I had dozed off by the time it was passing through local residential and industrial areas, but a characteristic smell I subconsciously associated with the city signaled our impending arrival before I even opened my eyes. Upon spending a few days visiting relatives and friends in Chicago, I boarded another train headed for Tacoma, Washington, which is located about twelve (12) miles from Fort Lewis where I had to report for duty in early September 1953. The 2140-mile trip from Chicago to Tacoma lasted forty-six and a half (46.5) hours along the rail lines of The Milwaukee Road. Their double decked "Hiawatha Scenicruiser" railroad car provided ample opportunities for enjoying landscapes and sights along the way.

At Fort Lewis, I was assigned to Company E of the 123rd Infantry Regiment, which was housed in ivy-adorned brick barracks with easy-to-buff tiled floors. My fellow GIs and I were now part of the 44th Illinois National Guard Division that was de-activated in January 1955 when the colors of the 2nd U. S. Infantry Division were brought back from Korea and "permanently" based at Fort Lewis, Washington. As of that time, the former constituents of the 44th Division were summarily transferred to the 2nd Division. Its distinguished performance in combat carried over to us as well so that we became entitled to brandish the National Defense Service Medal. Eventually, I was also awarded the Army Good Conduct Medal.

While I was unpacking things at my assigned bunk in a third-floor room, the first sergeant had me summoned to the Orderly Room just prior to his imminent departure for another assignment. With reference to my linguistic aptitude reflected in my records on his desk, he asked whether I wanted to attend the U. S. Army language school at Monterey, California. I said, "yes, but what's the catch?" His response was, "you'll have to sign up for an extra year of service." Being fresh out of wearisome basic training, I truly had no desire to extend my time in the army at all. If I had only known then how bored I was going to be while undergoing advanced infantry training for the next year and then some! In the back of my mind, I was hoping to be sent to Japan, which never happened. In any case, I failed to take advantage of the excellent offer at hand.

As things turned out, I was retained at Fort Lewis where I ended up digging many foxholes on maneuvers while getting soaked during notoriously frequent periods of local precipitation. On many subsequent occasions, I honestly regretted not opting for language school where I would have enjoyed regular hours indoors instead of having to trudge through wet underbrush in wooded areas around Fort Lewis during odd hours pursuing imaginary enemy forces! Acquiring knowledge of an idiom like Russian or Chinese also would have provided me with an added asset toward my eventual career as a university language professor, which was as yet unforeseen even by me at the time.

Leisure time activities at service clubs on army posts constitute excellent opportunities for gaining glimpses of cultural differences among soldiers of different social, regional, and racial backgrounds. American-born acquaintances of mine expressed surprise at my willingness to spend 25 cents for a cup of soup that seemed like flavored water to them. While they were not accustomed to having soup at all, it happened to be an integral part of my European diet. I truly missed it in the service where soup was never on a menu. Other differences in eating habits manifested themselves through use of salt and pepper, which seemed to be added to food by many Americans before they even tasted it. Where I came from, people were more apt to use paprika rather than pepper if more spicing was desired. Ketchup was something I had never even seen before I came to the United States. Peanuts and peanut butter were also new to me and it took a while before I developed a taste for them. Root beer, on the other hand, turned out to be a beverage I liked right away, unlike ginger ale or tonic water, which were only palatable when mixed with whiskey or gin, respectively.

The first patrons to arrive at the Fort Lewis service club I frequented after lunch on Sundays tended to be Caucasians. People of color seemed to take a siesta before going there. Meanwhile, most pool tables and ping-pong tables were occupied. On one occasion, a black soldier approached a couple of Caucasian players and said, "I'll play the winner." When the two Caucasians had finished their game, they put down the paddles and started to walk away whereupon the black GI asked, "what's the matter, ain't I good enough for you?" One of the Caucasians explained, "it's just that the two of us want to spend time together." The incident made me aware of the ever-present possibility of having peoples' particular behavior misconstrued as being racially motivated or biased.

On another occasion, I encountered a couple of Caucasian GIs at the service club who struck up a conversation with me and seemed interested in learning how I was getting along in the U. S. as far as adjustment to a new way of life was concerned. I pointed out some differences that I had observed and also showed them a deviation I had noticed on a 1909 penny that had the initials S. V. D. B. engraved on it. One of the fellows got visibly excited over it and said that he had wanted one of those for a long time. He began to stammer around and wanted to give me a dollar for the penny. When I asked what was so special about it, the two chaps became evasive. I finally told them to keep it as a present since I knew nothing about numismatic worth then. Years later, I became aware of the fact that the value of such a coin exceeded a hundred dollars even for a used specimen! It made me understand that although ignorance is said to be bliss, it is also liable to cost a pretty rare penny.

One autumn night in 1953 while we were out on maneuvers in damp weather, I was just getting into my sleeping bag under a big tent when the mail was distributed. Upon reading the letter I received from my sister Rose under scanty lighting, my body temperature instantly changed from chilly to balmy. I was overjoyed when I read the happy news that she had located our youngest brother Tony at the home of unrelated Mrs. Elisabeth Etzel whose married name used to be STEIGERWALD. We had lost touch with Tony when our family became scattered as a result of Tito's 1945 confinement of Yugoslavia's German minority to concentration camps. In response to our search efforts, the Red Cross had informed us that Tony joined his mother in Philadelphia, Pennsylvania, in 1950. Since the three of us were present when our mother died at home in Banat-Topola on November 10, 1944, the message from the Red Cross did not make sense at all.

As things panned out, Yugoslav orphanage officials had gotten identities mixed up and sent Tony to America in lieu of someone else. By pure chance, Rose had learned of the arrival of two children from Yugoslav orphanages. Upon attempting to inquire whether they happened to know our brother, the boy turned out to be Tony himself! The incredible coincidence confirmed the old adage that truth is stranger than fiction. As indicated in Chapter 6, the mix-up served as the plot for a one-hour television presentation by the Armstrong Circle Theater under the title "H. R. 8438 - The Story of a Lost Boy" that was aired on June 12, 1956 with John Cameron Swazey serving as moderator.

Another important milestone was reached when I became a naturalized American citizen on December 7, 1953. I was sworn in at the U. S. District Court in the State of Washington. According to concurrent U. S. regulations, a non-citizen who had completed at least ninety (90) days of active duty in any branch of this country's armed forces was eligible to apply for citizenship. I filed my papers soon after I arrived at Fort Lewis in early autumn 1953. Having been a stateless person since Tito summarily stripped the constituents of Yugoslavia's German minority of all civil rights as of November 29, 1944, it felt great to enjoy a home country again. Now I was able to partake of the freedoms stipulated in the Bill of Rights. At long last, I was better off than I would have been in Yugoslavia where citizens unfortunately had to endure oppressive conditions time and again.

An impressive range of educational opportunities available to all GIs was offered through the United States Armed Forces Institute (USAFI) at Madison, Wisconsin. The array of about 400 USAFI correspondence courses had already been brought to my attention at Camp Breckinridge, Kentucky, where I successfully completed my high school equivalent general educational development (GED) test in May 1953. It covered five (5) areas: a) English Grammar, b) Social Science, c) Natural Science, d) Literature, and e) Mathematics. Upon subsequently completing my first college-level correspondence course in English Composition, I passed the GED equivalency test for the first year of college on July 2, 1954 at Fort Lewis, Washington. Luckily, it did not include a mathematics component that would have proved to be my Achilles' heel. By comparing the corresponding respective U. S. percentile levels, it can be seen that my English had improved quite a bit in the meantime:

	a) Engl. Grammar	b) Social SCI	c) Natural SCI	d) Lit	e) Math
My H.S. %iles	27	54	69	27	24
My Coll. %iles	43	43	50	36	NA

Opportunities to enroll in evening courses that were offered at Fort Lewis through educational institutions of the area also presented themselves. As of March 4, 1954, I participated in a non-credit Typing class. On September 7, 1954, I enrolled in a Speech class that was offered right on the army post through the University of Washington. Mr. Walberg Tonstad was our instructor and we used the 3rd edition of the textbook *Principles and Types of Speech*, by A. H. Monroe. I also registered for a college-level USAFI course entitled "Journalism II." In addition, I was accepted as an amateur player for the role of Paul Sycamore in the drama "You Can't Take It with You," by George S. Kaufman and Moss Hart.

111

My active educational pursuits prompted a first sergeant to suspect that my real motivation was to get out of having to perform regular military duties. Some non-commissioned officers openly disliked GIs who had been to college as well as those of us who were anxious to get into one. GIs apparently were only supposed to concentrate on soldiering and following orders deferentially. The best single qualification for giving orders seemed to be a loud voice, which I may have had as a child but not as an adult. Nevertheless, I was promoted to Private First Class (PFC) as of January 19, 1954. My previous rank as of August 4, 1953 was that of a Private E2, which meant that I was an enlisted soldier who had completed basic training. Individuals who had volunteered for active service had the designation RA (Regular Army) instead of an E.

At Fort Lewis, there were several Hispanic-Americans in my squad. They visibly enjoyed using Spanish all day long. In quite a few cases, my knowledge of English already exceeded theirs even though they were born in the U. S. and I had only lived here for two years. While trying to continue my study of French, which I had begun in Austria, it dawned on me that I really should take up Spanish now and benefit from the prevalent supplemental linguistic environment. On my next visit to the PX (Post Exchange), I invested 35 cents in a pocketbook entitled *Spanish through Pictures.* Upon reading the introductory part about sounds, etc., I began to do the exercises and after a while I was able to test my pronunciation while addressing native speakers around me. By the time I was released from active duty, I had gained enough of a head start to earn top grades in the Spanish language course I subsequently took at the University of Illinois.

My interaction with Hispanic-American soldiers also helped me to establish friendlier relations with them; however, that tendency was reversed when I became an Acting Squad Leader (without extra pay). Like most soldiers, the Hispanics were generally accustomed to doing as little as they could get away with in the barracks or on maneuvers. Consequently, they had to be prevailed upon to make an extra effort toward achieving results that were more satisfactory in the eyes of our cadre. In response, they gave me the cold shoulder treatment and avoided communicating with me as far as possible. Their unfriendly behavior saddened me, since I derived absolutely no benefit from having been put in charge. Instead of being able to just fend for myself as before, I now had to keep an eye on everyone else's performance. If something was not done as expected, I was the one liable to be called on the carpet! I either had to straighten things out personally or risk incurring the wrath of those who did not care about adequate results in the first place.

Upon having been deployed on maneuvers one day, I divided the squad into groups of two and assigned each pair of soldiers an imaginary sector of fire. Prior to going back to the CP (Command Post) for the password, I told the members of our squad to dig in and to keep a low profile so that we will not attract the attention of an officer who might be in the area to check on things. By the time I returned from the CP, it was dark already and our orders had not been carried out as expected. What could have cost us most dearly though, was the fact that no one was vigilant. So-called "aggressors" could have easily taken control of our sector and we would have been blamed for letting them "break" through! Once again, I was prompted to ask myself where I went wrong to be caught in such a predicament.

Why was there such a big discrepancy between my expectations and the reality with which I was faced? The four Mexican-Americans in our squad had not even attempted to dig in; instead, they were sitting under a couple of ponchos draped over some fallen timbers. Their glowing cigarettes could be readily seen from beyond our peripheral area and it sounded like they were going to start singing at what was supposed to be an inconspicuous front line sector! The loquacious fellow of Polish descent, who was paired up with a GI of Irish ancestry, had not even taken off his backpack yet! His partner had merely used the entrenching tool to mark the outline of what was going to be their foxhole. One of the two black fellows in our squad had gone on sick call in the morning and the other one had indeed dug in nicely; but he was sound asleep in his foxhole beneath his poncho when I went to inform him of our password.

I came to the conclusion that due to my upbringing as a pliable and obedient person, I was not unlike hapless German GIs who wound up following orders unquestioningly, because they considered it their duty to do so uncritically. In an environment of freedom where each person can choose to march to his own drummer, my inclination to conform to prescribed rules was entirely out of place! Until I had a chance to reorient my disposition, my intuitive responses were bound to be inappropriate most of the time in my contemporary setting. I realized that I had no business trying to lead people who had grown up with an unencumbered carefree outlook on things. Soon afterwards, I asked my platoon sergeant to put another person in charge of our squad.

113

As Nicholas of Cusa (1401-1464) explained it, rational orientation entails movement from premises held to be valid to conclusions yet to be tested. Up to that point, my premises had largely been based upon traditions and common beliefs in my former environments; thus, they often did not entirely jive with tenets held by people here and elsewhere. What tended to confound things even more, happened to be the perception that the opposite of every truth is true also.

Another aspect to be considered in dealing with concepts of truth has to do with the extent to which average members of a given society generally tolerate deviations. What baffled me right off the boat for instance, was the subtitle of the *Philadelphia Bulletin* that touted it as "The World's Largest Newspaper" even though *The London Times,* among others, happened to be even larger! Upon seeing my first edition of the *Chicago Tribune,* I noticed that it had the subtitle "The World's Greatest Newspaper." Were such unfounded claims meant to alert the readers to take the respective paper's contents with a heap rather than just the proverbial grain of salt? The pervasive U. S. phenomena of commercial and political exaggeration that would have been seen as perfidious where I grew up, interfered with my ability to properly assess things for conducting my affairs positively. As products of a U. S. environment, fellow Americans only had to react to situations on the bases of their conditioned reflexes while I had to expend time and effort to sort things out in light of my dissimilar background and orientation.

Meeting a variety of soldiers from different parts of America proved quite conducive to my acculturation. Naturally, I remember some fellows better than others. My best pal with whom I used to converse for hours turned out to be of the Mormon faith. His name was Wendell L. Roberts and his hometown was Tremonton City, Utah. Before I met him, I knew nothing about Joseph Smith and Nauvoo, Illinois, or of Brigham Young and his followers' trek to the area of the Great Salt Lake where The Church of Jesus Christ of Latter-day Saints established a permanent realm of operations. Wendell and I took a trip to Mount Rainier around the time when Robert Mitchum and Diana Lynn were being filmed in segments of "The Track of the Cat." However, we never saw either of these stars in person. The depth of the snow up near the lodge where some scenes were filmed dwarfed the buses and trucks parked in cleared areas.

Wendell and I used to share a tent on maneuvers. On one occasion, we were trucked to an area in the Yakima Valley

114

of the State of Washington that was characterized by sage-brush in powdered lava soil where jackrabbits and rattlesnakes seemed to be the only regular inhabitants. With every step a person took, a cloud of dust would rise as one's boot sank into the loose top layer ankle-deep. It was impossible to keep rifles and other equipment clean. The nerves of everyone tended to be high-strung under given circumstances, too.

One night, Wendell and I woke up when two GIs with unfamiliar subdued voices were arguing near our tent about tossing a live rattlesnake inside. One chap was saying, "how do you know it's not going to bite Roberts? He's an American! I don't want to see him get hurt." Without offering an appropriate answer, the other GI just wanted to carry out his intention knowing full well that it could result in tragedy. Luckily, the con-cerned person prevailed and they left without doing any actual harm. Although I had also become an American by that time, some GIs obviously did not regard me as an equal. The inci-dent reminded me that one did not need to be among depraved Nazis to run into murderous prejudice.

During another maneuver, Sergeant Dennison from Kentucky intervened to keep me out of harms way. He was married to an American of Russian-German descent. When he first told me to make myself scarce in the field during the up-coming tactical exercise, I thought he was just trying to give me a break. Upon selecting a slightly elevated spot, I prepared a sleeping area with my entrenching tool and provided for water runoff. Then I placed some long sticks across the dugout and unfolded my poncho over the main area. My tent section was used to cover the ground beneath me. Finally, I placed branches over the whole enclosure in a random manner with some dried grass as additional camouflage. In the absence of further orders, I crawled under the contraption and reached for a copy of the *Reader's Digest*. I always liked to carry the latest edition in a pocket of my field jacket.

By deliberately going for chow and water after all others had already eaten, I was hoping that the sergeant would not see me. One night, I woke up, as one of the squads from our platoon happened to pass by my position without them knowing it. One GI of Dutch descent, whose voice I recognized, was saying, "I just wanna see him bleed." I could not help but won-der whom he meant. While I was walking through a grassy clearing around mid-afternoon the next day to get something to eat, I heard a couple of rifle shots while something had whirred past my right ear and shoulder. Instinctively, I went down on my knees in the tall grass whereupon I heard someone shout triumphantly at a distance, "I got 'em, I got 'em!"

I crawled into the nearby woods for better cover and eventually reached the field kitchen where I ran into an unfamiliar GI who was startled upon reading my nametag. Wide-eyed he said, "you're the one they were shootin' at back there," as if he were surprised to see me among the living. I replied, "yes, would you be willing to give testimony about it?" He began to stammer something like not wanting to get involved and left hastily. Now I understood why Sergeant Dennison wanted me to remain out of sight!

I tried to relate what happened there to manifestations of ethnic bias I had witnessed while growing up in a multinational East Central European setting; however, it eluded my comprehension why my blood was to be spilled impulsively by American GIs with whom I was faithfully serving the same country! I wondered if the Dutch-American and the Polish-American who fired the shots figured that their motives for hurting me were more legitimate than those of nazi criminals had been who harmed people on racial or religious grounds. It occurred to me that these GIs may have had latent urges to avenge their ancestral countries for having been invaded by Germany. In their twisted minds, it did not seem to matter that the ethnic "kraut" they had targeted was born in Yugoslavia and in no way accountable for Hitler's excesses.

One summer-day in 1954, I was among a work detail assigned to help unload provisions at a regimental Ration Break Down facility. I enjoyed performing useful labor for a change, so I asked if there was a chance for me to become a member of their regular crew. It so happened that Corporal Orenstein, the person in charge, needed someone in the meat distribution section. To test my suitability for the job, he had me cleave a solidly frozen block of ground beef at a designated point. Due to lots of wood chopping practice in Austria, I happened to hit it right where he wanted it split. That proved to be helpful in being accepted as a regular worker at the place. Upon transferring to the Service Company, my classification as an infantryman was changed to that of a Supply Records Specialist. As of that time, I no longer had to be out in the boondocks, nor did I have to march in parades.

Upon due reflection, I found it peculiar how varied soldiers' lives turn out to be right in the same place! It was also quite sobering to see how readily another could replace any of us. As time passed, I began to make plans for the future. Uppermost in my mind were hopes of attending a university under the "GI Bill" (Public Law 550).

In order to be able to enroll for the 1955 Spring Semester at the University of Illinois, I was granted an early release from active duty. My regular obligation was shortened by three months so that I was ready to leave Fort Lewis as of January 21, 1955. At that juncture, I was transferred to the Army Reserve to complete the remainder of a total of eight (8) years of service. My eventual honorable discharge certificate was issued on April 29, 1961. On the basis of proficiency tests taken and course credits earned, I was admitted to the University of Illinois as of February 7, 1955 with 30 semester hours of advanced standing. Thanks to opportunities provided through the U. S. Army, I had been able to advance from a freshman status in high school to the level of a college sophomore while simultaneously completing my active military tour of duty.

Two years of the University of Illinois' undergraduate division could be completed at the Navy Pier when I commenced my studies there on February 7, 1955. The campus at Chicago Circle was not even on the drawing board yet. To be eligible for payments of $110 monthly under the GI Bill, I had to carry at least fourteen (14) semester hours at a time. The money barely covered room and board payments of $25 weekly. While taking classes at the Navy Pier during the spring semester and the summer session in 1955, I needed transportation so I purchased a 1950 Studebaker Champion. Since I did not have time for gainful employment, I had to keep on dipping into my insufficient savings to cover additional expenditures.

In order to stretch the GI Bill payments so that I could continue to study on a full time basis without getting a side job, I decided to go abroad. It so happened that some foreign currency equivalents of the money I received enabled me to get by, thanks to a highly favorable exchange rate. My goal was to get into motion picture production. A college in Scotland and a conservatory in Austria where offering suitable programs. I opted for Vienna where I attended the Academy of Music and Dramatic Arts from autumn 1955 until summer 1957.

A couple of months before leaving for Austria to continue my education abroad, I was destined to see Marie at one of the German dances in the Social Turner Hall on Belmont Avenue west of Lincoln and Ashland where we had originally become acquainted not quite three years earlier. When I inquired right on the dance floor about the state of affairs in her heart, she responded by saying, "frage nicht" (don't ask) while squeezing my hand in a way that rekindled feelings I thought to have outgrown since our previous date a couple of years earlier! Upon giving Marie a ride home, we decided to meet and go out on dates again. Now that we had both matured some and I had completed my military service, she might have been amenable to a marriage proposal, but I was focused on attaining qualifications for a well-paying job that I could enjoy, too. - Our subsequent ten-month courtship was conducted by mail with hundreds of letters crossing the ocean both ways.

Meanwhile, my brother Tony joined me at Chicago, from Pennsylvania. He also wanted to enter the University of Illinois. We were now both living with Uncle Nick and Aunt Katharina, whom relatives called "Bäsl Kathi." Their rented apartment was on the third floor at 2056 N. Halsted Street. After a forced separation of ten (10) years, Tony and I had bonded again when I spent my 1954 summer furlough in Pennsylvania where he was living with our sister and her family since May 1954.

Our older brother Josef (1926-1977) and his family were living near Salzburg, Austria. I went to see them shortly after I commenced my studies at Vienna as of October 1955. I crossed the Atlantic on the French liner *Liberté*. The weather was much calmer than what I had experienced on my initial ocean voyage. The journey also proved to be much more enjoyable because the accommodation in cabins was better and the world-renowned French cuisine turned out to be like a symphonic culinary experience with each succeeding course attuned to what was served before and next. Although it all tasted so good, I never had a feeling of being stuffed and I never got seasick. *Vive la France!*

For Christmas 1955, I traveled from Vienna, Austria, to Weinsberg near Heilbronn, Germany to visit my half-brother Michael STEIGERWALD (1923-1956) and his family. I had not seen him since 1944 when he was on furlough in our hometown of Banat-Topola as a soldier in the *Wehrmacht* (regular army). Toward the end of WW II, he suffered some combat injuries and was sent to a hospital at Trier from where he was placed into a French POW camp before he had fully recovered. French military authorities released him to his home state of Yugoslavia where he was confined in another POW camp until 1948. In that year, Tito finally closed the concentration camps where the remainder of the country's German minority was confined since 1945. Michael and his family wanted to move to Germany; however, officials at Belgrade did not consent to that until years later. Meanwhile, he was inducted into the Yugoslav army to train recruits even though his lung injuries had not healed properly under prevalent inadequate nutritional, sanitary, and quiescent conditions. His premature death in January 1956 was the ultimate result that rendered his wife Susanne (*1931), née SCHULZ a widow with two children, Hildegard (1952-1976) and Jakob (*1955), to care for.

Around Christmas 1955, I wrote to Marie and asked if she was willing to come and live with me in Vienna. From her mother's side, strong religious influences had permeated the family environment of my wife-to-be. Five aunts were nuns in Romania, for example. In observance of our respective family traditions, we made wedding plans for September 8, 1956 in the Church of Saint Lambert at Skokie, Illinois. In the interim, I had asked my brother Tony to sell my Studebaker automobile, which had just been sitting on the street unused. He had his own car, a 1946 Chevrolet in mint condition. When the school year ended, I boarded the Dutch liner *Nieu Amsterdam* and returned to Chicago in early June 1956 via New York. Until our wedding in September, I worked as a carpenter's helper for the Holt Construction Company that was owned by Marie's brother Peter.

Over 200 people attended the wedding reception at a rented hall and we did not get back to the house of Marie's parents until the wee hours. By the time we had our luggage ready and the presents sorted for storage, it was almost time to go to the station downtown Chicago where we took a train to New York. We arrived there quite tired after having spent a second night without much sleep. Nevertheless, we went to see the Empire State Building, Radio City Music Hall, and other sites before spending the night at a hotel. We barely made it to the dock on time the next morning to board our ship. Originally, we had booked passage on the Swedish vessel *Stockholm,* but since it was heavily damaged in a collision with the Italian liner *Andrea Doria,* we had to make other plans. Luckily, we were able to book passage on the Greek ship *Arosa Kulm* through the American Council on Education for about $160 per person - one way. On the *Stockholm,* we would have had to pay $220 each. The *Arosa Kulm* had a German-speaking crew and there were only about 89 passengers aboard the chartered vessel. We had quite a leisurely cruise. During a dance contest in the middle of the Atlantic, Marie and I won the waltz prize.

As a married student, I received $135 monthly under the GI Bill. The exchange rate fluctuated some, but we usually received 25.92 Austrian shillings for one U. S. dollar. Our monthly total amounted to more than what my brother Josef and his wife Ritzi, née LINZNER, had to get by on with a couple of children! As a student, I received free tickets to operas and theatrical performances as well as discounts at museums, etc. Marie and I also went to see a lot of movies, but she still got homesick after a while. She had never been away from her family for any length of time. It hurt my ego that she was not as happy with me as I was with having her by my side.

At home, Marie had lived in a new house, but at Vienna we could only locate and attain partial use of a 3rd floor apartment in a pre-WW I edifice where we had to go out in the hallway for running cold water and to use the toilette. There was no bath on the premises, but our rent only amounted to about $5 a month! Our address was Adamberger Gasse 1a in the 2nd district of Vienna also known as *Leopoldstadt*. Our kind elderly landlady's name was Maria Szapak; she hailed from Czechoslovakia but lived in Vienna since she was seventeen.

What probably perturbed Marie right from the beginning in Vienna was the fact that I had to be in the hospital for about a week when I had an appendectomy. It left me with a diminished capacity to digest sausage casings, apple peals, and other cellulose food substances. Prior to my operation, Marie did not have time to make the acquaintance of any local people. My brother Josef came from Salzburg when I was just coming out of my narcosis, which affected me more adversely than the operation itself. I literally had been knocked out with ether. As I was subsequently told, patients normally fall asleep while counting to around thirty-nine or so. I still heard myself counting upon reaching 117 and then I passed out. The Austrian doctors had not taken into account that my occupational exposure to all sorts of paints and coatings in America had increased my resistance to ether. Toxic coatings were not as extensively used by house painters in Austria, as they happen to be in the United States.

Even as a foreign student attending an Austrian institution of higher education, I received free medical treatment at the general hospital (Allgemeines Krankenhaus) in Vienna. I only would have been liable for a partial payment if I had wanted a private or semi-private room. As it turned out, I shared a wardroom with about a dozen Austrian patients. Several of them were former waiters with leg problems. They had interesting and funny stories to tell.

In the bed next to mine was a man who had lost both legs. One of his stumps failed to heal up completely, which caused him to spend much time in hospitals. One night, I happened to wake up as he rustled through his night stand drawer in the dark and then slid toward the other side of his bed so that he could slip some something into my glass of tea, which stood on a night stand between our beds. Naturally, I did not touch the beverage again.

After waking up in the morning, he looked at me and at the glass to see if I had consumed its content. When I asked the nurse for a fresh drink, he was quick to point out that my glass still contained liquid. Thankfully, the nurse brought me another drink in a different glass and removed the contaminated one. I kept wondering what the chap had put into my glass and shuddered at the thought of what might have happened if I had unknowingly taken a drink from it. The thought occurred to me that the lowly fellow might have wanted to take revenge on an American whose countrymen may have caused his disability during the war. It was also possible that he was mad at anybody who still had his legs to walk with. Needless to say, I did not trust the louse afterwards and I was glad to be released from a place where a person could be a target of malice while immobilized in a hospital bed.

Another type of ordeal Marie and I were in for coincided with our 1956 Christmas visit at the house of my brother Josef and his family. They had just completed a room addition where a wood-burning stove was emitting smoke at the wrong end. Their children Maria and Josef Jr. already had bad coughs when we got there and they slept right next to us in the same bed! Their incessant coughing combined with the frigid room temperature kept us from sleeping, too. We wanted to leave as soon as possible under the miserable circumstances but they insisted that it would hurt their feelings if we left before the holiday period ended. Luckily, we had purchased tickets for the famous Viennese Strauss concert on New Year Day, which justified our earlier departure; however, we were already in for nasty colds anyway.

What must have also frustrated Marie was that her strong desire to be constructively involved had no suitable outlet. She obviously could not really help me with my studies since my topics did not coincide with her own interests. It was also hard for her to relate to my pursuits, because I myself was not quite sure where I was headed. I was still haphazardly trying to sort out my career goals while she was anxious to know what lay ahead. It only added to my predicament when she questioned whether I was ready for married life. I was truly unable to give her even a hint, let alone a blueprint, regarding our future. For years to come, I honestly did not know what career I would eventually wind up pursuing. All I knew was that I had immigrated to America in efforts to better myself. Having to settle for anything less would have been tantamount to self-deception.

When my two-year course on motion picture production ended with the spring semester 1957, Marie and I booked passage on the nearly new Dutch liner *Statendam* for the return voyage to New York. With whatever money that was left, we only got as far as my sister's house in Pennsylvania. From there, Marie's parents and my brother Tony picked us up in the Chevrolet station wagon of her brother Alex who happened to be in the U. S. Army at the time. Upon arriving in the Chicago area again, I did not have to spend time looking for a job right away since my brother-in-law Peter promptly re-hired me as a carpenter's helper. For the time being, Marie and I moved in with her folks at 3935 Harvard Terrace in Skokie, Illinois. The used 1954 Plymouth Plaza we purchased before long had a built-in flaw: Whenever the temperature fell below twenty-five ABOVE zero, the car needed to be jump-started.

We were not the first couple who returned broke from their honeymoon. While spending time in Europe, we had visited all of our relatives except those who were living behind the iron curtain. The two of us had also been sightseeing in London, Paris, Zurich, Lucerne, Innsbruck, Graz, and at other places. We had even traveled to St. Peter's Square in Rome to hear Pope Pious XII (1939-1958) deliver his 1957 Easter message. While in Rome, we went to see Marie's former school chum Maria Tozzi, née Pipping, who prepared a savory Italian pasta dish for us as a treat. Upon taking the train to Venice, we marveled over its location in a lagoon. At Trieste, we were disappointed by their poor-tasting version of pizza and upon hearing some visiting Yugoslavs speak Serbian within earshot, I got chills up and down my back as it reawakened memories of scary moments I had experienced at the hands of uncouth partisans under Tito's regime.

After working for the Holt Construction Company from June until August 1957, I got a job as a messenger/chauffeur at Kling Film Studios on West Washington Boulevard in Chicago; thus, I was closer to Columbia College where I continued my studies during evenings as of the fall quarter. I had one year to go toward a B. A. degree in Speech and Communication Arts.

IV. IN PURSUIT OF DOMESTIC AND CAREER GOALS

10. Family Growth and Further Education

To maintain my eligibility for a scholarly stipend under the GI Bill (Public Law 550), I had to resume my education at an institution that granted full credit for the studies I had completed abroad between 1955 and 1957. At Northwestern University and at the University of Illinois I only would have gotten credit for courses that also happened to be among their own offerings. Another problem I would have been faced with at these institutions concerned scheduling. Since I had to work full time, it was essential for me to be able to get all the courses I needed during evening hours; therefore, Columbia College, then at 207 South Wabash Avenue in downtown Chicago, turned out to be my best overall option. I had already made the acquaintance of the College President Mr. Mirron Alexandroff before I went to Vienna. He and his staff were very accommodating. Carrying a full program of study evenings while working full time during the week was hard, but it had to be done since I wanted to graduate from college without undue delays.

As of summer 1957, Marie returned to work in the Stock Transfer Department of City National Bank at 208 South La Salle Street, Chicago, where she was able to benefit salary-wise from her accumulated seniority. To increase my own lower earnings, I quit my ($70.00 weekly) job at Kling Film Studios in October 1957 and went to work for Dallas Jones Productions on Wells Street near North Avenue for $80.00 a week. In addition to earning a little more money now, I was gaining experience related to motion picture production. Initially, I worked in the Ektachrome still-photo processing laboratory and later in the film editing room.

One night after work, I stopped at a hardware store on North Avenue a couple of houses east of Halsted Street. Since the meter where I had parked our 1954 Plymouth did not need to be fed after 5:00 p. m., I left the car right there and walked a couple of blocks to the house of my Uncle Nick BARBA and Aunt Katharina on 1829 N. Dayton Street. She always had delicious baked goods along with refreshing libation on hand. I enjoyed some beer and we talked for a while. Before I made it back to my car, darkness had set in outdoors. As I came within sight of the vehicle, I noticed that someone was hiding behind one of the nearby steel supports beneath the elevated train tracks. Upon having spotted the tips of the person's shoes, I paused and looked around, but the nearest human being I

123

could see on deserted North Avenue was about a block west by a subway entrance.

Before resuming my walk, I reached into my pocket as though I had something I could use to fend off an attacker. The next thing I knew, a squad car suddenly pulled up from nowhere with its lights off. A black police officer jumped out and quickly shackled the practically hidden black man who evidently was up to no good. Addressing me, one of the two black peace officers present exclaimed: "Hey man, I ain't never seen nobody come as close to dyin' as you just did!" The constable's energized tone of voice gave me ample cause for sustained reflections about life. Mine apparently might have ended then and there if it had not been for timely action by vigilant law enforcement agents.

Productions at Dallas Jones included commercials for the Sunbeam Corporation, the National Athletics Association, the Swift Meat Company, the Carrier Corporation, and others. What made me terminate my employment there in November 1958 were the high dues I had to pay to a motion picture workers' union. In addition to a $6.00 monthly liability, I had to contribute 2 percent of my gross earnings! It struck me as ludicrous that I should have to pay anybody for holding down a job where I only earned a pittance to begin with. Undeniably, the opportunity to work in that field was regarded as an auspicious jumping board to something more lucrative; however, my immediate financial needs were too compelling for me to stick around in anticipation of a remote chance to do better. Without personal connections and/or investment capital, the likelihood of achieving higher earnings was quite slim.

Meanwhile, Marie and I had moved from her parents' house in Skokie to a 3rd floor one-bedroom apartment at 1533 W. Cornelia Avenue in Chicago. Doing so reduced the commuting time to our respective jobs and to the classes I attended. In the meantime, we also had traded in our unreliable light blue 1954 Plymouth Plaza for a brand new 1958 Verona-green Opel Rekord. It cost over $2100 but turned out to be a real gem that we kept for a decade! Its 4-cylinder engine was so straightforward that I was able to perform a tune-up in the moonlight one evening without a flashlight when the car conked out on a country highway while our family was returning home to Urbana, Illinois, from Bloomington, Indiana.

On June 21, 1958, I was awarded my B. A. degree in Speech and Communication Arts at Columbia College. In view of impending academic regulations under which prospective teachers were going to be required to complete a professional sequence in addition to their subject specialty, President Alexandroff wanted me to apply for a teaching certificate even though I was not planning to use it as of then. Following his advice would have proved advantageous because pretty soon schools around the country were hiring increasing numbers of foreign language instructors when the National Defense Education Act (NDEA) of 1958 called for upgraded curricula after Russia's successful sputnik launch in October 1957. Being a native speaker of German and having studied in Vienna, Austria, would have undoubtedly enabled me to begin my language teaching career a lot earlier; however, the low starting salaries of high school teachers did not entice me at all.

Since I had to give up hope about advancing to a better-paying job in motion picture production, I figured international business would be a good area to get into; therefore, I enrolled in two applicable evening courses at Roosevelt University during autumn 1958. One was on Export Trade Practice and the other one a Survey of Foreign Markets. Predictably, my efforts in that direction did not lead to any job prospects either because American firms were unwilling to offer extra remuneration to employees with a knowledge of foreign languages. Most company officials were afraid to lose control unless English remained dominant in negotiations.

Just before the Christmas shopping season in November 1958, I was hired to work at the downtown Chicago department store of Carson, Pirie, Scott & Company as a sales clerk in the men's department. After the holidays, I was retained as an assistant to Mr. Robert Ward who was the buyer in the yard goods and draperies department. Since my salary was quite low and because under prevalent bank rules Marie had to quit working when it became apparent that she was expecting a baby, I had no choice but to go back into house painting to match the joint level of income we had gotten used to. Still without a career and woeful about my troubled childhood, I was not at all sure that I wanted to bring children into this world. It just did not appear to be a comely place for them; however, Marie would have felt unfulfilled without having at least two. Earning more money for a decent living became even more important when our son Carl was born on June 18, 1959, during our third year of marriage.

My primary reason for never wanting to remain in painting emanated from trepidation that continual exposure to some of the materials used would bring me to an early grave. My suspicions were substantiated when it came to light that test benzene, which we regularly used for thinning oil paints as well as for cleaning brushes, rollers, and spattered skin areas, turned out to be a carcinogen! In recognition of health hazards, most coatings now come with warnings as follows:

'Repeated and prolonged exposure to solvents may lead to permanent brain and nervous system damage. Eye watering, headaches, nausea, dizziness, and loss of coordination are signs of high solvent levels.'

It was no wonder that I used to come home, after having painted indoors all day in residences around Chicago, with my taste buds so vastly numbed that I could not savor the flavor of what I was eating. Having my palate constantly impaired was not the way I visualized partaking of America's cornucopia when I left my post-war ration cards in Austria and opted for the green card of a U. S. immigrant.

Our son Carl was about five months old when Marie and I purchased our first home in Chicago. It was a 2-family frame house located at 2842 North Albany Avenue. We paid $18,000 for it. Avondale Savings and Loan Association held our first mortgage of $14,500. The previous owner extended us a second mortgage amounting to $1,500. Marie's parents lent us $600 and my employer Louis Wesserle gave me an advance of $500. The rest, plus expenses, came from the $1,800 Marie and I had saved. The 2-bedroom 1st floor apartment was rented out to a tenant for $80 monthly and the 2nd floor apartment became our own abode upon completion of major cleaning and remodeling tasks. We painted or wallpapered all plaster areas and refinished the wooden floors. Trim around doors and windows as well as the baseboards were grained to look natural. In the kitchen, we added a row of upper and lower cabinets and we also modernized the bathroom that still had an old cast iron tub on legs. By the end of December 1959, we were able to move in even though a lot of work remained to be done.

While working as a house painter full time, I got myself a side job at the Joseph Funk Realty Company on 2237 Irving Park Road in Chicago. I became a duly licensed Real Estate Salesman who never sold any homes other than our own. While contacting people over the telephone and in person, I managed to get some listings and a few leads but no sales transaction ever materialized. One prospective couple said, "we enjoy working with YOU, but we don't want to have any dealings with your broker." When my painting boss found out that I was moonlighting, he offered to give me extra work on weekends, too. He evidently did not realize that I had my fill of painting and would have loved to switch to another occupation.

In my state of unhappiness as a house painter, I decided to go back to school evenings for more education so that I could eventually qualify for a safer job where I would earn a comparable living. When I applied for readmission to the University of Illinois in the early 1960's, I was informed that I had deficiencies to make up in algebra and geometry before my application could be considered. The new requirements reflected rising educational standards all around the country.

Before remedying the deficiencies at two Chicago City Junior College branches between 1961 and 1963, I also enrolled in a six-month evening course to study Electronics at DeVry Technical Institute on Belmont Avenue in 1962. As of the Summer Session 1963, I was able to reenter the University of Illinois at Chicago's Navy Pier and in autumn, I began to attend classes on the main campus at Urbana. Early that year, we had an addition to the family when our daughter Ellen Susanne was born at Grant Hospital in Chicago on January 24.

During autumn 1963, we rented out our cozy flat at 2842 North Albany Avenue in Chicago and temporarily moved into a house at 1307 Westfield Drive in Champaign, Illinois. Meanwhile, a prefabricated National Home was being built for us at 411 Glenn Drive in Urbana, Illinois, under a 30-year FHA-insured loan. The new 3-bedroom house with a hardwood floor over a crawl space cost $11,900. By doing the painting ourselves and upon payment of $500, our mortgage came to $11,000 on which we paid $91 monthly. To earn our keep, I worked as a freelance house painter on weekends and early evenings while attending morning and early afternoon classes on the main campus of the University of Illinois. My genuinely concerned brother-in-law Peter Norman HOLT rightfully questioned whether I was being gutsy or foolhardy to resume full time study at my stage in life.

To further illustrate my vexing inability to arrive at a career choice in this recognized land of opportunities, I should mention that I initially enrolled in Pre-Journalism upon entering the University of Illinois on February 7, 1955. When I went to Vienna later that year, I had decided to study music and motion picture production. My studies at Columbia College (1957-1958) also tied in with that area. After transferring to Urbana in fall 1963, I wanted to major in Agronomy; however, I soon learned from classmates that even most descendants of American farmers could not see a future for themselves in agriculture. It made me ask myself, how I was to attain a competitive edge in that field to hold my own against others who were born into it.

127

Upon losing faith in the program that I was pursuing, I decided to major in a subject area where I knew I had an advantage as a native speaker of German; thus, I embraced the idea of becoming a foreign language instructor. I completed corresponding studies in 1965 and was awarded my B. A. degree in Teaching German. By continuing studies toward an M. A. degree, which I obtained in 1967, I raised my earning potential. Meanwhile, I even got licensed and gained a year of teaching experience at Edison Junior High School in Champaign, Illinois, when my predecessor Marie Dresch unexpectedly resigned her position to get married upon having attended the 1966 summer session at Middlebury College in Vermont.

My gross salary for the 1966/67 academic year was $6,161.00 at Edison Junior High School. As a freelance house painter, I would have earned $7,800 during the same time period at my going rate of $5 an hour if I had worked forty hours weekly. My first year of teaching proved that I needed to earn a higher degree to boost my income as a teacher. I also learned that, with my varied international background and on the basis of my personal inclination, I was better suited to work with adult students than with teenagers whose mood shifts can often be infuriatingly disconcerting.

Just before Christmas 1965, our second son Richard Peter was born. Although we had not planned to have a third child, his arrival proved to be a true blessing as things turned out. False symptoms made us go to the Carle Clinic in Urbana about a week too early so that Marie's mother Magda, who had come to be with us, was really getting nervous by the time Rick actually made his appearance before Christmas eve, with me watching the event. Holding a scalpel in his right hand, the doctor almost dropped the baby when it suddenly slipped onto his left arm as a result of a final push by Marie. Another anxious moment was caused by the fact that her hemorrhoids were ballooning so very near the point of incision that a tiny slip with the sharp instrument could have jeopardized her own life while she was delivering a new one! Thank goodness, nothing bad happened and the suturing turned out fine also.

Now that I was finally within reach of formal qualifications toward a viable career outside the hazardous house painting business, greater opportunities ironically began to open up for me in that line of work as well, thanks to the support of a number of local townspeople. Among my first benefactors was Mr. Charles Zipprodt, then Secretary of the Urbana Chamber of Commerce and later mayor of the city. He hired me to do some painting at his own house and also put me in touch with Mr. Henry Green, a local banker who owned various properties where painting work was needed. I also became acquainted with Mr. Fox, the owner of three local laundry and dry cleaning plants. I was able to paint there unperturbed during evening hours and on weekends when the facilities were not in operation.

Before it was opened for business, I was also hired to do some painting in the office of the new Carter Travel Agency. While occupied out of sight behind the large paneled counter that I had stained in a spiffy turquoise hue, the owner came by with a guest. Upon praising my work, he asked his companion, "what are we doing wrong in this country that we can't keep craftsmen with great expertise working in their own fields? The guy who is doing this project wants to go into foreign language teaching!"

A homebuilder who hailed from the "Sudetenland" in Czechoslovakia was another local patron of mine. He said, "why don't you stay here? I'll put 'em up, you paint 'em, and we'll both make money." Somebody else suggested that I hire painters from abroad and have them work for me so that I could take it easy. Ever since my disappointing army experience as an acting squad leader, I knew better than to take charge of a motley crew whose constituents would carry on as they pleased in no time at all.

On June 27, 1968, Marie and I sold our 2-family frame house in Chicago. Its upkeep had proven to be quite a chore as time went by. It had also prompted repeated quarrels between us: Instead of being able to just visit with her folks at 7929 N. Linder Avenue in Morton Grove, Illinois, Marie and I wound up having to carry out clean-up work and small repairs at our rental property. Tenants could not be expected to maintain the premises on top of having to pay rent! On one occasion, a tenant even asked us to come from Urbana, a distance of 140 miles, to light the pilot on the hot water heater. Luckily, we knew that the local gas company attended to such matters routinely; so we got that problem solved immediately. Other things that needed our attention usually turned out to be more time consuming.

The value of the house in Chicago had undoubtedly appreciated because of momentous improvements we had made during our nine years of ownership. Nevertheless, we wound up selling it for the same price we had paid for it. Upon deducting the realtor's commission of six percent, we were left with $16,920 out of which we had to pay off the remainder of the mortgage and defray other applicable fees and expenses including the prorated property tax. We learned that selling a home from a distance tends to diminish expectable proceeds quite a lot.

Subsequent dealings with realtors taught us that the outcome is never quite as prearranged with them. Even when we agreed to accept a lower offer in order to have the buyer meet specific timelines, it never worked out as bargained for. Over the years, we gained the distinct impression that realtors, though acting as a seller's agent, are far less mindful of vendors' deadlines than about getting a prospective buyer to make an offer! Lenders often cause additional delays. As sellers, we were naive enough to accurately inform realtors of our agenda expecting to have our timeframe actualities observed. Unfortunately, our stipulations always turned out to be like so many words spoken into the wind. In the end, the purchaser's circumstances wound up being the determining factors as far as the consummation of sales was concerned! The only thing that any of our realtors ever did without losing time was to promptly collect their commission. Based on experiences with the five homes we owned so far, I cannot recall a transaction where serendipity did not outweigh the contributions of the realtors involved.

In 1968, Marie traded in our 1959 Renault Dolphine on a brand new 1968 Volkswagen Squareback, a move we were contemplating anyway. The abrupt acquisition became necessary when the oil-burning Renault nearly left her in a lurch while she was driving to her folks in Morton Grove, Illinois, on the very day when rioting had unexpectedly broken out in Chicago as a result of the assassination of Martin Luther King (1929-1968). Her mother was a nervous wreck by the time Marie and our kids got to her house in Morton Grove and the Renault turned out to be on its last leg also! Ever since we had acquired it for a mere $90, we had to prime it before it would start and then it usually only ran on two of its four cylinders. One day, when Marie gave our son Carl a ride to school in the sputtering red sedan at a speed of five miles per hour, he said wearily, "let me off mom, I'd rather walk."

Miraculously, Marie and her brother Al HOLT were able to drive the decrepit Renault to a VW dealer in Evanston, Illinois. They were granted $46 toward the purchase of our VW Squareback that cost around $2,800. The compact Granada red station wagon proved to be our most versatile vehicle yet, because of its hatchback-accessible expandable cargo space inside. With the rear seat folded down flat, all three of our children could stretch out and sleep on long trips and during travel

130

at night. The car remained part of our family for twenty (20) years whereupon we sold it to a carpenter in Winona, Minnesota.

Several of our family trips in 1968 were prompted in connection with our relocation from Urbana, Illinois, to Cincinnati, Ohio. My award of a fellowship under the National Defense Education Act (NDEA) for pursuing doctoral studies in German at the University of Cincinnati caused us to move there. With most of the proceeds from our house in Chicago and a mortgage of $9,000, we purchased the single-family red brick house at 3076 N. Hegry Circle in Cincinnati, Ohio, for $14,000 on August 1, 1968. It had hardwood floors, two bedrooms, a living room, kitchen with breakfast nook, and a bath on the main floor. The attic was unfinished but it sported two dormer windows in the front that came in handy when we built two additional bedrooms up there. The one-car garage was under the house along with the basement area. Our lot fanned out toward the back, because we were situated on the outer periphery of an oval street, which was nice for our children who liked to ride bicycles. Being able to enter the basement through the garage, also proved advantageous when we bought an 800-pound used upright Starr piano that we just rolled in behind the furnace. Carl got lots of practice on it after he began to take lessons from Mrs. Helen Berger on Veazey Street in January 1969.

Our home in Urbana was sold in August 1968 for a total of $14,000. We rented the biggest truck available and, with the greatly valued help of my brother Tony and his wife Martha, we managed to get all of our possessions on it before we hit the road as the saying goes; by then, it was beginning to get dark already. Tony and I were in the truck with me driving while Marie, Martha, and the children took off in two different cars.

Our wives and respective progeny reached the house in Cincinnati in good time even though the women had to fight sleep while driving. Tony and I started out with the truck gauge showing a full tank of gas. After having driven for a while, the needle was at the half tank mark as we passed a filling station along Interstate 74. I figured we could go farther before refueling; however, soon afterward the truck began to sputter and we had to pull off the highway and onto the shoulder. Trying to restart the engine proved to be futile. We just sat there in the dark for a while hoping that a patrolman might come by who could help; however, the only vehicle that stopped to offer assistance happened to be a car full of black folks. Since unmistakable fumes of liquor streamed toward us as they were talking, we

131

thought it best to forego whatever aid they might have been able to provide.

Since cell phones were not available for years to come, Tony and I had no way of calling anyone; thus, I decided to walk back until I got to a gas station. While driving, one seldom realizes how far apart stations can be! It took quite a while before I reached an open one on foot. The attendant on duty was good enough to provide me with a 2-gallon can of gasoline and a policeman drove me to our rented truck. As soon as we poured fuel into the tank, it did not take long to get the engine started again.

With the police officer guiding us across the median, we turned around and went back to the station for more gasoline. When the tank was about half full, the needle already pointed to full; thus, we realized that we could not trust the gauge any more than we should have trusted the rental agency! It had not only cheated us out of a half tank of gas but also of about five hours of sleep. After this experience, I knew that one should make it a point to pull up to a pump and top off the tank before taking a rented vehicle on the road. If the gauge is off, it is best to have the agent make a note of it right then and there because getting an adjustment later is much more complicated. Even approved claims never actually include compensation for lost time.

Instead of arriving at Cincinnati around midnight, we did not get there until dawn. Fortunately our wives were too tired to just sit in the house and worry; they went to sleep with the children. After taking a nap, Tony and I got up and began to unload the truck with help from Marie and Martha while the children were reconnoitering our new neighborhood. There was a small grocery store nearby on one end of the circle drive where they could buy soda and candy. On the other end, there was a discount store named Chinatown, which made shopping quite convenient. What became a favorite place close by was a restaurant where La Rosa's pizza was available. Another excellent local brand a little farther away turned out to be Pasquali's pizza.

Between October 1968 and June 1971, I was able to complete all required courses at the University of Cincinnati toward a Doctor of Philosophy (Ph. D.) degree. In addition to focusing on the German language itself, we studied literary examples of the Old High German period, representative Middle High German writings, and works in High German right up to contemporary belles-lettres categories. Upon completing long reading lists by April 18, 1970, I passed my preliminary doctoral examination covering the literature from 750 to 1600. As of August 14, 1970, I had passed the one on the literature from 1600 to 1850. On March 19, 1971, I was informed that I had also passed the examination on the literature from 1850 to the present.

Thanks to the $360 monthly fellowship payment my family and I received during the first of three years, $380 monthly during the second, and an even $400 during the third, I was able to devote all of my time to studying. We also enjoyed meeting quite a few new people at Cincinnati and we were lucky enough to have excellent neighbors, too. The Kleemeier family lived on one side of us and the Pfalzgraf family on the other. The "children" of the Kleemeiers were all grown up, but those of the Pfalzgrafs were of the same ages and genders as ours, which worked out well for the kids also.

The climate around Cincinnati is considerably milder than in the Chicago area; however, it can get just as muggy at that particular "gateway to the South," which Winston Churchill referred to as the "Queen City of the West." A white Christmas is never a sure thing at Cincinnati either; snow is apt to melt soon after it falls. The mild weather conditions also result in other benefits for local residents. Right across the Ohio River on the Kentucky side, one can harvest the juiciest peaches in large orchards and take them home for making preserves or to conserve them in jars. One day, when our whole family was picking the best peaches we could find, the ladder our son Carl was standing on happened to shift so that he lost his balance and got ready to jump to the ground. In the last second, he noticed that there was a rusted old plow where he was going to land. Amazingly, he managed to propel himself off the ladder in such a way that he narrowly cleared the junk heap as his feet reached the earth surface. I still shudder at the thought of injuries he could have sustained!

A local facility that also proved to be greatly beneficial for our family was the Findley Market where fresh vegetables and fruits could be bought from area growers as well as from states like Michigan and Georgia for instance. Meats, breads, seafood, and delicatessen could be purchased there as well as live chickens for example. Weekends and Wednesdays were the busiest shopping days until around mid-afternoon when vendors had already met expectations and were left with little produce that they usually sold for a lot less than the regular price. We were able to stretch our budget considerably by timing our shopping accordingly.

Our leisure activities included area sightseeing trips and attendance of suitable events sponsored by local German clubs. One favorite outing involved taking the Anderson Ferry across the Ohio River to Kentucky and returning via the John Augustus Roebling suspension bridge near the stadium downtown Cincinnati. We also liked visiting friends like Inge and Sofus Simonsen who lived on Chickasaw Street with their five boys while Sofus attended the university as I did. The family had a ping-pong table in the basement that attracted other classmates and some staff members, too. The Simonsens' house parties were also well liked by fellow students. Other friends of ours happened to hail from my birthplace. John (Hans) Konrad and I went to school together back in Yugoslavia. His older brother Michael and sister-in-law Eva were active in the Danube Swabian club. The men's sister Magdalena and her husband Willy Miess of Transylvania used to own a local so-called "pony keg" where beverages, delicatessen, and snacks were sold along with knickknacks.

In summer 1970, our family of five was invited by Tony and Martha to spend a two-week camping vacation with them at the Nicolet National Forest in Wisconsin east of Eagle River. My brother and his wife owned an Apache pop up camper in which Marie, Martha, Ellen, Rick, Kristine and Lisa were able to sleep. Carl, Tony, and I slept in a tent borrowed from Martha's sister and brother-in-law Marianne and Bob Stefczak. Since we had not anticipated that the temperature would go down into the thirty-degree range on the Fahrenheit scale, we found ourselves in a campground at Long Lake with only light clothing. Nevertheless, we went canoeing and caught quite a few small perch, but big ones eluded us, which was partly due to the fact that a raccoon had eaten all but one of our minnows right out of a covered bait bucket.

Using food morsels as bait, we could observe the reactions of the fish in the clear, shallow water. When one of us dropped in a baited hook close to the edge of the canoe, we could see little fish going for it and tugging at it but their mouths were too small to actually grab the bait. Sometimes they pulled or knocked it off the hook though whereupon a big fish would dash for it with a swift sweep of its tail. The big ones seemed to have learned when it was safe for them to imbibe food that was not common to the area. The immature larger fish proved to be much more active, voracious, and reckless; consequently, some of them wound up getting hooked as they promptly darted for the bait in efforts to beat others to it. The behavior of the fish was reminiscent of human conduct in a number of ways.

Evenings, we would sit around a campfire conversing, laughing, and singing while I played familiar tunes on a Hohner "Marine Band" harmonica. One night, we just sat and talked when someone with a flashlight approached our site and a woman's voice asked, "aren't you going to play tonight?" Having been made aware that others were listening also made me more self-conscious of my performance. It inadvertently detracted from its spontaneity, but I tried to play as well as I could in my preferred key of G. Unfortunately, the reeds of the instrument were no longer entirely in perfect tune either. Enjoyable music must come from a person's heart or from well-trained performers. On that dreary evening of the requested encore, I did not feel that I was able to meet expectations either way, but fortunately no one complained.

If we had extended our camping time, I might have also learned to engage in a dialog with chipmunks. When I started our VW Squareback for our departure after it had been parked at the site for about ten days, an excited ground squirrel ran up to the open driver-side window and reproached me in panic with rapid-fire screeching utterances. I got the drift of the critter's denunciation, but I had no idea how I had triggered it. For the moment, it seemed like an apology was definitely in order on my part; as I verbalized it, the tiny creature actually seemed to calm down a bit. The rationale for its outburst became evident when we stopped at a gas station for fuel. Upon checking the oil, we found a neat chipmunk nest right on the engine manifold! The sudden vibration of the motor and the sound of the internal combustion must have shocked the poor thing out of its mind and to make things even worse, someone was in the process of driving away with its domicile! - We were fortunate that the tinder-dry nest did not catch fire on the searing hot exhaust manifold.

One of the hardest aspects of my doctoral studies at the University of Cincinnati concerned the selection of a topic for my dissertation. I would have liked to treat a subject related to my ethnic group known as Danube Swabians; however, there was no one among the senior faculty who was sufficiently familiar with this ethnic-German minority. Consequently, I was compelled to select an area of studies in which a tenured staff member was competent. I decided to focus on the 18th Century period of Enlightenment. It coincided with the time when most Danube Swabian forefathers migrated from different parts of the Holy Roman Empire of the German Nation to the Banat in Hungary, which eventually wound up under Romanian and Yugoslav jurisdiction when the Austro-Hungarian empire was dismembered after WW I.

135

The professor who offered to work with me was Gottfried Merkel, a graduate of the University of Leipzig. He had a number of scholarly publications in German and English to his credit. His academic standards were very high, which made it difficult to meet his expectations and it definitely prompted me to work much harder. To start with, he had me write short papers on different topics to find out how my studious attributes and leanings could be applied most advantageously in the drafting of my dissertation. I also owe him a considerable debt of gratitude for having stressed the importance of choosing words according to their primary rather than ancillary meanings. It results in a more precise depiction of what one is trying to say.

I ended up treating Johann Christoph Gottsched (1700-1766) and the most gifted prospective writers among his students at the University of Leipzig who were striving to improve literary taste and modern usage of language. In accordance with widespread contemporary practice, their initial writings were published anonymously. Based on the title of the journal in which many of the young authors' trenchant literary creations appeared, the group became known as "Bremer Beiträger" in German literary history. The two associates, who eventually achieved the widest recognition under their own names, were Christian Fürchtegott Gellert (1715-1769) and Friedrich Gottlieb Klopstock (1724-1803).

When I accepted a teaching position in Minnesota in 1971, I had to defer work on my dissertation for a couple of years. It took a lot more research and repeated revisions of individual components, before I was able to complete and defend the final version in December 1974 whereupon I was awarded a Ph. D. degree in German Language and Literatures in 1975.

11 Job Searches and Relocation to Winona, Minnesota

In anticipation of completing my course work at the University of Cincinnati by June 1971, I began my job search as of fall 1970. Since the number of openings for doctoral candidates in foreign language teaching had diminished considerably, I decided to send out queries regarding other types of work also. Firms I contacted in vain about non-teaching positions included:

Cincinnati Milacron,
Crown Publishers Inc.
Dover Publications Inc.
Dun & Bradstreet International,
E. I. Du Pont de Nemours & Company,
Encyclopedia Britannica Educational Corporation,
Glidden-Durkee Division of SCM Corporation,
Holt Rinehart and Winston Inc.
Litton Educational Publishing Inc.
The Procter and Gamble Company,
The Sherwin-Williams Company
The Viking Press Inc., an affiliate of Weston Woods Studios.

In addition, I sent fruitless inquiries to the following governmental agencies: Department of the Army - Defense Language Institute, Federal Trade Commission, General Services Administration, National Security Agency, U. S. Civil Service Commission, U. S. Department of Commerce, and the U. S. Information Agency.

In response to the more than two hundred (200+) queries I mailed to universities, colleges, and community colleges, I received about one-hundred forty-two (142) letters of regret and over sixty (60) addressees chose not to reply. I even contacted some vocational institutions to see if they could use an instructor with my background in the building trades and agriculture.

In language departments around the country, staff cuts were generally carried out after Princeton University led the way in dropping foreign language requirements for admission as of 1968. Two years later, on January 4, 1970, *The New York Times* (E 9) reported: "Suddenly Ph. D.'s Are 'A Glut on the Market'."

Overproduction in manpower training exacts a price from individuals who get caught in the process; however, it benefits society in at least two ways: 1) Educating and training

137

extra people provides employment for professors, teachers, instructors, and support personnel among others. 2) Having an oversupply of applicants, ultimately results in greater productive output since go-getters and those with better qualifications tend to be selected for employment while many who are not chosen wind up enhancing their skills through more training and education.

It took me almost a lifetime to realize that "crisis management" not only entails finding solutions to problems but it also involves the precipitancy of conditions that make people try harder to surmount difficulties, be they imposed or natural. "Putting out brush fires," as one college dean phrased it, really is only part of the process; the corollary calls for agitation, coercion, provocation, cajoling, enticements, force, etc. to elicit hustle and bustle and to promote wear and tear which tend to enhance economic activities. This modus operandi does not come into play much in socialist societies where each constituent is supposed to derive benefits according to his or her needs while only having to contribute according to their abilities. Since socialists regard incentives for the augmentation of one's abilities as a type of exploitative bribe, individual productivity remains low and the means to provide for everyone's needs are perpetually scarce; thus their maxim may look good in theory, but it proved to be utterly impractical.

As a prospective applicant with all but the dissertation completed toward a Ph. D. degree, I also considered it relevant to mention my multiplex work background in my letters of inquiry. Filling out application forms for employment tended to frustrate me because none of them had appropriate spaces for listing all of my occupational experiences that extend back to my childhood and adolescence in different countries! Even if I could have detailed them adequately on paper, it is doubtful whether personnel managers might have had the inclination or corresponding erudition to match my vocational attributes with respective employers' needs, for mutually beneficial alliances. More often than not, the atypical entries on my applications probably irked screening agents who were attuned to processing forms with cut and dried data.

A chronological listing of my employers and their locations as well as the type of work I performed from childhood to retirement stacks up as follows:

a) Time:	b) Employer & Place:	c) Type of Work Done:
1945	Labor camp, Yugoslavia	General farm work
1945-1947	Nicholas Frecot, Romania	General farm work
1947-1948	Michael Artner, Austria	General farm work

1948-1951	Josef Neureiter, Bad-Ischl	House painting
1951-1952	Walker-Jimieson, Chicago, IL	stock clerk
1952-1953	Louis Wesserle & Son, Chicago, IL	Hse paintg
1953-1955	U. S. Infantry, Fort Lewis, WA	Food distrib
1956&1957	Holt Construction Co., Skokie, IL	Carpentry
1957	Kling Film Studios, Chicago, IL	Chauffeur
1957-1958	Dallas Jones Prod., Chicago, IL	Film editing
1958-1959	Carson, Pirie, Scott & Co., Chicago	Retailing
1959-1960	Funk Realty Company, Chicago, IL	Salesman
1959-1963	Saffran/Wesserle/Pharher, Chicago,	Hse paintg
1963-1968	Self-empl'd, Urbana/Champaign, IL	Hse paintg
1966-1967	Edison Jr. H. S., Champaign, IL	Teacher
1971-1992	Winona State University, MN	Lang. Prof.
July, 1980	FEMA (Cuban influx) Ft. McCoy, WI	Interpreter
1980-now	Self-employment sideline: Translating & bk sales	
1992	Retired; continuing translating work+book sales.	

Other manifestations of achievements not generally requested or taken into account on job application forms include certificates and honorary awards of which I received the following:

1. Honorary Awards:
a) Graduate Club membership card of the Americanization and Adult Education Division of the Chicago Board of Education sponsored by the Illinois Society of Colonial Dames of America and granted in June 1952.
b) Delta Phi Alpha. Deutsche Ehrenverbindung. Kapitel Pi granted February 25, 1965.
c) Chi Gamma Iota, Veterans Scholastic Honor Society. Alpha Chapter granted March 15, 1966.
d) Pi Delta Phi. Société d'Honneur Française, Chapitre Pi, granted April 23, 1979.

2. Extracurricular Spanish Language Courses:
a) Instituto de Filología Hispanica, Saltillo, Mexico, 1972
b) IMCI, Guadalajara, Mexico, 1981
c) Eurocentro de Madrid, Spain, 1984.

3. Certification as a Qualified Translator in the following languages and specialty areas on the bases of examinations by the National Translator Certification Service, 28089 Pine Drive, Evergreen, CO 80439 as of 1978:
a) General and Commercial German
b) German - Engineering and Physical Sciences
c) German - Medical and Life Sciences
d) General and Commercial Hungarian
e) General and Commercial Spanish.

4. Certificates for Completing Seminars and Workshops:
    a) 1975 summer program on "German Literary Existentialism," sponsored by the National Endowment for the Humanities at the University of Minnesota in Minneapolis.
    b) 1977 participant in Fulbright program on German Culture, at Bonn and Berlin.
    c) 1986 participation in "Micro-Computers for Teachers," a workshop offered by IBM at Winona State University in Minnesota.
    d) 1987 attendance of a "German Script Seminar" held at The Moravian Archives in Bethlehem, Pennsylvania.
    e) 1988 attendance of a workshop on "The Setting for Computer Supported Writing," offered at the University of Minnesota in Duluth.
    f) 1989 completion of a program on "Using Technology in the Modern Language Classroom," given at Rochester Community College in Minnesota.

    My dossier of credentials was available to prospective employers from the placement office at the University of Cincinnati and from that of the University of Illinois. I anxiously awaited the biweekly "Vacancy Bulletin" from the latter. The edition of April 9, 1971 listed an opening at Winona State College in southeastern Minnesota for a Ph. D. or near Ph. D. candidate in German with a strong backup in Spanish. Along with my response of April 12, 1971 to Mr. Jordan V. Hodgson, Acting Head of the Department of Foreign Languages, I sent a copy of my résumé and the following information:

a) German is my native language.
b) My knowledge of Spanish was initially acquired through self-study and practical exercises with some Mexican-Americans and Puerto Ricans at Fort Lewis, Washington, where I was stationed for 17 months.
c) Upon my release from active military service, I took Spanish at the University of Illinois. It was my best subject at the time.

    In his response of April 15, 1971 Mr. Hodgson informed me that I qualified for the position that they were hoping to fill as of the fall quarter. He also gave me the titles of the respective textbooks used at Winona State in Elementary German and Spanish. I responded to his informative letter on April 20, 1971 and told him that I was willing to go to Mexico for a booster course in Spanish during the summer of 1972. In a letter dated May 10, 1971 Mr. Hodgson asked whether I was still available; he also spoke to me over the telephone on that day to see if I could come to Winona, Minnesota for an interview. I drove there from Cincinnati and the outcome was positive. In a letter dated June 3, 1971, I was offered an appointment at the rank of Assistant Professor with a salary of $10 400 for the academic year starting September 10, 1971 and ending on June 3, 1972. The offer was open for two weeks but I did not need that long to decide to accept it since nothing else was in the offing for me as far as I knew. Eventually, I learned from Mr. Hodgson that I was chosen for the position because none of the other applicants had a backup in Spanish. - If someone had only given me advance notice to that effect, I would have taken additional applicable classes ahead of time!

In early June 1971, Marie and I put our Cincinnati home on the market and made plans to go house hunting in Winona, Minnesota. My brother Tony and his wife Martha were kind enough to let us use their Apache camper so that we did not have to stay at costly motels. The distance from Cincinnati, Ohio to Winona, Minnesota is just less than 600 miles along interstate highway routes. By spending a night at Marie's parents in Morton Grove, Illinois, we only had to drive for six hours at a time to cover half the distance before getting some rest.

Along with a "welcome letter" dated July 30, 1971, Dr. Robert A. DuFresne, President of Winona State College, sent us a campus and city map; he also asked me to pick up my orientation program from his Administrative Assistant Mr. Ray K. Amundson on September 10.

When I informed Mr. Hodgson of our relocation status on August 18, we still had not concluded the sale of our house in Cincinnati. There was a delay in the FHA approval process since the wife of our buyer's buyer had been in a mental institution. Thus, our $20 000 deal could not be closed until September 8 - two days before I was scheduled to report for work at a location that was almost 600 miles away! Upon paying off the remainder of our mortgage and after deducting the realtor's commission plus minor other expenses, we were left with a net amount of $10 055.86.

Our house hunting efforts at Winona, Minnesota, a city of about 27 000 inhabitants, had turned out to be problematic. Whatever dwellings local realtors were able to show us turned out to be rundown overpriced dumps that had been poorly "remodeled" or subdivided into rental units for students. One higher priced option would have been the acquisition of a brand new 3-bedroom home near the West End Shopping Center for $27 000. I was ready to go for it when we became aware of another possibility through the trust department of the Merchants National Bank of Winona. The bank had just cleared all the hurdles towards the sale of the former Lillian Perkins home at

355 West Fourth Street that happened to be vacant since 1967 while the estate of the childless deceased owner was being settled in probate court.

Our $16 500 offer on the house, dated June 17, 1971, was accepted and the people at Merchants Bank were even kind enough to rent the place to us until our real estate transaction at Cincinnati was completed. The rent from August 15 to September 1 amounted to $55. It represented 8 percent interest on the purchase price of $16 500, which came to $3.67 a day. In efforts to get the house ready for occupancy, the bank hired a plumber to replace some pipes that had ruptured during a winter freeze. Other manifestations of neglect were evident all over the two-story frame building. Outside, the paint was peeling off gutters, eaves, and the wooden drop siding. The steps to the open front porch were rotten and needed to be replaced soon for safety reasons. Inside, parts of wallpaper had separated from wall and ceiling areas. The double-hung windows were in need of fresh coatings and new ropes. The varnished maple floors were quite scratched up and the linoleum in the kitchen looked rather shabby. The bathroom fixtures were as ancient as the well-worn cast iron kitchen sink. The house was built in 1915 when Winona was primarily a lumber town. Thankfully, timbers used for its construction were of excellent quality but time had taken its toll on manmade home components.

Exposed areas along brittle insulation on electrical wires were evident in the basement, and the entire edifice only had a 30-amp service capacity. - Instead of having been enabled to get to work on the house in Winona, we had to while away the summer at Cincinnati, because of the delayed closing. Our acceptance of a lower bid for a quick transaction had been in vain! I still reproach myself for having been stupid enough to put credence in promises by people who were in no position to determine the actual consummation of the sale either! I believe we paid for this lesson to the tune of several thousand dollars plus the loss of irretrievable time for getting a head start in Winona.

We arrived at Winona with all of our possessions in a rented truck on Sunday, August 22, 1971 without having completed the sale of our residence at Cincinnati, Ohio. Two months earlier, we had made a binding offer on the house at 355 West Fourth Street that became our home for the next twenty-six years.

As of September 1971, Merchants National Bank of Winona granted us a 15-year mortgage at 7 3/4 percent in the

142

amount of $10,000. It took us years of hard work to get the house into good enough shape to make it cozy and presentable. Marie's father, Mr. Frank HOLT, a retired carpenter, built new steps in the front and some years later in 1983, he and his wife Magda, née THEISZ, helped us install siding all around. On August 11, 1972, I got a permit to upgrade the electric service from 30 amperes to a 100-amp capacity. We also replaced the gravity type coal furnace that had been converted to oil. We opted for a forced air gas furnace from Montgomery Ward, which gave us excellent service until the house was sold in 1997. The scores of work projects we completed during twenty-six (26) years of residence there included the following:

A. Exterior
1) Repeatedly painted the outside before siding was applied
2) Installed siding in 1983
3) Replaced old storm windows and storm doors
4) Enclosed the front porch and replaced its gutters
5) Had new roof shingles installed
6) Tuck-pointed the chimney
7) Had metal flue liner installed
8) Replaced all down spouts
9) Installed iron railings in front, back and on the balcony
10) Lined top surface of the balcony walls with sheet metal
11) Replaced steps by the front porch
12) Installed exterior grade electric outlet
13) Insulated underside of front porch and the façade above it
14) Added a central air conditioning unit

B. Garage
1) Extended electrical ground wire to the garage
2) Installed two electric outlets
3) Replaced existing light and switch including the old wires
4) Shielded foundation against seepage with sheet metal skirt
5) Applied roll roofing to unfinished back side
6) Painted the exterior of the 2 1/2-car garage
7) Had new roof shingles installed
8) Reinforced cracked rafter
9) Raised the corner post and placed a stone support under it
10) Adjusted doors for free movement by trimming bottom

C. Yard
1) Reestablished the lawn
2) Planted birch, linden, maple, and mulberry trees
3) Planted purple and white lilac bushes
4) Planted flowers and vegetables
5) Replaced stone sidewalk with concrete
6) Replaced cracked concrete in front of garage

7) Built checkered patio area with blocks
8) Added drain and walkway by the garage
9) Installed exterior light by the garage
10) Installed exterior lights by front and back porches

D. Inside front porch
1) Installed two electric outlets
2) Reinforced the swing hooks with chains above the ceiling
3) Painted the walls
4) Installed indoor/outdoor carpeting

E. Vestibule and guest closet
1) Added a set of folding doors
2) Installed light and switch
3) Installed second shelf and clothes rod
4) Painted the ceiling and papered the walls
5) Installed a heat register
6) Refinished the maple floor

F. Living room
1) Removed old wallpaper from ceiling and wall areas
2) Applied 2 coats of paint to ceiling and re-papered walls
3) Installed additional heat register
4) Added two electric outlets and one coaxial cable outlet
5) Added Venetian blinds and drapes
6) Refinished the floor and later installed wall-to-wall carpet

G. Dining room
1) Removed old wallpaper from ceiling and wall areas
2) Replaced ceiling-plaster with drywall and painted it
3) Added two electric outlets
4) Added Venetian blinds and Belgian lace curtains
5) Refinished the floor and later installed wall-to-wall carpet

H. Solarium
1) Re-papered the walls and painted the ceiling
2) Added an electric outlet
3) Installed Venetian blinds and curtains
4) Refinished the floor and later installed wall-to-wall carpet

I. Butler's pantry
1) Installed Formica countertop
2) Added two electric outlets
3) Applied ceiling tiles
4) Replaced light fixture
5) Re-papered the walls
6) Added Venetian blinds and curtains
7) Installed a vinyl floor

J. Back porch

144

1) Added insulation to outside wall areas
2) Applied ceiling tiles
3) Installed two electric outlets
4) Replaced the light fixture
5) Built shelf and added hooks for hanging cleaning utensils
6) Added Plexiglas window panes and curtains
7) Installed wall-to-wall carpeting

Kitchen
1) Built soffit and installed new cabinets
2) Applied canvass to ceiling and painted it
3) Replaced cast iron sink with a sink cabinet
4) Added a dishwasher unit
5) Installed three Formica countertops
6) Added five electric outlets
7) Installed two light fixtures
8) Installed a ceiling fan
9) Added a range hood with light and fan
10) Re-papered wall areas
11) Built a corner bench
12) Added Venetian blinds and curtains
13) Installed vinyl floor

L. Landing by the side entrance
1) Installed recessed light fixture with two 3-way switches
2) Enlarged the toilet nook, installed a light and small shelves
3) Re-papered the walls and painted the ceiling
4) Installed a vinyl floor

M. Stairway to the basement
1) Built new steps including a landing
2) Added a window sill and curtains
3) Re-papered wall areas
4) Installed stair treads
5) Attached a slate blackboard above the landing

N. Fruit cellar
1) Patched and painted the wall areas
2) Added two electric outlets and a ceiling light with a switch
3) Built additional shelves
4) Painted the concrete floor

O. Basement hall area
1) Added two electric outlets and two ceiling lights
2) Installed a phone jack
3) Painted the wall areas
4) Built shelves beneath the stairs
5) Installed a forced air natural gas furnace
6) Installed vinyl floor tiles

P. Laundry room

1) Replaced all accessible electrical wire
2) Installed 100-amp service box with circuit breakers
3) Replaced old sink with a new double bowl laundry tub
4) Installed a cold water filtering device
5) Extended natural gas pipes to connect a clothes dryer unit
6) Modified plumbing to accommodate new washing machine
7) Installed three double electric outlets
8) Installed two ceiling lights with switches
9) Extended heating ducts and added registers
10) Painted ceiling and wall areas

Q. Basement family room

1) Dismantled the old octopus-type furnace to get rid of it
2) Added ductwork and two heat registers
3) Installed Styrofoam ceiling
4) Added one single and three double outlets
5) Installed 3 ceiling lights with switches including a dimmer
6) Installed paneling with built-in book shelves
7) Textured wall areas with patching plaster and painted them
8) Installed two Formica countertops
9) Installed a base cabinet and added a set of shelves
10) Extended coaxial cable to the TV corner
11) Installed vinyl floor tiles

R. Basement workshop

1) Got rid of large oil drum and cleaned out coal bin residue
2) Installed ceiling light and wall outlets
3) Painted the ceiling and wall areas
4) Installed shelving along all wall areas
5) Installed heat register

S. Stairway to second floor and upper hall

1) Replaced parts of cracked ceiling plaster with drywall
2) Painted ceiling areas and re-papered the walls
3) Replaced ceiling light fixture
4) Added phone jack and an electric outlet
5) Installed wall-to-wall carpeting

T. Northeast front bedroom (smallest)

1) Replaced fallen ceiling plaster with drywall
2) Added three electric outlets
3) Installed coaxial cable and telephone jack outlet
4) Enlarged the clothes closet and installed sliding doors
5) Installed additional shelves and an extra rod
6) Painted the ceiling and re-papered the walls
7) Sanded and refinished the maple floor

U. Master bedroom (northeast)

146

1) Replaced the ceiling plaster with drywall
2) Installed two sconce outlets
3) Installed a ceiling fan
4) Added two electric outlets
5) Installed a light in the closet
6) Painted the ceiling and re-papered the walls
7) Installed a coaxial cable and phone jack outlet
8) Sanded the maple floor and refinished it.

V. Rear bedroom (southwest)
1) Paneled the cracked ceiling in the closet
2) Installed a closet light
3) Added two electric outlets
4) Re-papered the walls
5) Sanded and refinished the maple floor

W. Main bathroom
1) Replaced all fixtures
2) Added two linen closets
3) Installed ceramic tiles on some wall areas
4) Painted ceiling, woodwork, and remaining wall areas
5) Installed three new light fixtures
6) Added electric outlets
7) Added Venetian blinds and curtains
8) Installed a vinyl floor

X. Attic bedroom
1) Paneled wall areas along two beds
2) Installed four electric outlets
3) Installed two light fixtures
4) Painted the woodwork, walls, and ceiling
5) Built a large counter in study area
6) Installed a phone jack
7) Installed wall-to-wall carpeting

Y. Attic closet
1) Installed light
2) Built shelves
3) Created access to covered storage areas
4) Installed carpeting

Z. Attic bathroom
1) Installed Melamine paneling on vertical wall areas
2) Painted the rest of the drywall and woodwork areas
3) Installed a new light fixture
4) Added an electric outlet
5) Installed vinyl floor tiles.

It seemed to be worth every effort for us to carry out whatever improvements we could on the old residence right

147

from the time of our arrival at Winona, Minnesota. Even if my annual work contracts had not been renewed, we probably would have recovered our investment if it had become necessary to sell the house and to look for employment elsewhere. Before giving in to the latter thought, I made every effort to translate my probationary position into an enduring one.

V. MEETING PROFESSIONAL DEMANDS

12. Good Performance Is Just One Requisite in Academe

In retrospect, it appears that my arrival at Winona State in September 1971 coincided with the end of what turned out to be part of the proverbial "good old days." Some of the wholesome ways in which new faculty members used to be made to feel truly welcome simply faded out of the picture as of then. One valued feature of the customary routine was the dinner to which the college president treated new faculty members and their respective chairperson. Another part of the tradition entailed invitations to the homes of prominent community members for hors d'oeuvres prior to attending the annual "President's Ball" in formal attire for dinner and dancing. Proceeds from the payment of $25.00 per person were earmarked for academic scholarships. Of course, quite a few among the faculty who were subsequently hired gave the noticeable impression that wearing a coat and tie was not part of their lifestyle. Be that as it may, the old customs definitely facilitated becoming acquainted with members of the local establishment and new colleagues.

Another circumstance that initially resulted in closer contact with other faculty members was attributable to the fact that several departments that moved to the newly constructed Minné Hall in 1973 were still housed in Somsen Hall where my office was located also. After their relocation, I regretted not seeing some colleagues as often as before. Opportunities for good interaction between faculty were also provided through optional leisure activities like bowling for instance. I got along very well with my three teammates: Dr. Richard Behnke (Athletics) Dr. Brice Wilkinson (Theater Arts), and Dr. Roger Carlson (Geography) whose congenial wife Beth used to join him at the Student Union for moral support.

My first year at Winona State went well enough for me to have my contract renewed. To fulfill an earlier promise, I went to Saltillo, Mexico and completed a Spanish course at the Instituto de Filología Hispanica during the summer of 1972. My family and I stayed with the Cepeda family who happened to have a Nash Rambler auto dealership. On one weekend, they were kind enough to take us out to the country for a picnic where we gained a better insight into the natives' way of life. We were truly impressed by the integrity of the Mexican people, which also manifests itself through the respect they accord their elders. Some Mexicans expressed concern over modern

149

American influences that tended to get in the way of established local middle class mores.

Upon concluding a booster course in Spanish, I took my family on a sightseeing tour through the American West in our 1968 VW Squareback. Places we visited included the Petrified Forest, the Grand Canyon, Jackson Hole, Yellowstone National Park, Mount Rushmore, and the Badlands in South Dakota. Jumping into the warm pool at Huckleberry Hound Hot Springs was a new experience for all of us. By morning, our bathing suits had frozen solid on a makeshift clothesline, but we were able to keep warm with sleeping bags in our "Western Field" tent from Montgomery Ward. Our entire journey proved to be quite enjoyable.

One year after my arrival at Winona State, Mr. Chuck Dietrick was hired as of fall 1972 to fill a vacancy in Spanish. He hardly had time to settle in before a directive came down from Chancellor Mitau's office in St. Paul calling for the elimination of ten (10) Winona State College (WSC) faculty positions. The action was apparently called for to compensate for drastic declines in enrollment at Mankato State College, which was part of the Minnesota State College System along with our institution as well as others. According to administrative practice, staff members who were hired most recently were the first ones to be let go when necessary; thus, Mr. Dietrick wound up getting a December 1972 notice of termination of employment at WSC, effective as of June 1973.

The imposed faculty cutbacks also threatened to nix President Robert A. DuFresne's plan to start an External Studies Program at Winona State for which he had counted on the availability of extra staff. Since the allotment of funds by the College Board was enrollment-based, new instructional endeavors could only be launched at the expense of existing programs that were quietly short-changed at least temporarily. Mr. Dietrick asked to have a talk with President DuFresne whereupon it was decided that he would officially be retained in the Department of Foreign Languages during 1973/74 but 2/3 of his time was to be spent serving the new External Studies Program (ESP).

In the summer of 1973, I conducted dissertation research in a number of academic libraries. Upon visiting the Joseph P. Regenstein Library at the University of Chicago via local transit facilities, I became aware of its location in a neighborhood notoriously threatened by hooligans. At Cornell University, I searched for applicable library holdings while camping near Ithaca, New York. Libraries at the University of Minnesota

150

in Minneapolis and at the University of Wisconsin in Madison could be reached in the span of day-trips from Winona, Minnesota. The primary works most conducive regarding my dissertation topic were at Yale University's Beinecke Rare Book and Manuscript Library in New Haven, Connecticut. My doctoral dissertation has the descriptive title, "Die Bremer Beiträger: Ihr Verhältnis zu Gottsched und ihre Stellung in der Geschichte der deutschen Literatur" (University of Cincinnati, Ohio, 1975). It is written in German and focuses on a prominent group of writers and their relationship to Johann Christoph Gottsched (1700-1766), a fundamental theorist in the Eighteenth Century. Their efforts were directed toward enhancing German literary standards by emulating works of highly regarded foreign authors.

In order to be able to teach additional Spanish courses as of Winter Quarter 1973/74, Mr. Dietrick managed to get his obligations in the External Studies Program reduced to 1/4 time. Due to his corresponding efforts, I wound up serving part time in that program as an adviser; in addition, I found myself teaching an evening course at Rochester, Minnesota, without extra compensation. Besides additional preparation and time, it entailed a 50-mile commute each way in a vehicle provided. - Though it appears rather dubious whether employers in the private sector would have tried to pull something like that, it evidently was not uncommon in civil service realms.

For the following year, the newly established Department of External Studies (ESP) received funding of its own on the basis of credits that had been generated in its behalf through locally reapportioned productive resources. Since part of the "output" of its faculty was credited to the newly launched External Studies Program, the Department of Foreign Languages registered a decline in its productivity while its constituents had worked harder than ever! As far as the College Board was concerned, local administrators were at liberty to reassign allocated assets within the overall scope of operations.

To counteract disgruntlement among faculty members who paid attention to what was happening, local administrators intimidated some faculty by brazenly trying to apply the College Board's arbitrary allotment formula as an overall yardstick for gauging each department's "productivity." The Board's neutral formula was not aimed at a particular academic discipline. It was conceived on a hypothetical basis of "full-time equivalencies" (FTE's) whereby the Board arrived at a dollar amount for each campus within the system. As a convenient mathematical expedient, the Board assumed a 19:1 student to faculty ratio per credit hour involved in determining respective campus appropriations.

In their deliberate misapplication of the 19:1 ratio as a general productivity yardstick, local administrators generally disregarded distinctions to be made regarding feasible class sizes in respective academic disciplines. Departments in subject areas where large lecture-type courses are common (e. g., Business, Sciences, and Sociology) easily exceeded the quota; however, departments with classes involving instrumental or vocal music could not have achieved a 19:1 ratio even if the instructors concerned had been able to work around the clock! Since foreign language class sizes have to be kept within practical limits also, fulfillment of the illusory quota was never entirely attainable either. Consequently, we were generally expected to feel grateful for not being cast off altogether as an "expendable frill."

One might have expected some help from foreign language teachers' organizations in this struggle against misapplied rationales. However, instead of addressing the issue head on, self-flagellation was on the agenda at professional meetings and in applicable journal articles. Many spokespersons advocated notions of overcoming problems unilaterally by contrived so-called "innovative" approaches to classroom instruction! Under given circumstances, foreign language major requirements wound up being trimmed to a bare-bones minimum with counterproductive results. Since language qualifications rarely come into play on job applications in America, the situation did not precipitate a general outrage by employers either. It is as though we as a nation actually prefer to employ money instead of idioms other than English to achieve good things in international dealings.

If part of the local administrators' reasoning in arbitrarily applying the 19:1 ratio was to divide and conquer the faculty, it must be said that they succeeded. The lunacy was carried far enough to make departments with large class capacities accept the idea that they had to settle for less than their share of allotments in order to "support" departments that could not generate enough credits on their own. The destruction of faculty morale under such circumstances was predictable and may even have been deliberately precipitated by some of the administrators in hopes of being able to exercise greater control.

Normally, a full time faculty member was expected to carry twelve (12) credit hours per quarter, i. e., 36 credit hours per academic year. In the Department of Foreign Languages, each full time member carried forty-four (44) credit hours per year when I arrived at WSC and forty-eight (48) credit hours a short time later. The gross inequities in pay and workloads began to be equalized when the faculty became unionized during the late 1970's under President Robert A. DuFresne. Prior to that, periodic pay raises that often did not even match inflation rates (see Appendix C) consisted of across the board increments by a certain percentage. This simplistic approach resulted in a widening of the gap between faculty with higher pay and those with less bargaining power and concomitant lower compensation even though many among the latter had earned higher degrees! The unreasonable practice accentuated inequities and lowered staff morale.

To help improve our department's productivity profile even under contrived full-time equivalency (FTE) criteria, I asked for permission to reintroduce courses in Elementary French at Winona State, which had been phased out as of the end of Spring Quarter 1971. Previous enrollment figures indicated that interest in the language even exceeded that in German. From my perspective, the disreputable tactics of our devious administrators proved to be of appreciable benefit to them, because they exacted expenditure of greater efforts among faculty members. I for one was prompted to go out on a limb professionally at no cost to Winona State by reintroducing Elementary French even though my formal qualifications in the language amounted to less than an academic Minor.

If I had fallen flat on my face teaching French, my supervisors would have had a good excuse to replace me as an inept faculty member! Fortunately, I had begun to take private lessons in the language way back in Austria. In Illinois, I was able to improve my knowledge in a conversational evening course and at the University of Cincinnati I enrolled in "French Readings" as part of my preparation toward passing the required additional language examination in partial fulfillment of the requirements for my doctorate.

I was glad that no problems arose with me serving as the sole instructor of the first-year French sequence at Winona State for the next four years from 1974-1978. I told my students, "if you want to learn from me, you should enroll in German, but if you are willing to learn with me, you can take French." Fortunately, enough students opted for the latter so that the three-course annual sequence became a permanent part of departmental offerings. However, as far as the misapplied FTE production ratio was concerned, our department never would have achieved a 19:1 ratio even with every constituent staff member carrying uncompensated overloads, which we had done for years prior to union-invoked equalization! It might just be that administrators were ultimately shamed into quitting the underhanded practice of using the demoralizing formula whimsically as a perpetual menacing device.

Upon returning from dissertation research in Europe at the end of summer in 1974, I was anxious to familiarize myself with the materials I intended to use in my Elementary French sequence. To my horror, I noticed that the publisher in New Jersey had failed to send us the promised tape recordings to accompany the textbook *Perspectives de France*, Shorter Revised Edition, by Arthur Bieler, Oscar A. Haac, and Monique Léon. It so happened that I had to take our son Carl to Massachusetts anyway, where he was awarded a 4-year scholarship from Deerfield Academy as a proficient carrier of the Minneapolis Tribune. Thus, I decided to personally stop at Prentice-Hall headquarters in Englewood Cliffs, New Jersey, to confront Jim Carson with whom I had corresponded about getting the recordings to Winona State on time. To my great disbelief, a receptionist at Prentice-Hall informed me that "Jim Carson" was a code name. Consequently, I never did get to the person who had let me down! I was compelled to swallow my anger and to regard my personal efforts that involved going out of my way as payment for a lesson in shirked responsibility under a corporate mantle.

My family had accompanied me to Europe in a chartered airplane that landed at Amsterdam, Holland, on June 23, 1974. Most of the passengers were members of the National Education Association (NEA) who had arranged for reduced fares. When my family and I checked in at Chicago's O'Hare Airport, most seats had already been randomly assigned in a manner that left no block of adjacent seats available for my family of five. My wife and our children aged 15, 11, and 9 had never traveled by air before. The scattered locations where we were placed included two seats in the smoking section despite the fact that we were all non-smokers including three minors. One would have thought that the people in charge of seat assignments might have noticed that there was a group of five passengers on the list with the same last name who had paid for the tickets with a single check! Obviously, the money we saved on that charter-flight did not make up for the thwarted joy of our first flight as a family. The occurrence amounted to one of those experiences in life that one pays for without eventually benefiting from lessons learned in the process.

From Amsterdam, we took a train to Marie's Uncle Peter THEISZ (1907-1977) at Meldorf in Schleswig-Holstein. Our kids

154

were amazed that everybody spoke German there and that the delicious goodies, which they used to be able to acquire on rare trips to Kuhn's Delicatessen in Chicago were available all over. After spending a few days visiting, we took another train to Bonn where the American Association of Teachers of German (AATG) held its annual convention in 1974. We met several colleagues there from Cincinnati and to our pleasant surprise also Dr. Kurt Kiesinger (1904-1988), the former German Chancellor who attended a reception sponsored by Schiller College to which AATG members were also invited. While camping by the Rhine River, my family and I walked around some, but rainy weather made it quite unpleasant. Our "Western Field" tent from Montgomery Ward just did not seem to be designed for successive daily downpours without some sunshine in between. By comparison, local brands of tent equipment came with an additional deflecting roof; they also sported solid rubber floors with a 5-inch dado all around. When Carl's sleeping bag got soaked because of seepage through our poorly impregnated tent floor, we could not find a drier large enough to get it dried out.

After purchasing a used Fiat Autobianchi automobile for about $800 from a local streetcar conductor, we drove to the university library at Würzburg and made an excursion into the Steigerwald forest from which our family name was derived. Next, we drove to Weinsberg near Heilbronn to visit my sister-in-law Susanne STEIGERWALD, née SCHULZ and her son Jakob. Upon pondering our itinerary, they felt that our trip was more like a tour de force than a vacation! While looking for the university library at Heidelberg, we were shocked to see so many wall areas inside and outside of campus buildings defaced with graffiti. We thought that people who are drawn to a place like this would strive to find better ways and formats to make use of their freedom of expression.

At the "Haus der Donauschwaben" in Sindelfingen, we saw informative displays concerning our Danube Swabian heritage, but their library holdings were not organized yet for targeted research. In Stuttgart, we were able to visit friends of ours and to spend a couple of days with them. From there, we drove to Geislingen on the Steige River where Emilie Wörz, the widowed mother of my sister-in-law Martha resided. The elderly woman was very kind to us and we enjoyed watching the German "Hit Parade" on her TV set. Upon driving to Ulm on the Danube, we were able to walk up to the steeple of the impressive Gothic cathedral for memorable panoramic views and corresponding photographs. Ulm happened to be one of the cities from which Danube Swabian ancestors departed for Hungary during the Eighteenth Century.

We also drove to Freiburg im Breisgau where my niece Hilde STEIGERWALD (1952-1976) was attending the university. The few hours we were able to spend with her turned out to be our only contact, since she became the victim of an unresolved homicide two years later. From Freiburg, we took a side trip to Colmar in France. We walked around some in the Market Square until it started to rain whereupon we entered what appeared to be a sizable hardware store. As we looked around, it was interesting to hear native Alsacians communicate in their Germanic dialect among themselves, but when I approached an employee in German for some information, he automatically responded in French. It was like a conditioned reflex that had evolved in the disputed Franco-German border region.

Upon getting back to our car later that afternoon, we were unable to start it. In pouring rain, I opened the hood to see if I could do something to make our return to Germany possible where communication would not have compounded the problem if a trip to a repair shop had become unavoidable. Luckily, I spotted a wire that seemed to have gotten loose. Upon taking a chance on reconnecting it, the car started but the motor did not run smoothly at all. Nevertheless, we made it back to our tent that was pitched at an inn near Freiburg.

From southwestern Germany, we drove to Liechtenstein's capital Vaduz. We gazed up at the prince's hilltop residence and looked around among some kiosks where souvenirs and many stamps were available for collectors. The principality is too small to support mints of its own for money or postage so they maintain special corresponding arrangements with neighboring Switzerland and Austria. The nearest sizable Austrian city along our route was Feldkirch in the province of Vorarlberg. After only a brief stop, we drove on to Innsbruck in Tyrol. Two prominent landmarks in the Town Square are the "Pestsäule" monument from the Middle Ages and an edifice with a bay that sports a gilded roof. Sights of alpine mountain ranges around Innsbruck are breathtaking, but they also struck me as restrictive barriers circumscribing views of the horizon and impeding mobility. Unobstructed vistas in flatlands like those of the Banat where I was born still endow me with a greater sense of freedom and elbowroom.

From Innsbruck, we headed for Salzburg where my brother Josef STEIGERWALD (1926-1977) and his family resided. Marie and I had not been at their house since our honeymoon in 1956 about eighteen (18) years earlier. Josef and two of his five children, Josef Jr. (*1953) and Heidi (*1956), had come to visit us in Minnesota in 1973; however, the rest of his family had yet to meet our children and we had never met his two youngest sons Hans-Peter and Alfred either. We got the red carpet treatment at their house. My sister-in-law Ritzi (1931-1981) thought that our kids would only drink soda pop so she really had stocked up in that sector. We explained to her that many children in America prefer water, juices, or milk, which are less harmful to teeth for instance.

One of our excursions around Salzburg was to the Untersberg Mountain from where the view was awesome. Another side trip took us to nearby salt mines. After standing in line for hours to get tickets, we eventually descended into the mountain via wooden slides from one level to the next. On some levels, there were small pools of water that were reminiscent of the kind one encounters in caverns. The air had a sulfur scent and irritated the throat somewhat. A few tourists suffered from spells of claustrophobia but the only way out was by finishing the tour. The visitors hailed from different countries; we also met some from the U.S.A. who mistook me as an Austrian, because I sounded like a native.

Our next destination was Munich where we visited my uncle Josef MARTIN (1912-1977) and aunt Lissi (1912-1990), née SCHWARZ, as well as cousin Peter STEIGERWALD (*1926) and his family. Among sights we saw downtown was the Rathaus (city hall) with its famous Glockenspiel, St. Peter's Church, the Michaelerkirche (St. Michael's church), and the Frauenkirche whose steps we climbed all the way up to the steeple for a panoramic view. We also looked in at the renowned Hofbräuhaus whose waitresses carry three heavy oversized glass mugs full of beer in each hand! We also went to see the "Olympia Stadion" where the American swimmer Mark Spitz won several gold medals in 1972. The architecture of some structures was quite unusual with big steel cables and cone-shaped plastic roofs like those of some tents. Years later, we were able to observe similar construction features at Denver's International Airport (DIA).

On our way back to Salzburg, we stopped at Berchtesgaden where we could only cover some of the sights, because of a shortage of time. From Salzburg, we also paid a visit to my uncle Anton MARTIN (1915-1980) who resided just outside of Bad Ischl, Upper Austria, with his wife Justina, née FESTINI, and their son Anton Jr. On the way there, we passed through some scenic areas within the region known as Salzkammergut. We also drove into the city of Bad Ischl where I used to live before I immigrated to America in 1951. Among local landmarks is the Kaiservilla, a summer residence of Emperor Francis Joseph I (1830-1916), which is now a museum. Another local museum used to be the former residence of Franz Lehár (1870-1948), the renowned composer of waltzes and operettas including "The Merry Widow," "Zarewitsch," "Das Land des Lächelns," and others. The place name "Bad" means 'spa,' which refers to salt baths and thermal wells in this case. Ischl is the name of one of the two rivers encountered here. The other one, whose water is too cold for swimming, is called "Traun."

Next, we began to visit some of Marie's Austrian relatives. Our first destination was Leoben in Styria where my Uncle Anton MARTIN (1915-1980) worked in a coal mine briefly during WW II. Marie's cousin Terri, née HOLECSEK was living there at the time of our visit with her husband Bert PEINT-INGER. From Leoben, we drove to Knittelfeld, Styria where Marie used to live before she immigrated to America with her family in 1949. Her Uncle Anton HOLECSEK (1901-1987) and his youngest son Helmut were still living there, but her Aunt Amalia, née PARTELYI (1903-1967) had passed away. We took walks with the men in the scenic environment and conversed off the cuff. From Knittelfeld, we drove to Graz where Marie's cousin Marie, née THEISZ (1916-1984) was living with her daughter Tini, née GIEL.

Marie's cousin Hedi MITTER was employed as a beautician at Eisenerz in Styria. We paid her a visit also before heading for Höflein near Bruck on the Leitha River to visit the family of Richard Artner, the son of my former employers Michael and Katharina Artner, née Sailer. Mr. and Mrs. Richard and Angela Artner received us cordially and their children invited ours to the public pool. It was fun to see our kids blend in and interrelate until some local youngsters suddenly exhibited xenophobic sentiments and asked ours to leave. - The dialect spoken in this area is not the same as the German our children had learned from us and at schools in the U. S.

Returning to the town where I had spent about seventeen months as a teenager was rather agreeable for me personally. Having some of Richard's home grown wine with him lent itself well for reminiscing about bygone days when I used to work for his parents as a stateless refugee from May 1947 until September 1948; Richard was only about six years of age then. At the time of our visit in 1974, he was working for the Austrian railroad. His farming activities were pretty much limited to wine growing. I do not recall seeing any livestock around either. The residence had been completely remodeled and modernized.

From Höflein, we drove to Vienna where Marie and I had spent the first ten months as a married couple. We showed our kids parts of the city before finding a campground in the outskirts where my brother Josef and his wife Ritzi decided to pay us a surprise visit. Upon spending the night in tents, we returned to Salzburg. A couple of days later, we drove to Regensburg with a stopover at the new university campus to distribute some student recruitment posters for Winona State University. Our next destination was Berlin via the university town of Göttingen where we spent the night at an inn. Listening to the natives speak their customary Plattdeutsch among themselves, we could only understand a word now and then; therefore, we communicated in High German with them in which they were equally fluent of course and their pronunciation was truly exemplary.

The trip to Berlin involved driving through part of what was called the German Democratic Republic where communists were in control. Clearing the checkpoint at either end of the autobahn route to the free City of West Berlin was frightening. The West German license plates we had on our car were not valid in the communist part of the country so they had to be temporarily replaced for a small fee. While waiting for our papers to be checked, we found ourselves looking into rifle muzzles that were trained in our direction from guard towers close by. What the communist regime seemed to fear most was enlightenment of its citizens. Consequently, even the Western newspaper fragments that we happened to have in our car were confiscated. The unfriendly conduct of the border guards was weird enough to remind a person of some equally chilling scenes in works of the Austrian novelist Franz Kafka (1883-1924).

In West Berlin, we attempted to visit the parents of Hanne, née SCHELLER who is married to Marie's brother Al HOLT. Unfortunately, her folks were not at home, but we were enabled to sleep in their apartment by a cooperative custodian. Upon driving around a bit on our own, we left the very next day in the direction of Amsterdam from where we were scheduled to fly back to Chicago. Prior to our departure from Holland, we tried to sell our Fiat Autobianchi for any amount, but nobody was interested in buying it. After having driven the car around Europe for about eight weeks, we wound up having to abandon it on the lot of a used car dealer who reluctantly accepted it gratis only after being assured that the vehicle was in running condition. On the morning of our departure for the United States, we packed our belongings including the tent and took a taxi from the camping area at the Amsterdam ice hockey rink to Schiphol Airport. Our bagged metal tent poles caused officials some anxiety at security checks; they seemed to think we were transporting armaments. Before landing in the U. S., it was our turn to experience anxiety when our plane was diverted from Chicago to Milwaukee for some reason.

As I look back, I am still amazed how I managed to get my dissertation finished along with having had to contend with the extra preparations involved in teaching an additional language. Somehow, things worked out OK thanks to Marie's typing and retyping of parts of the manuscript in efforts to get it ready for submission to the evaluation committee at the University of Cincinnati. We were all very happy to hear that it was finally accepted and I was given the opportunity to defend it during Christmas recess in 1974. Everything went as well as could be expected and in a letter dated December 19, 1974 my Academic Dean at Winona State, Dr. Dan Willson, was officially notified of my completion of all requirements for a Ph. D. degree, which was awarded at the June 15, 1975 commencement.

One immediate result of having completed all requirements for my doctorate was a small increment in salary; in addition, I was now eligible to be tenured. Under the rules in effect at the time of my arrival at Winona State, I would have reached that point after only three years, but new regulations called for the attainment of one's terminal degree. As soon as I had completed my formal education after so many years, Marie entered the Winona Area Technical Institute in August 1975. She completed a secretarial course by June 1976 in preparation for getting a part-time job at the laboratory of the local Community Memorial Hospital (CMH) where she wound up working for twenty years.

The expediency-based modus operandi at Winona State had so dispirited my department chairperson Dr. Hodgson that he no longer even saw any point in submitting recommendations regarding my prospective promotion and tenure. Luckily, Dr. Richard Behnke, a member of the Committee on Promotion and Tenure knew of my eligibility in both areas, but he did not find any corresponding papers in my behalf among those that had been duly submitted; therefore, he contacted my academic dean for clarification. In a handwritten note to my chairman dated May 12, 1976, Dean Willson stated that I would probably be tenured with the next contract unless there were objections. In his reply of May 18, 1976 to a memorandum from Dr. Behnke, my chairman Dr. Hodgson indicated that I was not only eligible for tenure but he was also recommending me for promotion to the rank of Associate Professor. In a letter dated July 1, 1976 President DuFresne informed me that I was granted tenure in the Department of Foreign Languages effective September 7, 1976. This was good news for my family and me, because it provided more job security.

On March 14, 1977, I suffered the premature loss of another close family member. My brother Josef (1926-1977), an elementary school teacher at Maxglan near Salzburg, Austria, had just been appointed to a position as school principal when he was diagnosed with a terminal illness in the summer of 1976. Despite the immediate commencement of treatment, he died within about ten months, leaving five descendants behind along with his wife Ritzi (1931-1981), née LINZNER, who literally lost her will to live and followed him to the grave within a few short years. To know what losing someone close feels like, it may help to visualize oneself as a figure on a chessboard comprising the world. Suddenly, a gaping void looms large at a spot where there used to be a co-extension of oneself.

As of the end of Spring Quarter 1977, Dr. Hodgson resigned from his position at Winona State. Meanwhile, the institution had adopted a new name and became officially known as Winona State University (WSU). In a letter of April 6, 1977, which sported the new logo, President DuFresne appointed me Department Chairperson effective September 6, 1977. Unfortunately, my new title did not entail a raise in salary even though it augmented my responsibilities.

13. Bumpy Continuance in Action at Winona State University

Starting in 1975, a series of meetings were held by administrators and faculty members concerning a close cooperative arrangement between the foreign language departments of the three colleges in Winona. Officials at each institution appeared to envision a combined operation under which the College of Saint Teresa (CST) would assume responsibility for a degree program in French, Winona State (WSU) for one in German, and Saint Mary's College (SMC) for a Spanish one. Theoretically, it looked like money could be saved by avoiding duplicate course offerings and by sharing foreign language staff that was expected to cooperate. Unfortunately, many justified reservations expressed by various faculty members about different aspects of such an arrangement had not been acted upon by administrators when the ill-fated Tri-College/University agreement was officially launched as of December 1, 1977. Since the plan was impractical from the students' perspective, it never achieved full implementation; instead, it was used as an administrative excuse for keeping the respective departments involved from reaching the potential to function better on their own.

Some of the problems predicted by faculty members related to the following realms among others:

1. Calendars of each institution differed under various organizational frameworks: WSU was on a quarter system, CST on a trimester schedule, and SMC on a semester plan.
   a) WSU-students who considered enrollment in a language class at SMC for example would have had to be in town before they had access to dormitories at their home institution, since classes at SMC started earlier and breaks did not coincide with those at WSU and CST either.
   b) An SMC-student enrolled at WSU would have had to stay in town beyond his/her institution's completion of the school year. This was critical for students who were planning to get a summer job.
2. For optimal use of staff and campus facilities, classes were going to be scheduled throughout each day Monday to Friday.
   a) Since many WSU students worked for a living, they could only enroll in classes that ended by early afternoon. Late afternoon classes were never as popular as earlier ones.

162

b) Students were known to avoid Friday classes altogether.

3. Enrollment considerations:
   a) Each institution had separate criteria for allowing its students to take courses elsewhere, but even the adoption of modified rules in the early 1980's did not alleviate related problems entirely.
   b) Since students could save money by attending a state university to begin with, why would those paying higher tuition at private colleges wish to commute to WSU for some requirements! Although many WSU students chose to take classes at the private colleges without having to pay extra, very few CST and SMC students reciprocated in the foreign language area.

4. Transportation between the three campus areas was facilitated by expanded bus service, but
   a) distances were too great to permit back to back scheduling of classes at different institutions without allocation of a period in between for commuting;
   b) students with cars of their own could not count on finding a vacant parking space readily to make it to class every time at another institution without being tardy.

5. Routing faculty between colleges and having them give rides to their students was also suggested as a possibility, but among details never worked out, there were questions concerning
   a) the provision of vehicles with corresponding insurance coverage and
   b) office space and time periods for student consultations.

By insisting on the adoption of the Tri-College/University program against overwhelming odds, local administrators were reacting to pressures they were under within budgetary constraints. As of 1976, Chancellor Gary Hayes froze Minnesota State College budget allotments at the existing levels in ANTICIPATION of declining enrollments predicted on the basis of applicable early 1960's birthrates alone. Since such forecasts proved to be erroneous as far as developments at Winona State were concerned, one might have thought that the sagacious Chancellor or the College Board would have had the decent impulse to remedy the situation with retroactive compensations; however, nothing like that ever came about. Adjustments for inflation alone would have justified lifting the freeze by the end of the decade. To boot, 1980 enrollments at Winona State increased by 17 percent over the previous year! - The rates of inflation during the period of the budget freeze were as follows: 1976: 4.9 %, 1977: 6.7 %, 1978: 9.0 %, 1979: 13.3 %, 1980: 12.5 %, 1981: 8.9 % adding up to an 11.06 percent erosion of the value of state allotments. Faculty and staff inadvertently made up for much of it "out of hide," but the ways in which students wound up being short-changed by this myopic and unjust policy precipitated an incalculable perpetual loss to society.

It was highly doubtful whether the unpopular Chancellor would have espoused the same rationale along with commensurate increases in funding if a rise in enrollments had been anticipated! Other factors were among reasons why declines in enrollments did not occur as predicted. For one thing, the nation's economy was such that many employees decided to return to colleges for educational updates and higher degrees. A substantial percentage of those who did that chose to attend public institutions of higher education for financial reasons. The increased presence of older students on many campuses favorably rounded out the enrollment picture. It remains beyond my understanding how Mr. Hayes was able to short-change public colleges and universities in Minnesota on a sustained basis! He seemed convinced that declines in enrollment would occur until the 1990's. Unfortunately, funding continued to be woefully inadequate under his successors Jon Wefald and Robert L. Carothers also.

In a *Winona Daily News* editorial of October 22, 1981 (p. 4), Adolph Bremer indicated that the "Decline Hasn't Touched State University System." In another *Winona Daily News* editorial of December 21, 1983, which was entitled "The Revolution on the Campus," Adolph Bremer was able to report again that "the decline hasn't happened" (p. 8). On October 2, 1979 an article in the *Winona Daily News* (p. 11a) had the title "Enrollment Decline Seen for 1984." On October 25, 1984, the *Winona Daily News* reported that "the 1984 fall quarter head count at Minnesota's seven state universities shows an increase of 437 students over fall quarter 1983" (p. 11). On September 24, 1985 the *Winona Daily News* reported: "Record Enrollment at WSU" (p. 3); a year later, on September 24, 1986 the *Winonan*, vol. 64, No. 4 (p. 1) reported that "WSU Fall Enrollment Makes New Record." In the *Winona Daily News* of May 1, 1986, (p. 1) Patrick McIlheran was confident enough to announce that "WSU Braces for Freshman Storm." In the *NEA Higher Education Advocate*, vol. 5, No. 7 (February 15, 1988), it was conclusively observed that "the projected enrollment decline in higher education has not occurred." However, the money and services people were left without at colleges and universities remained permanent compounded losses for which no one ever had to answer.

In his article "Deadwood v. Dry Rot," which appeared in *NEA Higher Education Advocate*, edited by Sheilah Vance (November 1981), p. 8, H. D. Rowe suggested that:

> "A study of the history of education would probably characterize the 1970's as the decade in which administrative ineptitude struggled to get itself explained as faculty incompetence... but the principal problem in higher education is not faculty deadwood. It is administrative dry rot."

Professor Rowe who taught English at South Georgia College since 1975 also said,

> "to the faculty member, nothing is more destructive than an administrative style that results from an administrator's insecurities and suspicions. This poisons the milieu in which teaching and research take place."

With all their untidy hype concerning anticipated declining enrollments and concomitant shortages of funding, administrators were also responsible for declining interest in college teaching. In the *NEA Higher Education Advocate* of March 17, 1987 (p. 4) it was reported that "the proportion of college freshmen who want to teach college has dropped nearly 75 percent in the past 20 years."

Under the incessant budgetary squeeze to which Winona State had been subjected for too long, negative developments left the Department of Foreign Languages with only two full time German instructors and some temporary part-timers in Spanish. In efforts to upgrade and strengthen the only remaining viable foreign language major, I introduced over a half dozen new courses between Winter Quarter 1972/73 and Spring Quarter 1977 including the following. - The course number listed in parentheses next to the title can be looked up in respective catalogs and corresponding class schedules:

a) Current Issues in the German Press (G335),
b) Exploring Foreign Languages (FL200),
c) German Lyrics, Ballads, and Folk Songs (G370),
d) Germania, USA (G350),
e) Hermann Hesse (G450),
f) History of the German Language (G351)

During the summer of 1977, I participated in a Fulbright seminar on German Civilization and Culture, which was held at Bonn and Berlin. Upon returning, I created a corresponding course in English (G250). It constituted a general elective in the Humanities area.

Upon seeing the names of the recipients of merit pay for 1976-1977 in the faculty newsletter, I asked Dr. Dan L. Willson, my Academic Dean, how I could have qualified for the honor also. He had no specific answer but he indicated that the reason I was not included had something to do with the foreign language department's reluctance to endorse the administration's Tri-College/University cooperative arrangement. What compounded my material loss was the fact that merit pay did not just constitute a one-time bonus, but it raised a recipient's salary permanently. In a consolatory vein, Dr. Willson said that he had me on his list for promotion to the rank of Associate Professor. However, one member of the committee making recommendations to the president felt that the decision should be held in abeyance in my case until it becomes apparent how the new cooperative venture with the private colleges was working out. The unnamed committee member who blocked my advancement with coercive intent was Dr. Donald Warner, Vice President of Academic Affairs. As a staunch supporter of the ill-fated Tri-College/University arrangement, he expected foreign language staff to support it even against their better judgement.

In a letter dated April 14, 1978, I was notified of my promotion to the rank of Associate Professor effective September 5, 1978. The letter was signed by the new president Dr. Robert A. Hanson, successor of Dr. DuFresne who went back to teaching on a part-time basis after having served as president for ten years. Dr. Hanson was a soft-spoken man whom I approached about retroactive overtime pay. He indicated how difficult it was to adjust past budgetary concerns but he asked Dr. Sheila Kaplan, the new Vice President of Academic Affairs to look into the matter. According to her understanding, carrying extra courses was "normal" in my area before the faculty became unionized as of 1975/76. She did concede however that I may indeed be owed the $64 meal allotment to which I was entitled during an off-campus course offering at Rochester, Minnesota, but she had no suggestions on how I could actually obtain the money.

In retrospect, I realize that it would have behooved me to approach the new administrators about merit pay on the basis of my successful reintroduction of Elementary French at WSU and for having introduced seven additional courses. At the very least, it would have made them aware of my resourcefulness and achievements for a more accordant rapport with them. My failure to apply for such an award serves as another indication of my lacking attributes as a salesman. Yet, even without applicable training beyond foreign language instructional expertise, I was expected to actively "sell" functional aspects and merits of linguistic proficiency as if they constituted failsafe tangible derivatives of our departmental offerings rather than qualifications individually attainable only through sustained personal efforts.

Many of us who chose to pursue a career in teaching were resigned to earning less in exchange for greater job security, compared to people in business for instance. Yet, by having us constantly "justify" and extol our programs, we wound up devoting considerable time to promotional activities at much lower rates of compensation than advertising or marketing agents could command! The clever administrative exaction was quite presumptuous and I looked in vain for a segment of my graduate school training that might have prepared me as a program wholesaler or retailer, too. Ultimately though, I did wind up designing colorful departmental posters along with flyers announcing new course offerings. - If all that does not demonstrate the effectiveness of my superiors along with my obliging pliancy, I do not know what might.

Thanks to successful negotiations by the Inter Faculty Organization (IFO) and its affiliate, the National Education Association (NEA), with the Minnesota State University Board, every unit member was brought to within four (4) steps of his/her calculated experience-based place on the salary scale in 1980/81. This clearly shows how far some of us lagged behind in our remuneration! In succeeding years, we continued to hear about lack of funding, the need for retrenchment, accountability, continuing preparation, etc., etc. An article by Sue Saarnio in the *Winona Daily News* of January 19, 1982 may serve as an example of further administrative shock treatments. The item had the following title: "WSU May Lay Off Up to 14 Instructors." The group included faculty members with tenure, but some of them were retrenched instead. Even though I was not directly affected, I believe the fact that I was hospitalized for kidney stones as of July 2, 1982 had something to do with related stress.

In due course of time, faculty evaluation forms were further expanded and detailed. Eventually, they covered the following broad areas:

I. Demonstrated ability to teach effectively or perform

167

effecively in other current assignments.
II. Scholarly or creative achievement or research.
III. Evidence of continuing preparation and study.
IV. Contribution to student growth and development.
 V. Service to university and community.

In addition to individual faculty evaluations, there were annual departmental self-studies. Every five (5) years, a major administrative review of each program was conducted. The five-year review also determined whether or not a program received accreditation. Every ten (10) years, Winona State was subject to a review by outsiders representing the North Central Association of Colleges and Schools. In 1980 and in 1990, Dean Bernard O'Kelley from the University of North Dakota happened to be the reviewer of the Department of Foreign Languages. In both reviews, the need for additional staff was emphasized, but it took what seemed like forever before noteworthy positive action was finally taken under the administration of President Darrell W. Krueger as of the early 1990's.

The contract between the Minnesota State University Board (MSUB) and the Inter Faculty Organization (IFO) was renegotiated every other year. New agreements were rarely reached on time and every so often the faculty had to issue notices of their intent to strike before things were finalized at last. Frequently, it was hard not to suspect the Board negotiators of deliberate foot dragging, because payments that eventually had to be made retroactively never included dividends or interest! Consequently, whatever earnings had accrued on the money in the meantime amounted to a bonus for the Board at faculty expense. - Good faith bargaining is not always what the name implies!

During the summer of 1980 when President Jimmy Carter admitted many Cuban refugees and expellees to the United States, I served as a Spanish interpreter at the Fort McCoy processing center in Wisconsin from May 24 to June 25. I worked long hours and slept in one of the barracks for which I paid $1.30 a night. My stay brought back memories of my army days, but things were more hectic at Fort McCoy with people coming and going at all times. One day, when I stopped in at the NCO-Club for a refreshment after work, I almost fell victim to some macho GIs in camouflage fatigues who were eager to demonstrate their guerrilla skills on an unsuspecting civilian like me. Fortunately, their sergeant kept his departing squad under control.

When asked about their most recent address, quite a few Cubans named some prison where they had been subjected to interrogations by committees that also included persons who might have hailed from the Soviet Union or from the communist German Democratic Republic for example. One of the aims of the interrogators seems to have been to identify Cuban nationals who were deemed unfit for life in a communist society. Citizens whom Fidel Castro wanted to eject included mentally impaired persons as well as hardened criminals.

After a month of 12-hour shifts at Fort McCoy including four hours of overtime daily, I yearned to go home and rest. Most personnel involved in processing the Cubans seemed to be civil service employees. Temporary extra help was hired by FEMA, the Federal Emergency Management Agency. My remuneration was based on the GS-5 annual salary scale of $11,243. The hourly rate of earnings only came to $3.84 for straight time; overtime added up to time and a half, i. e., $5.76 an hour. FEMA employees were not paid a night differential. Obviously, translation and interpretation work is not among high paying jobs either.

By the time my three-year term as chairman of the Department of Foreign Languages ended in 1980, we had a new dean of Liberal Arts: Dr. Helen Popovich. She arrived at Winona State in 1978 and replaced Dr. Dan Willson in the area indicated. Her work experience at other institutions included administrative and teaching duties. She had earned a Ph. D. degree in English at the University of Kansas. Since Dr. Popovich declined to allot more than two hours of release time for my chair responsibilities, I chose not to run for reelection whereupon Dr. Hodgson's 1978 replacement, Dr. Ronald M. Mazur was elected to the post. Some of the extra time I gained thereby was devoted to increased research and publication efforts.

In June 1981, our son Carl graduated from Winona State University with a degree in Business. His part-time job as a teller at Merchants National Bank of Winona was expanded into a full time arrangement. He gained valuable practical experience in different departments through on-the-job training and was well liked by coworkers and bank patrons alike. From there, he continued his career in finance at BankWest in Pierre, South Dakota as of 1984. Before long, he was promoted to head the Commercial Loan Department as their youngest Vice President ever. An enticing offer from Don Pratt, a bank president in Illinois, prompted Carl to relocate to Rockford in June 1986 where his knowledge of finance was further enhanced while working at the First National Bank and Trust Company as Vice President and Commercial Banking Officer. Upon undergoing a name change to First Community National Bank, Carl continued to serve the institution as Vice President in the areas of Credit Administration and Commercial Lending. After a couple of years, he successively worked for AMCORE as a Mortgage Loan Originator and as an Account Executive at Norwest Mortgage, Inc. As of April 6, 1996, he became a Financial Consultant at Merrill Lynch. In November 1999, Carl began to work as a Financial Advisor at First Union Securities in Rockford, IL.

In efforts to improve my knowledge of Spanish further, I flew to Mexico City in the summer of 1981 for some initial sightseeing at the country's capital. From there, I took a bus to Guadalajara and enrolled at the Instituto Mexicano de Cultura Internacional (IMCI) in a 4-week Spanish course. The bus trip itself was a cultural experience since some passengers not only took pets along but also live chickens, piglets, and lambs. While attending classes at IMCI, I was provided with room and board at the home of a Mexican family along with other students from the U. S.

In 1983, I published an anthology containing fifteen of my articles that had appeared in German periodicals and newspapers. In the 130-page paperback edition, I provided summaries in English, an historical introduction, observations for further studies, and two maps. The esteemed Danube Swabian scholar Josef Volkmar Senz contributed a Preface. The book has the bilingual title *Donauschwäbische Gedankenskizzen aus USA - Reflections of Danube Swabians in America. Aufsätze - Articles 1968-1982*. Most of the 500 copies printed at Winona State University for a total of $591.60 sold for $8.95 each; quite a few of the books were distributed gratis until supplies ran out.

My book was listed among the events of the congressionally declared "Tri-centennial Anniversary Year of German Settlement in America," which coincided with the 300th anniversary of the inception of the ethnic group that came to be known as Danube Swabians. The 1982 edition of the *Directory of American Scholars*, edited by Jaques Cattell Press (Bowker: New York and London) also included my name on pages 506-507 of volume 3.

In December 1982, our daughter Ellen Susanne was among the Winona State students who went to Ingolstadt under a program offered through St. Cloud State University. Most students returned home to Minnesota after completion of two academic quarters in Germany. Ellen opted to stay there and even managed to find work while continuing her studies at Munich toward a special language diploma entitled "Kleines deutsches

170

Sprachdiplom," which she was awarded in 1984. Prior to her return to the U. S. at the end of summer after having spent twenty (20) months in Europe, she joined me at Madrid, Spain, where I had completed two Spanish courses at the Eurocentre in conjunction with my Sabbatical Leave in 1984/85.

Upon some quick sightseeing at Madrid, Ellen and I took an overnight train to Paris for more sightseeing and to enjoy the renowned French cuisine. To my surprise, she thought that some of the crêpes Suzettes she had enjoyed in Munich tasted even better than local ones. Ellen walked a lot faster than I could without being short of breath. On one occasion, she was far enough ahead of me to cross a busy street before I even got to the curb. She dashed across the traffic lanes like a chased filly, and if drivers of oncoming cars had not applied their brakes hard enough to make tires squeal, she would have been hit for sure. I was terribly horrified and pleaded for celestial redress in face of what looked like imminent disaster. One driver actually stopped and got out of his car bewildered by what might have happened! Ellen's sheepish glance toward me showed her embarrassment, but she did not wait for me to catch up so that I could read her the riot act right then and there.

Before returning to the United States, we went back to Ingolstadt by train where Ellen introduced me to some of her acquaintances and friends. From there, we took a train to Munich in order to visit relatives, especially my cousin Peter STEIGERWALD and his wife Anni who graciously let Ellen stay with them while augmenting her knowledge of German. On the following weekend, we were joined by some of my nephews and nieces from Salzburg, Austria, for a picnic at the home of my cousin Peter and his family who resided at Hölzlweg 5 in the suburb known as Freimann. Upon returning to Winona via Trier, Germany, Luxembourg, and Chicago at the end of summer 1984, Ellen went back to work at K-Mart and got ready to resume her studies at Winona State University from where she graduated magna cum laude in 1986 with a double major in Business and German.

From December 14, 1984 until January 10, 1985, Ellen and I joined the family of my brother Tony for a trip to Brazil. We visited my godfather Jacob MARTIN (1909-1988), his wife Susanna (*1909), and the families of their sons Hans (1934-1999) and Peter (*1940). Ellen and I flew from Minneapolis to Miami where we stayed overnight before flying to Rio de Janeiro. From there, we were taken to Sâo Paulo by car. After a most cordial reception and upon getting acquainted, we had a good time sightseeing and swimming in the Atlantic at Guarujá where our relatives own a residence by the beach. My godfather, his wife, and their son Hans emigrated to Brazil from Yugoslavia on November 22, 1934.

My godfather had served an apprenticeship at a blacksmith and locksmith shop in Kikinda, Yugoslavia. After struggling along in Brazil for decades, he finally achieved economic success with the help of his sons, starting in the late 1950's when Brazil was beginning to become increasingly industrialized. Jacob MARTIN'S family founded a punch press operation that blossomed into concomitant laminated steel processing. Hans' son Joâo Enrique studied metallurgical engineering and eventually expanded the family business by building additional steel processing plants.

The first plant was named Indústria Metalúrgica "JotaeMe" Limitada. It used to be located at Rua Dr. Armilo 300, CEP 03269 Sapopemba, Sâo Paulo, but it was combined with FITAFER (mentioned below) in 1999. The acronym (in quotes) spells out my godfather's initials J. M. in Portuguese. Products manufactured include cup washers, undulated washers, square washers, clamps, angle braces, wedges, etc. The second plant is called INDAL Ltda. (Indústria de Aços Laminados). Peter MARTIN and his family own this business. Peter also owns a plant called StampTech. A fourth plant was built around the mid-1990's just outside of Sâo Paulo by the four descendants of Hans: Ana Maria, Joâo, Walter, and Sepp. Their business is called FITAFER Indústria & Comércio Ltda. The address is Rua Miguel Segundo Lerussi, 53 - Parque Industrial - Franco da Rocha - Sâo Paulo, Brazil CEP 07780 - Caixa Postal 64. The respective owners keep investing in their plants by adding new machinery all the time.

From Sâo Paulo, the six of us, i. e., Tony, Martha, Kristine, Lisa, Ellen, and I drove to the Danube Swabian colony Entre Rios near Guarapuava, Paraná, in a Ford Fairlane that we borrowed from our cousin Peter MARTIN. As part of a scholarly survey during my Sabbatical Leave in 1984/85, I wanted to compare the ethnic group's way of life in Brazil with what it used to be like.

Some of the highways on which we traveled had four lanes and some only had two. What happened to be different about the latter from what we were used to in the United States was the lacking road shoulder. It made driving more strenuous for Tony who came through for us all the way with flying colors. A few times, we were caught speeding, but the highway patrolmen were not at all averse to settling the matter right then and there for 50,000 cruzados, which amounted to about $22 in U. S. currency.

The Danube Swabian colony Entre Rios was established in 1951/52 and it consists of five villages: Vitória, Jordãozinho, Cachoeira, Socorro, and Samambaia. The initial colony included 2448 Danube Swabian settlers. Not all of them remained in the area; some went back to Europe and others relocated to cities like Curitiba, Sâo Paulo, and elsewhere. Some of those who stayed eventually intermarried with indigenous inhabitants, but efforts continue to be made to preserve the Danube Swabian heritage as much as possible. Matthias Leh, former president of the local agricultural cooperative Agrária served as our generous host. He passed away in May 1994. - The Bibliography includes sources of additional information about the colony.

From Entre Rios, we traveled to Iguassú Falls where the hydroelectric facilities impressed us greatly. The return trip to our relatives went smoothly until we got to Sâo Paulo where one of the tires deflated. Upon looking at it more closely in daylight the next day, we had reason to be grateful that we did not suffer a blowout on the road. Another anxious moment I was destined to experience occurred at Guarujá one morning when I was told that Ellen went hang gliding. I thought I was going to go into shock upon hearing about it. My brother Tony gave me a motorcycle-ride to the launching pad where I hoped to be able to talk her out of it. Luckily, the wind had shifted and prevented take-off! Lack of sleep and Ellen's risky intent made me feel quite shattered. She looked rather drawn herself and was more rebellious toward me than ever! Her nerves seemed to be frayed to a point of open revolt. She appeared to be under the influence of reckless demons.

On the eleven-hour flight back from Rio to Miami, my ankles swelled up again temporarily. Upon retrieving our luggage, I noticed that one suitcase reeked of alcohol. Half the contents of a bottle had either leaked out or someone had "sampled" the beverage leaving the flask partly unscrewed to suggest evaporation and to cover up for unauthorized rummaging. My offer to open the suitcase for the customs inspector at Miami was declined so I had to take care of the escaping booze later. In my drained physical condition, I was not even tempted to taste the stuff before securing it. - On the basis of my travel experiences, I would say that visits to relatives should be interspersed with solitary rest periods, but not all hotels or motels lend themselves to appropriate recuperative stays either.

My promotion to a full professorship (level 1) at Winona State University went into effect as of the fall quarter 1984. Dr. Thomas F. Stark was the university president at the time. What had kept me from being promoted earlier was due to at least a couple of different factors. Acting Dean Jim Spear who had succeeded Dr. Helen Popovich thought that I had not been in level 2 (Associate Prof.) long enough as of 1982. In 1983, Jim's successor Jonathan Lawson came to Winona State from elsewhere. He said that he needed more time to get to know me before he could arrive at a decision. Under an unwritten rule, administrators tend to promote faculty from level 3 to level 2 after about seven years and from level 2 to level 1 after about five years. I was an Assistant Professor (level 3) for seven (7) years and an Associate Professor (level 2) for six (6); the unwarranted postponement of my promotion to level 1 was at least partly attributable to the Tri-College/University program fiasco. My overdue promotion to level 1 might have been delayed some more if I had not informed my chairperson in all earnest that I was prepared to seek legal recourse in case of another deferral.

In 1985, I published a 61-page monograph on *Tracing Romania's Heterogeneous German Minority from Its Origins to the Diaspora*. The booklet provides an overview concerning the ethnic minority's varied background along with individual treatises regarding the main groups encountered, namely the Sathmar Swabians, the Transylvania Saxons, and the Banat Germans within a broader Danube Swabian context. Two Appendices and a List of References are also included. Persons interested in genealogy who frequently lament the relative lack of applicable sources in English ordered most copies of the opus. The 500-count run printed at Winona State for a total of $411.31 sold for $4.95 each. Quite a few were distributed free of charge and on October 17, 1989, I gave free permission to The Church of Jesus Christ of Latter-day Saints to make a microform reproduction of this publication for research purposes within the Mormons' library system.

Early in 1986, the Winona community was able to benefit from my knowledge of Hungarian when I conducted a lecture/discussion upon viewing the 1982-movie "Megál azüdö" (Time Stands Still). It was presented by the Winona Film Society in cooperation with the Minnesota Humanities Commission. A review appeared in The *Winona Shopper and Post* of January 8, 1986 on page 14. The film won the award for Best Foreign Film by the New York Film Critics and was praised as a breakthrough for Hungarian cinema in the West. Even with subtitles in English, much of the movie's symbolism was impossible to grasp entirely without the benefit of some historic background and cultural explanations that I was able to offer. Another contribution I made in 1986 was a 10-page unpublished manuscript on "Foreign Language Instruction at Winona State. An Overview: 1932-1985" (see Appendix B), which I drafted in consultation with Ms. Marion Davis, a staff member from 1932 until just before I arrived at WSU in 1971.

In 1987, I conducted a random survey concerning exploratory foreign language courses at American colleges and universities. One respondent remarked that a course like that could help students overcome apprehensions about enrolling in a foreign language course. Colleagues at Winona State suggested that an opportunity to explore languages could also help students discover in which idiom their chance of success might be greater on the basis of their particular aptitudes.

Building upon what I had learned while teaching a related course at WSU, I published a book in 1987 that has the title *Exploring French, German, and Spanish.* Of the 500 copies printed at Winona State University for a total of $932.04, some are still available in mint condition. The retail price is $11.95 a copy. For a time, the book was used in the Linguistics 3 Honors Course at West Virginia University in Morgantown. On September 2, 1989, I granted free permission to have the publication included in the ERIC database, which is the Clearinghouse on Languages and Linguistics of the Center for Applied Linguistics, Washington, DC, 20037. The microfiche call number at libraries around the country is ED 309 639/FL 018 110.

VI. THE BLOW THAT STRUCK AT THE CORE

14. Grieving Deferred in the Interest of Coping

At the young age of twenty-four (24), our daughter Ellen Susanne (1963-1987) succumbed to multiple head injuries on Wednesday September 9, 1987. She was hit by a 1978 Ford van while trying to walk across Oakton Street at Linder Avenue in Morton Grove, Illinois, around 6:50 p. m. The black model E 350 vehicle was driven by Joseph M. Jans (63) of Skokie, Illinois. He was headed west on Oakton Street with his granddaughter, age 5, as a passenger. Ellen had just gotten off a Nortran bus and was near the middle of the road at the time of impact. Her airborne body (127 lbs.) landed sixty (60) feet away and came to rest over the centerline with her head pointing south. It was never conclusively determined whether Mr. Jans was

a) blinded by the afternoon sun,
b) going too fast in the 30-mile zone,
c) under the influence of a debilitating substance, or
d) kept from stopping quickly, because of the presence of his granddaughter who may not have been wear ing a seat belt.

There were no indications of any mechanical defects regarding the van, which was registered in the name of a handicapped person. The vehicle's skid marks on the dry pavement measured 27 feet and 3 inches according to the supplemental police report of September 10, 1987 filed by Matthew Pankow, badge number 116, Morton Grove Police Department. There were no pictures taken at the scene since the police officer and the ambulance arrived simultaneously whereupon the victim was immediately placed on a stretcher and rushed to a hospital.

According to Mrs. Jackie (Bob) Jung who arrived at the scene shortly after the accident occurred, an alleged paramedic and a woman in an unmarked car tried to administer first aid. Other than placing a blanket under Ellen's fractured head, there seemed to be nothing they could do so they drove away. No additional information was ever obtained about, or from this couple. The ambulance of the Morton Grove Fire Department arrived shortly after the mishap at 6:56 p. m. The driver took Ellen to the Emergency Room of Rush North Shore Medical Center (formerly known as Skokie Valley Hospital). Doctors attended to her as of 7:08 p. m. Dr. Rosa Ignas pronounced her dead at 7:16 p.m. Ellen's body was identified by her uncle Peter N. HOLT and at 10:10 p.m., it was checked in at the Cook County Morgue for an autopsy performed by a Dr. Yuksel. While there was nothing incriminating found on her, no attempts were ever made to see if Mr. Jans who was instrumental in cutting Ellen's life short was equally unencumbered.

Marie's brother Peter (*1929) subsequently had the painful task of making the telephone call to Winona, Minnesota, to inform us of the tragic bereavement. All of us were totally devastated. Ellen had traveled all over Europe without sustaining so much as a scratch and now she was fatally injured only two houses from where she resided with her grandfather Frank HOLT (1904-1998) at 7929 Linder Avenue in Morton Grove, Illinois. Since nobody had expected anything like that, we did not know what to do next. We wondered whether she should be buried at Winona, Minnesota or at the All Saints Cemetery in Des Plaines, Illinois, where her maternal grandmother Magda HOLT (1905-1983) was laid to rest. Mr. Tom Martin, then a funeral director in Winona, prudently advised us that it would be more conducive to the grieving process if Ellen were buried close to home where we could visit her grave more often. Thus, our son Rick and I had the lamentable task of having to select a site for her at Woodlawn Cemetery in Winona.

The bitter occasion reminded me of a spontaneous observation that Ellen had made once when she and I were riding our bicycles past Woodlawn Cemetery; she ominously referred to her being buried there some day. Her remark to that effect shocked me and I asked her in dismay whether she wanted to ruin my day. She seemed genuinely sorry for having brought up the matter and I wondered what had prompted her to say something like that. As young as she was, Ellen tended to surprise me at times with her intuitive insights, a phenomenon not uncommon among women, which is also reminiscent of characteristics ascribed to female personages in classical mythology. By a strange coincidence, one of the last snapshots on the film inside her camera depicted a cemetery with a high chain link fence in the foreground on which there was a standard yellow road sign with the words "Dead End." Such foreboding signals suggest metaphysical links that cause a person to wonder about aspects of life transcending cognitive reality.

Ellen's achievements in her short life and the loss to society in terms of expectable further contributions she was apt to make become more apparent from excerpts of her résumé:

LAST EMPLOYMENT: Worked as a staff accountant for the Federal Deposit Insurance Corporation (FDIC) at Continental Illinois National Bank in downtown

Chicago since July 1986 upon successfully concluding an internship there. - The day after her unexpected demise, she was going to be informed by her supervisors of yet another promotion.

PRIOR EMPLOYMENT: K-Mart Store at Winona, Minnesota, as a salesperson in Cameras and Jewelry, from the time the store opened in 1980 until June 1986 (except for a period of absence while she was studying in Europe). Out of several hundred applicants of all ages for 70 fulltime and 40 part time jobs, she was one of only two high school students hired.

OTHER WORK EXPERIENCE:
a) Newspaper carrier in Winona, Minnesota,
b) Food service worker at Winona State University,
c) Baby sitter in the U. S. and nanny in Germany,
d) Maid at Munich-American Guest House.

FORMAL EDUCATION:
a) Graduated magna cum laude from Winona State University in 1986 with a double major. As an undergraduate, she had spent twenty (20) months studying, working, and traveling in Europe to augment her language skills. Prior to her untimely death, Ellen was enrolled as an evening student in an MBA program at DePaul University, downtown Chicago. In the three courses she completed there, she had earned two A's and one B.

b) At Winona Senior High School, Ellen elected to enroll in several challenge courses. She also played the b-clarinet in the Band and was a member of the Missteps Cheerleaders.

Ellen's high aspirations and her ability to stand on her own two feet were also reflected in her way of thinking. When Marie once observed that she could become the wife of a U. S. president some day, Ellen promptly replied: "The wife? No, I could BE president!" Her strong sense of independence also manifested itself in an interview she gave Brian Krambeer for an article in *Winona Campus Life*, No. 98 (July 22, 1985), p. 4 about how "Studies Abroad Expand Educational Experience." Before returning to the United States, she successfully passed the examination for the "Kleines deutsches Sprachdiplom" at the Goethe Institute in Munich as of May 8, 1984.

On many occasions, I recall being fascinated by Ellen's forthright deportment. At times, it was as though she had been placed in our care so that we could observe and learn from the way a human life unfolds. Marie and I marveled at how clearly she could already say words when she was only about ten months old. Her kind heart manifested itself in early childhood when she found injured birds for example that she tried to nurse back to health. She always wanted to do well and did not shy away from expending the necessary efforts to achieve her goals.

I felt privileged to have Ellen as a daughter and since she was taken from us, life has not been the same. Even the brightest of sunny days seems to be short of heart-warming dimensions without her! The magic of her unique character did not only register with loved ones but also with total strangers as demonstrated in the following excerpt from a letter of December 23, 1987 by Mr. Morton Paradise (67) of Skokie, Illinois, who made Ellen's casual acquaintance on a Nortran bus. He said, "you can both be proud of the impact she made on all who knew her." Thanks to Marie's efforts, an inscription of Ellen's name on a stone tier by the monument of Princess Wenonah at Windom Park in Winona also serves to keep memories alive among local residents who knew her.

Getting legal matters taken care of upon Ellen's unexpected demise turned out to be very difficult emotionally, and it proved to be a piercing educational experience, too. To begin with, we were at a loss in trying to locate an attorney who would resolutely seek answers to unexplained factors regarding our unfathomable loss. Looking back upon it now - over a dozen years later, I realize that even if we had found out that the accident was attributable to someone's negligence, it would have only deepened our agony since nothing short of having her back could have alleviated our pain! That may be why investigative procedures seem utterly superficial as far as dead victims' rights are concerned.

In an effort to get a good attorney, we asked relatives and friends for recommendations but none had applicable experience to draw upon. I consulted the Martindale-Hubbell Law Directory and wrote to The Association of Trial Lawyers of America in Washington, DC. One highly acclaimed attorney was named Leonard M. Ring. Marie and I, accompanied by our two sons Carl and Rick, went to see Mr. Ring at his office in Chicago. He made a favorable impression upon us so we decided to have him handle our case. However, what we had not anticipated was the fact that Mr. Ring immediately turned over the matter to an assistant named Gary D. Leigh whose attitude and experience in dealing with people did not measure up to our expectations.

Mr. Leigh lacked sensitivity and even became indignant with Marie over the telephone. He was tactless enough to refer to our case as trivial compared to others that involved larger sums of money. He evidently thought it was unreasonable for us to expect more than rudimentary attention, but we felt that seeking justice regarding the wrongful death of our only daughter merited more effort than he was willing to invest. Consequently, our agreement with the firm of Mr. Ring was terminated even though it set us back time-wise.

Through Mr. Duane M. Peterson, a fair-minded Winona attorney, we were put in touch with Mr. Tom Harvick in the Chicago area who agreed to handle our case. Mr. Ring had already informed us of the four-year backlog in Chicago courts. Due to time lost, our lawsuit was not actually initiated until June 30, 1989 when the Circuit Court of Cook County Illinois appointed Marie as Special Administrator of Ellen's estate. The legal settlement occurred nearly four years after that date, on May 19, 1993 - about five years and eight month after her wrongful death! While we were biding our time, we had gradually gained some insight into the workings of such matters. The process seems to be quite cut and dried as far as lawyers are generally concerned. Under a typical "Retainer Contract" one-third of the sum recovered plus expenses go to the attorney involved.

Not having had any dealings with attorneys before, we were under the mistaken assumption that upon hiring a lawyer, he or she will carry out the client's wishes just like a building contractor would for example. That proved to be a totally unrealistic expectation, because at the inception of a lawsuit it is still uncertain what route an attorney has to take to win the case. In the course of long, drawn-out proceedings wrought by legal counselors on both sides, clients' questions and concerns often remain entirely unanswered! Some aspects of the strategy of one's attorney may even appear to serve the interests of the opposition, perhaps in hopes of expected reciprocity or in anticipation of a possible kickback.

On one occasion, Marie and I were summoned to Chicago for a recorded deposition in the presence of attorneys representing Mr. Jans and his insurance company. We did not understand why we were deposed at all, since our daughter was not a minor and the disaster had occurred three hundred miles from where we were living at the time. Lacking better explanations, we wondered whether these legal solicitors wanted to find out

> a) whether Ellen had grown up in unhappy surroundings, which might have made her reckless or suicidal,

> b) about our state of mind and the extent of our resolve in seeking justice,

> c) whether we harbored feelings of vengeance toward Mr. Jans that might have jeopardized his safety,

> d) anything that could have been used as a basis for having Mr. Jans and/or his insurance company successfully deny liability in court.

We waited in vain to be apprised of some of the contents of the deposition of Mr. Jans about which our attorney told us nothing at all. In due course of time, we found out that upon learning of an impending lawsuit against one of their clients, insurance companies declare the applicable amount of liability as a tax-deductible business expense and place it in escrow where it earns interest for the company concerned. Then, they gather whatever data they can to gauge their chances of winning if they decide to let the matter get to court.

Even with no chances of emerging victorious themselves, insurance companies find it profitable to wait until the case in question is about to come up in court. At that point in time, they offer to settle out of court to forego concomitant legal expenses; thus, the long backlog in courts results in extra interest income for insurance companies while they try their best to find ways to get out of having to pay anything. Factors such as these clearly show why they defer settling even obviously legitimate claims for as long as possible! Other motives for deliberate foot dragging include expectations that appellants kept waiting for years may die or become willing to settle for less to assuage attendant anxiety and pain.

The total amount of liability insurance Mr. Jans happened to have was $50,000 of which our attorney's standard take was one-third plus expenses. Without being offered an option to the contrary, we were told that no additional recovery could have been obtained even if the matter had gotten to court. In some ways, it might have helped to know how our attorney had arrived at that conclusion, but on second thought, it also might have compounded our grief! When it is considered that many people get six to eight digit sums for personal injuries, one cannot help but be baffled that the out-and-out return on a human life can be so downright insignificant! Thus, compensation proffered to family left behind for their loss of companionship, comfort, and hope regarding prospects of grandchildren, nephews, and nieces often only adds insult to injury.

Ellen's unexpected death upset Rick so much that he thought of terminating his formal education. On second thought, he realized that his sister would not have wanted that to happen so he stuck with it. On May 28, 1988, he graduated from Winona State University with a Bachelor of Science degree in Business. After trying unsuccessfully to find suitable employment in Winona, he decided to join his brother Carl in Rockford, Illinois. Rick wound up working as an Assistant Production Manager at Arachnid, a company that made plastic products including dart boards. Rick felt that he had to work hard to prove himself so that his older brother Carl, on whose recommendation he had landed the job, would not be disappointed. He tried to do his level best and made himself available at all hours during the day and even at night. In doing so, he overextended himself and began to exhibit symptoms of stomach ulcers; therefore, we had to ask him not to jeopardize his health even if it meant that he had to find employment elsewhere.

Luckily, Rick met amiable Dane OLIVER before long who proved to be a valuable companion right from the start. She was working at a financial institution where "absolutely free checking" happened to be featured on an outdoor banner to which Rick responded one fateful day. His frugal nature paid off doubly when she agreed to marry him in Las Vegas, Nevada, on August 19, 1990. I had the honor to be chosen as his best man and Marie was able to document part of the ceremony with an unfamiliar video camera. The newlyweds settled down in Lakewood, Colorado, and Rick began to work at the Aluminum Supply Company in Denver, which was owned by Marie's brother Al HOLT. When his uncle sold the business to NORANDEX in 1996, Rick began to work in the Denver office of The Equitable Life Assurance Society of the United States, which became affiliated with AXA Financial Advisors. On February 26, 2000, Rick received the National Leader Corps Award for 1999. A couple of months later, he was promoted to District Manager for AXA Advisors - Denver Branch. Since then, he became a Certified Financial Planner (CFP) upon passing the required examinations. His advancement to the position of Vice President - Rocky Mountain Region occurred as of January 2001.

Less than a year after our daughter Ellen had passed away, Dr. Thomas F. Stark, the well-liked President of Winona

State University died unexpectedly in 1988. John (Jack) Kane took over as Acting President until Dr. Darrell W. Krueger was hired to fill the post as of 1989. My status at Winona State under the stewardship of these men showed marked improvement somehow. After a decade and a half, I had apparently been there long enough to be regarded as one of the "regulars." In the *Winonan*, vol. 65, No. 25 (April 20, 1988), p. 11, I was featured in the "Variety" section of the student newspaper.

Through employee newsletter editions, I kept the WSU community apprised of reviews of my publications, my attendance at professional workshops or conferences, and of travel overseas. In a letter of April 18, 1990, President Krueger even penned a handwritten note saying, "I hear good things about you." At long last, Winona State University had a president whose genuine support of foreign language study manifested itself through an expansion of offerings and a corresponding addition of staff.

During the summer of 1991, I was a participant in the Annual World Congress of the Federation Internationale des Professeurs de Langues Vivantes, which was held at Pécs, Hungary. Before driving there in a car rented at Frankfurt/Main, Marie and I tried to trace my paternal ancestry in the Spessart forest whereupon we visited relatives at various locations in Germany and Austria. We also stopped at Lake Balaton on our way to Pécs. We were curious to see how half a century of communist rule had affected the Catholic country; promoting uniformity may have been good for some things, but in the area of culinary arts, it was disastrous. When I ordered Debrecen-style sausage in a Hungarian restaurant, I was served an ordinary hot dog! I had to ask myself, 'is this what I traveled thousands of miles for?' Luckily, sausage manufacturers in Vienna, Austria, still know how to make some that taste genuine. Let us hope that genetic engineering and the trend toward lean meat will not rob consumers of the traditional goodness either.

At Pécs, Marie and I participated in a sightseeing and wine tasting tour by bus. We also had a chance to listen to an indigenous group that sang German folk songs for us. One of our stops was in an open area where budding sculptors had a chance to test their artistic skills. Along a stretch of highway, the bus was traveling close to the Croatian border where the recent conflict with Serbs had not entirely subsided. Some of the firearm projectiles had landed on Hungarian territory.

When the foreign language teachers' conference at Pécs ended, Marie and I drove to Budapest for more sightseeing. People at the Hungarian capital were in the process of getting ready for a visit by Pope John Paul II. While taking a tour by taxi, it was enlightening to see how the facades of government buildings of the imperial era were still riddled with bullet holes and shrapnel from WW II. The communists evidently had no interest in allocating funds for their renovation. Conversely, the populace lost no time in demonstrating its dislike of communist street names: They painted a red X over them and restored the historic nameplates. Monuments and icons depicting communist heroes on bridges for example were wrapped in gunnysacks; their relevance was no longer applicable in a country that was free of political oppression at last.

As of the early 1990's, sanity in the operation of the Minnesota State University System began to manifest itself as realities were finally faced. In an editorial entitled "State's Love for Education Has Long History," *Winona Daily News*, April 14, 1991, p. 6A-7A, Gary Evans wrote:

> "Per student support in constant dollars declined by $1,000 since 1978 in the Minnesota State University System ... Resource allocation has emphasized the numbers game rather than the transfer of knowledge ... While post-secondary enrollments were forecast to shrink, they grew - at a rate almost beyond belief."

It was good to hear that past mistakes were finally recognized, but why no one was ever called to account for them remained an unanswered question in my mind.

On May 22, 1992, I was among seventeen (17) WSU faculty and staff members who were honored for twenty (20) years of service. One month before that in April 1992, I published a 154-page bilingual (German and English) monograph concerning my place of birth: *Banat-Topola's Schwaben: 1791-1945*, at Winona, Minnesota (L.C. card number 92-187274). Of the 500 copies printed at W & C Printing Company for $2,264.00, many were sold to interested parties in Europe and the U. S. Numerous copies were distributed gratis to libraries and as advertising samples. Some have remained in stock due to a diminished circle of concerned readers and a general lack of awareness regarding the ethnic minority treated.

During spring 1992, my wife Marie and I attended a dinner sponsored by the Inter Faculty Association of Winona State University. Dr. Paul Grawe from the Department of English happened to sit at the same table with us. He made a comment to the effect that some of us will be working for less than what we might get if we took advantage of the early retirement incentive that was offered by the Minnesota State University

Board at the time. Although Paul's observations probably were prompted with someone else in mind, they seemed to fit my situation also. Soon after that, I spoke with our personnel director and he referred me to a counselor of the Teachers Retirement Association (TRA) in St. Paul. Upon being presented with a couple of scenarios, I was rather inclined to accept the incentive offer that entailed an extra year's salary paid out over a five-year period. It also included an extra year of health insurance coverage under the state contract with Blue Cross and Blue Shield of Minnesota as well as Delta Dental of Minnesota.

Marie was quite surprised when I told her what I thought about the given window of opportunity for early retirement, but she went along with my judgment. To her, it was rather ironic that I was going to quit when I had finally reached the top (step 15) of the salary scale. It was a weird sensation for me to suddenly sever the ties that I had worked so hard to fashion and preserve for twenty-one years. However, with vivid memories of the infinite struggle for survival so hauntingly dominant in my mind, the prospects of letting go concurrently registered as relief that I craved. Thus, I submitted my resignation to President Krueger in a letter dated May 12, 1992. My last duty day at WSU coincided with my birthday on May 30, 1992. Commencement was the only official function scheduled and those of us who retired had the honor to sit on the stage with the usual dignitaries. It was heart-warming to hear President Krueger, a follower of the Mormon religion, say words of praise over the loudspeakers for our years of dedication and service to Winona State University.

Under the headline "Twelve WSU Faculty Members Are Retiring," the *Winona Daily News* of May 29, 1992 brought brief synopses of each of us concerned. Mine included the following points:

1. Served WSU for 21 years (1971-1992) in the Department of Foreign Languages

2. Chaired the Department from 1977-1980

3. Revised and updated language programs

4. Published a textbook on *Exploring French, German, and Spanish* in 1987

5. Published articles and books on an ethnic minority group

6. Was a consultant for John Wiley and Sons in the revision of the 4th edition of *Deutsch für alle*, for beginners.

7. Performed review of the German program at the University of Wisconsin-River Falls

8. Credentials: B. A. from Columbia College in Chicago, B. A. and M. A. from the University of Illinois, Ph. D. from the University of Cincinnati.

The German textbook mentioned is by Werner Haas, Doris Fulda Merrifield, and Gustave Bording Mathieu, *Deutsch für alle. Beginning College German.* Fourth Edition (New York: John Wiley and Sons, 1993) - citation under "Acknowledgments," p. xii.

15. Weighing Anchor at Winona and Relocation to Colorado

Prior to my quick decision to retire as of May 31, 1992, from my teaching position at Winona State University, Marie and I had not gotten around to making actual plans regarding our "golden years." Her father Frank HOLT (1904-1998) who was living by himself in Morton Grove, Illinois, wanted us to move in with him, because he was quite lonely and would have loved nothing more than to have family around him. Even if Marie had not wanted to keep working part time at the Community Memorial Hospital (CMH) in Winona, having us move in with her dad was not feasible for several underlying reasons. For one thing, it would have entailed the emotional stress of having to face the very site daily where our daughter Ellen had lain in the throes of death upon being struck down as a pedestrian in 1987 by a van. Moreover, relocation to the Chicago area would not have satisfied our desire to spend our golden years in a more favorable climate AND closer to family.

Without compelling reasons to make drastic changes in our way of life, we continued to reside in Minnesota for five more years, until Marie had accumulated over twenty (20) years of part-time service at CMH by 1997. Meanwhile, I kept busy with home maintenance, selective diminution of files, sorting of books for donations, personal as well as scholarly correspondence and by attending to my Translation & Interpretation Services. To keep in better shape physically, I frequented the "Eagle Room" at the local YMCA to which I had initially received a paid membership as a gift from my family. Under Marie's flexible work schedule, we were now also periodically able to catch up on paying visits to relatives and friends in Arizona, Colorado, Florida, Illinois, Pennsylvania, and Wisconsin.

In 1993, I took Marie to Seattle and to Fort Lewis, Washington, where I was stationed as an infantryman from 1953 until 1955. On the way there, we also stopped in Seeley Lake, Montana, to see friends. Prior to that, we visited Rick and Dane at their home in Lakewood, Colorado. They closed the deal on their first house as of December 30, 1991 and moved in on February 23, 1992. The ranch-style home has a two-car garage and is situated on an extra large lot; there are three bedrooms on the main floor and two more plus storage and a family room in the finished basement. Rick renovated the bathroom on the main floor and completely rebuilt the one in the basement including the addition of a corner shower stall. He also replaced the dark kitchen cabinets with natural oak units finished by Dane. In 1998, Marie and I helped him install vinyl siding and in 1999, he had new seamless gutters installed. Dane's abundant creative interior decorations reflect rural American and modern styles.

As of July 27, 1993, we enjoyed a rare visit by my sister Rose and her husband Joe KAPITAEN who came to see us in Winona, Minnesota. For Christmas 1993, Marie and I flew to Denver, Colorado, to be with Rick and Dane and with Al and Hanne HOLT. Carl caught us by surprise when he joined us for a visit, too. In 1994, we set out to see Marie's dad, our sons Carl and Rick as well as Tony and Martha. On March 11, 1995, Marie and I drove to her dad's house in Morton Grove, Illinois, to help celebrate the 82nd birthday of Marianne Kortanek, a good friend of Marie's father. The following Tuesday, on March 14, we flew to Naples, Florida, where we stayed at the condo- minium of Al HOLT'S business partner Chuck Smith. While there, we visited Marie's former coworker and friend Barbara Coriaci and her husband Joe on Marco Island. From Naples, Marie and I plus her brother Peter and sister-in-law Christine drove to Miami in a rented car as guests of Al and Hanne HOLT where we boarded the Norwegian liner "Seaward" for a cruise to Nassau. It was an enjoyable experience and provided us with insights into Caribbean lifestyles, too. We arrived back home in Minnesota on March 21, 1995.

From July 10-12, 1995, Marie and I visited our son Carl in Rockford, Illinois. Our next trip to his house took place in early October. From there, we flew to Las Vegas, Nevada, with Carl and his amiable bride Marzena. They tied the knot there on October 7, 1995 in a civil ceremony that was followed in 1996 by their church wedding in Poland - described below. The ceremony in Las Vegas was also attended by some of the newlyweds' friends from the Rockford and Belvidere areas. With quite a lot to see and do during our short stay at this city of lights, we eventually got back home a bit short on sleep.

In Winona, Marie and I had joined a dance group that met once a month at the Hilltop Ballroom near Arcadia, Wis- consin. On November 3, 1995, as we headed home around midnight, a male deer happened to cross Wisconsin highway 35 right in front of the hood of our 1988 VW Fox. We stopped abruptly but not before hitting the critter hard enough to expe- dite it into the ditch. Damage to our car's bumper, grill, head- light, hood, and right front fender rendered a repair bill ex- ceeding $1,200. Upon reporting the event to the police, we had the option to keep the young buck; but at that rate, we would not have enjoyed it. Our appetite for venison was never that great either.

On March 6, 1996, Dr. Daniel R. Barr of Winona diagnosed me as half blind on my right eye. It was impossible to say whether the deficiency was attributable to an injury I sustained near the left eye many years before or whether the liquid anesthetic that got into my right eye at CMH in 1982 had resulted in the serious impairment. I was hospitalized in Winona at that time for a kidney stone problem. The urologist Dr. Gilson Vieiralves had me put to sleep while he inserted some sort of harness through the urethra and up into my kidneys to enhance drainage. - While I have peripheral vision in the right eye, the center registers objects vertically as well as horizontally distorted and even bold headlines are illegible.

As of May 27, 1996, Marie and I left for Europe in order to attend the church wedding of our son Carl and his spouse Marzena, née Slusarska, at Pustinia, north of Debica, Poland. We were apprehensive about traveling to Eastern Europe, which had been pretty well off limits to Western tourists since WW II. Our relatives in Germany and Austria were also leery about going there for fear of being robbed. Auto rental agencies did not want to have their vehicles driven to Eastern Europe either because of theft problems. Luckily, our travel agent in La Crosse, Wisconsin, was able to get us a rental car without a restriction concerning Eastern Europe. The vehicle turned out to be a brand new 1996 Opel Astra station wagon. The GM car handled so well that I would have liked to buy one upon returning home, but no such model was available for purchase in the U.S.A. - Subsequently, General Motors incorporated features of the Opel Astra in the design of its brand new Cadillac Catera model.

Marie and I picked up the Opel at the Munich airport and drove to the house of my cousin Peter STEIGERWALD (*1926) and his family. From there, we went on to Knittelfeld in Styria, Austria, to visit Marie's cousins Helmut HOLECSEK and Terri PEINTINGER, née HOLECSEK plus friends and acquaintances. The room rate at the local Best Western motel was higher than it would have been at an American counterpart. On the way toward Bratislava, Slovakia, we stopped at Neunkirchen, Lower Austria, to visit Dr. Gerd Schwendenwein and his cordial wife Dee of Trinidad, for a chat and lunch before resuming our journey.

Before entering Slovakia in early June 1996, we spent the night at an Austrian "Pension" (bed and breakfast type of lodging) near Bad Deutsch-Altenburg on the Danube River.

Romans already frequented the ancient site to partake of local sulfur baths. The prevalent pungent odor combined with high humidity also makes it a favorite place for mosquitoes. Luckily, we were conditioned for attacks by such insects because of our exposure to similar swarms along the mighty Mississippi River.

As we got deeper into Slovakia the next day, traffic became lighter and the landscape looked more pristine and less polluted. Efforts to do some research locally concerning one of Marie's ancestors named Wenceslaus HOLECSEK were unsuccessful, because of sketchy data to start with. Since we were not in possession of any Slovak or Polish currency, we wondered whether we could buy gasoline with American dollars, German marks, Austrian schillings, credit cards, or travelers checks. Fortunately, we were able to reach our destination in Debica with the tank of gasoline we had acquired in Austria! Just to be on the safe side, we tried in vain to buy gas at a station in Poland. None of our means of payment proved to be acceptable until we acquired Polish money at an official currency exchange in Debica.

The hotel where Marzena had made reservations for us used to be a retreat for athletes. Although the place had a four-star rating, its furnishings were rather Spartan by American standards. Besides a TV set, a table, and a couple of chairs, our room on the second floor had two wooden cots with very modest bedding on emaciated mattresses. Thankfully, it had a balcony from where we could keep an eye on our rented car. Adjacent to the room, there was a bathroom with a shower and a wardrobe for our clothes. By means of the color-TV, we were able to receive broadcasts in Polish and German. Breakfast was available in a dining room within the building and meals could be charged to our room. Finding someone who spoke English or German proved to be impossible, but the few words of Russian that I had picked up as a child from Red Army soldiers passing through my hometown of Banat-Topola in 1944 happened to go a long way.

Having arrived a couple of days before the wedding enabled us to help decorate the local community hall for the dinner and dance that followed the church ceremony, which was scheduled for 3:00 p.m. on June 8, 1996. Both events were well attended by relatives who had come from different parts of the country. Some came from Wroclaw and others from Tarnow and Rzeszow. Marie and I enjoyed the local customs that added special dimensions to the occasion. They evoked memories of respective childhood experiences in Romania and Yugoslavia.

Marzena's parents Eduard and Irena, along with their three sons Adam, Bogdan, and Jurek had pitched a large army tent in the courtyard of their house. There, guests could have congregated in case of rain, but the weather turned out to be rather nice and even a bit too balmy. The band of six musicians took up a position in front of the tent and played a song in honor of every guest that arrived. As a token of appreciation, guests inserted money through a slot in their base drum. Since the collected amount exceeded the honorarium agreed upon, Carl and Marzena were presented with the balance. When it was time to go to church right next door, the musicians led the procession while playing fitting tunes. To everyone's surprise, Carl managed to say his vows in Polish.

After the mass, everybody got into cars to head for the hall. Along the way, jesters halted the caravan to claim a ransom for letting us pass! The road ahead was "blocked" by an oxcart loaded with hay on which a goat was merrily nibbling. The scene was rather theatrical and somewhat suggestive of what it might have been like in medieval times. After money was collected from someone in every car, the road was cleared and we were able to proceed until we ran into another roadblock staged by masqueraded individuals who strung a rope across the way as we were approaching. Each of the four groups of ransom seekers was unique and amusing. The operator of the gates at the railroad crossing prompted our fifth stop but the ransom was courteously waived. Smiles from the bride and groom amounted to sufficient payment.

At the hall, there were additional symbolic customs in the offing. First, the newlyweds had to break bread jointly and "wash it down" with a shot of vodka. Then the chief cook officially welcomed the couple and in the process of raising a glass to toast them, she "accidentally" dropped it causing it to shatter whereupon Carl was given a broom and a dustpan to sweep up the debris. Meanwhile, guests were throwing coins toward the bride and groom (not rice), which the children eagerly picked up in the couple's behalf. According to traditional lore, the spouse who ended up with the most change would be in charge of household finances.

Upon taking our seats, delicious food was served including the best chicken soup imaginable! There were various reasons why the meals tasted so good: 1) Polish cuisine is world renowned for its excellence. 2) The bride's family had hired the best local cooks. 3) Marzena's father had raised the chickens himself. 4) The pastries were homemade and devoid of chemical preservatives. 5) Our taste buds were quite attuned to authentic East European culinary fare.

By way of courtesies extended to us, we were made to feel like royalty. Every time we returned from the dance floor, there was a fresh set of dishes in front of us. Men who asked Marie for a dance bowed their heads and kissed her hand afterwards. Dance sets were much longer than we were used to. Unfortunately, one of the two window fans was out of service, which made us yearn for refreshing breezes. Dancing continued until daybreak on both nights! It was 4:30 a. m. by the time Marie and I got back to our hotel and the birds were stirring in search of breakfast already. On the third "wedding" day, guests from out of town stopped by the house of the bride's parents again prior to leaving for home. Marie and I did the same before we left for a final night at the hotel. The next morning, we headed back to Austria to visit more relatives. After returning our rental car at the Munich airport, we caught a flight back to the U. S. and on June 18, 1996, we were back in Winona, grateful that the journey we had so reluctantly embarked upon, ended with nothing but pleasant memories.

On July 4, 1996, we made another trip to Marie's dad in Morton Grove, Illinois. July 6, we stopped by Tony and Martha's lake cottage at 5266 Sandy Beach South, near Belgium, Wisconsin. The following day, we headed toward Colorado's Front Range in search of the place where we were hoping to take up residence. We had already checked out places like Loveland, Greeley, Fort Collins, Longmont, Boulder, and Colorado Springs but in our hearts, we were drawn closer to Rick and Dane who were expecting our first grandson Nicholas. Upon having had the pleasure of welcoming Carl's adept wife Marzena into our family, we were now able to take the first member of the next generation into our hearts as well.

On Saturday July 13, 1996 Rick drove us to more areas with houses for sale until we came upon an enclave of new construction just south of the Southwest Plaza Shopping Mall. We had always expressed a desire to live near stores and now our wish was within reach of fulfillment. Thanks to Dane's welcome input, lot number 8 in section 14 was selected in the Sunset West subdivision of PrideMark Homes Incorporated. We signed for the lot on Monday July 15, 1996 and arrived back in Winona two days later. Our house on Estes Street is situated so that the view northeastward should remain quite unobstructed, since the South Branch of Lilly Gulch runs through the area.

For August 31, 1996, we drove to Wisconsin to celebrate Tony's 60th birthday at their lake cottage. The next day, we visited Marie's dad in Morton Grove, Illinois. Upon calling my second cousin Andrew WEISZMANN from there, we learned that his mother Magdalena was in a hospital. We went to visit her there on September 2, 1996, but she was already struggling with death. When she expired among family and friends around 3:10 p. m., it was like someone dear had just been yanked from among our midst; however, rather than pausing in deference of her departing spirit invisibly bidding us farewell, those present engaged in spontaneous chatter. It seemed strange that the distressing bereavement did not prompt venting of profound sorrow! Though Marie and I lacked appropriate clothing for the somber occasion, we remained in town to attend the funeral, too.

October 7, 1996, Marie and I headed for Wisconsin again and on the 8th, Tony and Martha took us to Door County for sightseeing. We enjoyed the scenery along with historic lighthouses and stopped to sample local culinary specialties. We spent the night in a comfortable rented condominium. The next day, we enjoyed more of the landscape as we headed back toward their place on Lake Michigan and from there, home to Winona again. On October 19, Carl and Marzena paid us a visit in Minnesota. October 23-28, Marie and I were in the Denver area again to see our handsome grandson Nicholas and to select the color schemes as well as the cabinet and woodwork styles for our new residence in Jefferson County, Colorado.

December 16-20, 1996, we spent with Marie's dad in Morton Grove, Illinois. Just prior to that on November 15-16, Marie and I helped Carl and Marzena move from an apartment to their extensively renovated two-story house on Hurlbut in Belvidere, Illinois. It is situated on a corner lot, has a two-car garage and an outdoor backyard swimming pool. As an older home, it came with a lot of nooks and crannies. Located on the main floor is the kitchen, an enclosed porch, a dining room, living room, plus another room where they keep the upright Starr piano that we acquired at Cincinnati, Ohio in 1969 when Carl began to take lessons at the age of ten. On the second floor, there is the main bathroom, three bedrooms, and a laundry room. The exterior of the house was completely repainted and brand new combination storm windows and screens were installed. A bathroom with shower was subsequently added on the main floor along with siding all around the exterior of the building. The old gravity furnace works like a charm and makes the house quite cozy inside even in sub-zero weather.

On January 11, 1997, Marie's coworker Sandy Bauer and her husband Bruce, who used to be a participant in one of my German classes at Winona State, looked at our Winona residence with the idea of acquiring it. Bruce wanted a fancier bathroom. The Bauers told their friends Paul Houdek and Sandra Kay Kauphusman about our roomy house. The couple came to see it on January 15, 1997. Paul and Sandra Kay evidently liked it so well that they surprised us by agreeing to pay the asking price of $96,500. It made me wonder whether our valuation was way too low! When they made a formal offer on January 26, 1997, we accepted their bid and took it to our attorney Mr. Steven Libera on January 29, 1997 for due processing since we had not engaged a realtor.

Realty-type information I had listed in a flyer concerning our house in Winona included the following:

On a 41X150 ft. lot, a 2-story frame building with Masonite Colorlok siding installed in 1983 and new asphalt roof shingles applied also.

Water and sewer: City of Winona. 1997 res. net taxes: $956.00.

Cole-Sewell painted aluminum storm doors, windows and screens. Detached 2-1/2 car garage is 19X21 feet with extra high entry: 7'8".

Interior walls and ceilings: Plaster with natural woodwork and hardwood floors.

4 bedrooms, 2-1/4 baths; 100% basement, gas forced air heat & central air conditioning; 100-ampere electric service with breakers. Living space: 1,708 sq. ft., plus enclosed porches and basement area.

MAIN FLOOR:
- Enclosed front porch (with windows and screens) 8X25 feet.
- Vestibule 4X4 feet plus guest closet.
- Living room 15X25 feet with brick fireplace, antique brass and frosted glass light fixture, wall-to-wall carpeting, two built-in oak cabinets, and coaxial cable TV jack.
- Dining room 12X14 feet with bay window and antique brass and frosted glass light fixture, wall-to-wall carpeting.
- Solarium 5X6 feet with antique brass and frosted glass sconce, wall-to-wall carpeting.
- Walk-through butler's pantry 5X10 feet with built-in cabinets, Formica countertop, telephone jack, and vinyl floor.

- Kitchen 10X12 feet, with built-in cabinets, appliances: dishwasher, refrigerator, 36-inch gas range with electric hood, corner bench, ceiling fan, vinyl floor.
- Enclosed back porch 6X8 feet with freezer chest and floor carpet.
- Side entry stairwell 3X12 feet with storage bin and toilet.
- Note: Venetian blinds on all first-floor windows!

SECOND FLOOR:
- NW bedroom 13X14 feet with hardwood floor 20-sq. ft. closet, ceiling fan, two sconces, combination cable TV and telephone jack.
- SW bedroom 11X13 feet with hardwood floor, 20 sq. ft. closet, and tiled ceiling.
- NE bedroom 9X12 feet with hardwood floor, 20 sq. ft. closet, and combination telephone and cable TV jack.
- Main bathroom 7X8 feet with two built-in cabinets.
- Hallway (excluding stairwell) 3X12 feet, with telephone jack and a 21 sq. ft. hall closet.

ATTIC (380 sq. ft., excluding closet and enclosed storage spaces):
- Bedroom 15X20 feet with telephone jack plus closet and additional storage areas.
- Bathroom 5X7 feet.

BASEMENT (722.25 sq. ft.):
- Fruit cellar (83.875 sq. ft).
- Laundry room 11X15 feet.
- Central area 11.5X11.5 feet.
- Recreation room 11.5X24 feet.
- Workshop 7.75X11.5 feet.

Remarks: Walk to schools, churches, YMCA, interstate bridge, Mississippi River, Windom Park, Winona State University, stores, restaurants, motels, gas stations, repair shops, etc., in the downtown Winona area.

Marie and I signed the house at 355 West Fourth Street over to Paul and Sandra Kay on February 3, 1997. Since they purchased the house with a VA loan, it was inspected on March 1, 1997. On March 3, Marie and I rented a U-Haul truck and loaded it with household goods that we did not need on a daily basis. On the 4th, we left for Denver and on the 5th, we arrived there and placed the goods into a rented storage facility on Jewell Avenue, near Garrison Street. On the 6th of March, we visited with Rick and Dane and on the 7th, we drove for about 16 hours until we got to Winona again. A week later on March 15, 1997 the christening of Nicholas took place at the Cathedral of the Sacred Heart in Winona, Minnesota. Just then, we had the heaviest snowstorm of the season - over 3 feet of the white stuff had fallen! When Rick, Dane, and the baby arrived, they first had to shovel the driveway before they were able to park their car. Worse came to worst when our two-stage 521 Toro snow thrower conked out, too!

The final closing on our house in Winona occurred at 2:30 PM on March 21 whereupon we began to load an even bigger U-Haul truck. Fortunately, Tony and Martha came to help us as they had at other times when we were moving; thus, we managed to get everything loaded. The next morning when we tried to get underway, the heavy truck kept spinning its wheels on the frozen ground. We had backed it up to the front porch for easier loading and now it was stuck on the front lawn. We wound up having to call a tow truck to pull us onto the street.

Before we actually got out of town, we lost even more time because a light kept flashing on the dashboard of the truck. Not knowing what the problem was, we headed back to the rental agency but the clerk on duty was not a trained mechanic either so he had to call another office after closing time, in efforts to reach someone who could clear up the mystery. As it turned out, the motor had to be allowed to idle for a while upon starting it, so that the compressed air system could get charged up before driving off.

Bravely, Marie also took her turns at driving the U-Haul trucks! We were moving right along in Nebraska on one of the two trips when we had to pull off Interstate 80 for a cargo check. In response to an inquiry by state patrolmen concerning the nature of our load, we told them we were carrying household goods whereupon we were permitted to resume driving without having had to open the back of the locked truck. One other thing we had to be mindful of as "truck drivers" entailed watching for filling stations that sell diesel fuel since not all of them do.

The final inspection walk-through at our new house in Colorado was scheduled for March 24, 1997 and the closing was on the 27th. With all that taken care of, we were entitled to move in. The second truckload of our belongings was parked in front of Rick and Dane's house. Upon driving it over to our new residence, Marie's brother Al HOLT thankfully helped us unload whereupon we were able to return the vehicle to the U-Haul agent on Garrison Street and Jewell Avenue within the allotted time period. The household goods we had in storage were transported home with our VW Fox over a period of time. We undoubtedly brought too much stuff with us from Minnesota, but one never knows exactly what will be needed at a new location. All in all, we had every reason to be satisfied, since everything went perfectly well with our relocation.

Our twenty-six (26) years of residence in the same house at Winona, Minnesota, represented the longest time we had stayed anywhere in the world; yet, neither Marie nor I ever grew roots there. To her, Chicago was the nearest thing to home for many years until altered circumstances and the loss of loved ones gradually abated emotional ties to that area also. Deep down, we both knew that Winona was not going to be our ultimate habitat; however, it may well turn out to be our final resting place, since we already paid for our gravesites next to Ellen's. Especially after our grandson Nicholas was born, we wanted to be closer to where we can interact with grandchildren more regularly than we could have from a distance of 916 miles between us. Meanwhile, we were blessed with another grandson named Matthew Joseph who was born on July 30, 1999. Thus, our reward for having moved to Colorado has doubled.

At times, Marie used to say that she did not want to "rot" in Winona where few relatives besides our sons and Tony's family would normally come to see us. It was correctly anticipated that in the Denver area we were bound to get more visitors including some from overseas. Marie's brother Al had observed one day that half of her family was in Colorado; therefore, moving to this state also made sense in that respect. Additional "bonuses" we now enjoy include:

a) Shorter winters with much less snow to shovel and rare concern for the wind-chill factor.

b) Very few mosquitoes ever bothered us in Colorado so far.

c) The humidity that used to sap our energy in Illinois and Minnesota for many years is much lower here.

d) During about 300 days a year there is at least some sun at our current location.

The only drawback experienced thus far has been a lack of time to explore all the options in our new environment! Some of the things that kept us quite busy initially with our new house involved:

1. Emptying the rented storage facility by April 14, 1997.

2. Having an electric garage door opener installed, a gift from Al HOLT, 4/16/97.
3. Buying a ceiling fan with lights for the dining room, 4/17/97.
4. Enjoyment of visits from grandson Nicholas as of 4/18/97 and since August 1999 from grandson Matthew, too.
5. Mapping out the yard for landscaping, 4/19/97.
6. Seeing back yard fence put up and rock areas established 4/22/97.
7. Installing drapery rods, picture hooks, and towel bars, 4/26/97.
8. Obtaining a lawn sprinkler system and kitchen ensemble, 4/30/97.
9. Having lawn areas sodded at 5960 S. Estes in Littleton, 5/3/97.
10. Installation of cabinet, dryer vent, and shelf in laundry room, 6/97.
11. Adding cabinet, shoe rack, and towel rods in master bath, 6/97.
12. Installation of railing and screen door at front entrance, 6/97.
13. Adding ceiling fan & venetian blinds in master bedroom, 6/97.
14. Installation of storage shelves and hooks in the garage, 7/97.
15. Placing grates over two window wells outside, 7/97.
16. Enclosure of garden level storage area, as of 7/29/97.
17. Having central air conditioning unit installed 8/21/97.
18. Re-routing of heating ducts for garden level bedroom, 8/97.
19. Installation of pocket door to garden level storage area, 9/97.
20. Additions of coaxial TV cables to two living room locations, 9/97.
21. Roughing in two closets and the garden level bedroom area, 10/97.
22. Installation of switches, outlets, and paneling in the area indicated, 10/97.
23. Adding tiled ceiling and Berber carpet in said bedroom, 10/97.
24. Installation of heating duct in lower level office area, 11/97.
25. Losing my left middle fingertip along with the nail when an aluminum duct strap wrapped itself around it while I tried to enlarge a hole with a drill on November 17, 1997.
26. Had skin grafted to the finger from my hip area on November 20, 1997 - stitches were removed on December 3, 1997.

The garden level office area was completed, except for the floor and the ceiling, on December 23, 1997. On January 16, 1998, we began to enclose the furnace area where we also installed a laundry tub. Construction of the lower level bathroom was started on January 30, 1998. On February 13, we connected the bathtub and the next day, we finished the room. By May 13, the paneling was done on the garden level and on July 29 at 1:30 PM, we were done with the suspended ceiling, too. After that, we were ready to have wall-to-wall carpeting installed as of August 17, 1998 on the major portion of the wooden floor over the vented crawl space area below.

Meanwhile, we had attended leisure-time functions of the Edelweiss Club, the Goethe Club, the Denver Turnverein, and the Swiss Society. We also traveled some and enjoyed visitors from Austria - Hans-Peter's family - at our house, but on August 3, 1998, we were bereft of Marie's father Frank HOLT who died at the age of 94. Prior to selling the parental residence on January 19, 1999, Marie and her brothers had the heart-wrenching task of sorting memory-laden personal mementos before clearing out and donating spare possessions. A few weeks after Marie's dad had passed away, our daughter-in-law Marzena lost her father Eduard Slusarski on August 29, 1998 in Pustinia, Poland. His untimely demise was at least partly precipitated by the fact that he had smoked cigarettes for many years.

In Littleton, Marie and I joined an AARP group nearby as well as the Jefferson County Retired Teachers Association (JCRTA) with whom we enjoy lunch once a month. The biggest problems relocated retirees like us are liable to be faced with apparently concern health and dental insurance. When my health and dental coverage through my former employer ended one year after I retired, I was able to stay with the same carriers but our premium rose considerably while out of state care was only covered up to fifty percent of the allowable treatment costs. Finding supplemental Medicare coverage at our new location was facilitated when I rejoined the National Education Association (NEA). In 1999, supplemental insurance proved to be useful when Marie had her gallbladder removed at Littleton Hospital on January 5.

While trying to configure this chapter in April 1999, I was continually distracted and quite upset by televised accounts of what was happening in Kosovo. Reports of the ruthless ethnic cleansing carried out there by Serbs under directives of Slobodan Milosevic brought back frightful memories of a similar ordeal under Tito to which I was subjected as a member of Yugoslavia's ethnic-German minority in 1945. What fellow Danube Swabians have steadily deplored in vain concerns the media's failure to even mention the contemptible earlier event! Consequently, lessons that might have been learned from ignored analogous criminal conduct fail to keep additional outbursts of racism from happening.

From the middle of July to early August in 1999, Marie and I visited relatives in Brazil with Tony and Martha. After some sightseeing in Rio de Janeiro with our second cousin Joâo, his lovely wife Rosa, and their son Felipe, we went to see Aunt Susanna MARTIN (*1909) at Sâo Paulo. She had invited us to come and help celebrate her 90th birthday. The formal event was held on July 25, 1999 at the elegant Lebanese Athletic Club with live music, excellent food, and imported German wines. The most important development was that Hans and Peter, the two sons of the nonagenarian, became reconciled after allegedly not having spoken to each other for seven years. That constituted the greatest birthday present they could have given their elderly mother who strives to keep the descendant families together. Sadly, Hans passed away only four months later on November 3, 1999.

Hans MARTIN (1934-1999) was married to Wanda JONIKA. They had one daughter, Ana Maria and three sons: Joâo, Walter, and Josef also called Seppi or Sesinho. Ana Maria is married to Abimael Ruiz da SILVA. Their children are Marcelo and Mariane SILVA. Joâo MARTIN and his wife Rosa Helena, née CAHALI have three children: Lúcia (*1984), Natalia (*1986), and Felipe (*1988). Walter married a girl named Marluci on May 29, 1999. Josef got married on February 17, 2001.

Peter MARTIN used to be married to Ivone GERALDO. They have a son Edson and a daughter named Elaine. Edson is married to Simone NAGEL. They have a daughter, Fernanda, and a son, Rodrigo. Elaine's son is named Guilherme.

A couple of days after the big party in Brazil, Marie and I flew to Buenos Aires to visit the descendants of my Aunt Theresa HUHN, née MARTIN (1904-1971). After checking into the Claridge Hotel, I called my Cousin Catharina HÄUSZLER (1924-2000) and we arranged to have a family gathering at her house a couple of days later. While visiting, younger relatives began to arrive whom we had never met. My cousin Susanna LEDERER (*1931) and her husband Willy also came. They both speak German very well but the young ones are most comfortable with Spanish. Adriana (*1965), the unmarried youngest daughter of my cousin Elisabeth ZOBAJI, née HUHN

(1922-1996) works as a grade school teacher. She is greatly interested in genealogy, which has prompted us to keep in touch more than with other family members. Though traveling can be quite strenuous, it is unequalled for connecting with family members one has never met in person. Of the relatives in Argentina, I had only met Cousin Catharina (1924-2000) and her husband Martin (1919-2000). He died on January 18 and she passed away on October 20. - The following schematic provides an overview of the descendants of my Aunt Theresa, née MARTIN (1904-1971) who immigrated to Argentina in 1924 with her husband Josef HUHN (1896-1968) and their child Elisabeth (1922-1996). Their second daughter, Catharina (1924-2000), and their third one, Susanna (*1931), were born in Buenos Aires Province.

In 1941, Elisabeth married Jacob ZOBAJI (1909-1979) at San Vicente, Province of Buenos Aires. They had four (4) children of whom all but one got married and had descendants of their own:

1. José Antonio ZOBAJI (1943-1980) & Blanca Esther CEJAS
   | (*1942)
   Darío Gabríel ZOBAJI (*1970) & Aída Zulma
   | | RODRIGUEZ
   | Daniela Anahí ZOBAJI (*1990)
   | |
   | José Antonio ZOBAJI (*1996)
   |
   Fernando Javier ZOBAJI (*1972)
   |
   Estefania Julieta ZOBAJI (*1989)

2. María Teresa ZOBAJI (*1946) & Juan TOMIC (*1938 in
   | Croatia)
   Mariana TOMIC (*1968) & Carlos Adrian STABILE
   |
   Antonio Lucas TOMIC (*1970) & Silvia Mabel
   | | SIMONETTO
   | Lara Matilde TOMIC (*1999)
   |
   Juan Pablo TOMIC (*1971) & Soledad Silvina Lujan
   | | BEOERRA
   | Juan Ignacio TOMIC (*1998)
   |
   María Matilde TOMIC (*1973)
   |
   Mario Lorenzo TOMIC (*1974)
   |

Marcos Emilio TOMIC (*1978)

3. Martín Eduardo ZOBAJI (*1952) & María Cristina
    | NAVASAL (*1951)
    Nicolás Eloy ZOBAJI (*1984)

4) Adriana Beatriz ZOBAJI (*1965)

      Catharina (1924-2000), the second daughter of my Aunt Theresa HUHN, née MARTIN (1904-1971), remained childless. Her husband Martin HÄUSZLER (1919-2000) hailed from Lie-bling, Banat, which is now part of Romania.

      The third daughter of Aunt Theresa, named Susanna HUHN (*1931), got married in 1951 at Banfield, Province of Buenos Aires to Guillermo "Willy" LEDERER (*1927). They have two (2) sons with descendants:

1. Guillermo Alberto LEDERER (*1952) & Mirta Mabel VIVAS
    | (*1955)
    Nicolas Guillermo LEDERER (*1996)

2. Eduardo Martin LEDERER (*1958) & Teresita Dionisia
    | FILIPELI
    Laura Silvina LEDERER (*1984)
    |
    Natalia Soledad LEDERER (*1988)

      The data provided above augments the information concerning my maternal ancestral branch covered in chapter 2 and helps to round out genealogical aspects. More research toward complementing our family tree may well be on the agenda following the completion of the current opus.

      A memorable family reunion occurred on November 4, 2000 on the occasion of the most impressive wedding recep-tion of Rob KUENN and my niece Lisa STEIGERWALD at the Wyndham Hotel downtown Milwaukee, Wisconsin. In addition to enjoying the company of the bride's sister Kristine plus that of their parents Tony and Martha, we had the pleasure of see-ing relatives from Illinois, Florida, and Pennsylvania. Sister Rose KAPITAEN and her daughter Brigitte were present and so were Cousin Lisa ARB and her daughter Hilda, née Tkacz-Weber who was accompanied by her husband John JULITZ. Others present included Hildegard Ann DRAPER with her son Eric, Andrew and Leni WEISZMANN with their son Ron, Ingrid and Mark OSINSKI, Sandi and Reimar BARBA, as well as our two sons Carl and Rick with their respective families.

      In recognition of having served as a reader in church, the newlyweds honored me with a special gift: A handsome journal from Italy and a Reflections-pen so that I may write my memoirs for "generations to come," as they expressed it. How nice! I had better get with it then, because it's always later than one thinks, as the saying goes.

To my great surprise, a medical examination in February 2001 revealed that I had experienced a heart attack without my knowledge. Together with other consequences, the diagnosis made me realize how fortunate it is to be able to oblige our grandson Nicholas when he declares, "Opa, let's play!" It provides us both with added reasons to count our ample blessings! Upon concluding one of various sessions of hide-and-seek in our garden-level recreation room during April 2001 for instance, he delightfully exclaimed, "this was the best since ever!" His little brother Matthew, who is just beginning to talk, has repeatedly proven himself to be an effective seeker also. - May their lives be less unsettling than mine often was!

VIII. TAKING STOCK

16. Reviewing the Impact of Americanization upon Conventional Danube Swabian Norms

Keeping a journal from the time of my emigration from Austria to the United States of America in 1951, would have prompted me to make useful notations concerning things that struck me as different, unexpected, strange, surprising, etc. Regrettably, I did not record any of my thoughts and reactions. As time went by and I adjusted to new realities, I forgot the very moments that gave me pause to think when I found myself confronted with new situations in unfamiliar settings.

Growing up in a particular cultural environment endows a person with corresponding traits that are reflected in his or her character and behavior. Cumulative wisdom and beliefs of most societies have found expression in common sayings that are passed on to successive generations informally by word of mouth within families as well as formally in schools and via the media, through literature, art, etc. In Danube Swabian realms, proverbs, aphorisms, and so-called "golden rules" also appeared in calendars that resembled almanacs. They had informative plus instructional value and included advice on optimizing crop yields, for example. A prototype "Donauschwaben-Kalender" has been published annually for over a half century now by Donauschwäbischer Heimatverlag, P. O. Box 1680, D-73430 Aalen, Württemberg, Germany.

By comparing Danube Swabian precepts with related truisms encountered in the United States, philosophical dissimilarities and perceptual differences often become quite evident along with concepts that are no longer valid in modern settings. Economic considerations also shaped prevailing respective attitudes, as can be seen in some of the following maxims of which a good number continue to be shared by speakers of German today. Many have been used as topics in church sermons, too. Surprisingly, only a relatively small percentage of the postulates actually have consummate English equivalents; therefore, the interpretive translations and appertaining commentary provided allow clearer distinctions between variations in Danube Swabian and American cognizance. They also call attention to modifications in outlook that group members are likely to have experienced as a result of acculturation.

1. Acquiescence - **Wer zur Gewalt schweigt, verliert sein Recht** (deference to force results in loss of rights). Danube Swabians learned this the hard way under at least two WW II dictators: Hitler and Tito of Yugoslavia.

2. Adaptability - **Wer nicht kann, wie er will, muss wollen, wie er kann** (a person who cannot do as he or she wishes, must be willing to do as he or she can). Being accustomed to doing as they pretty well please, Americans are not as set to resign themselves to imposed realities as Danube Swabians used to be of necessity.

3. Art - **Nutzbare Kunst gibt Brot und Gunst** (useful art provides a livelihood and invokes goodwill). Among Danube Swabians, creative activity that did not fulfill criteria mentioned was apt to be regarded as a waste of time.

4. Attire - **Vor schönen Kleidern zieht man den Hut ab** (attractive clothes command respect). Americans are generally less likely than Danube Swabians to put a lot of stock in being dressed nicely. It may well be, because the latter wish to make up for times when they lacked means for doing so.

5. Authorities - **Grosser Herren Bitten ist Befehlen** (requests from people with authority amount to commands). Surprisingly, this is even true in America where autocrats held sway over the people only briefly, until independence was achieved.

6. Betrayal - **Wer dich einmal betrogen hat, dem traue dein Lebtag nicht wieder** (a person who betrayed you once should never be trusted again). Danube Swabians regarded treachery and dishonesty as more repugnant than people in America seem to, which proves to be better for business, politics, and interpersonal relations in the New World.

7. Borrowing - **Mit anderer Sachen muss man behutsamer umgehen als mit seinen eigenen** (things that belong to others must be handled more carefully than one's own). In America, this may seem unrealistic, but Danube Swabians took it quite seriously.

8. Charity - **Allzumild hilft zur Armut** (Disproportionate generosity impoverishes many a donor). Compared to Americans, Danube Swabians seemed to let prudence override openhandedness.

9. Child rearing - **Lieber ungezogen Kind als verzogen Kind** (an untrained child is preferable to a spoiled one). Kids in America are generally raised more indulgently than Danube Swabian children used to be.

10. Conscience - **Das Gewissen sagt uns wohl, was man tun und meiden soll** (our conscience lets us know, what to do

or forego); however, people's sense of right and wrong is often overwhelmed in today's modi vivendi.

11. Consumption - **Arm ist nicht, wer wenig hat, sondern wer viel bedarf** (poverty is not determined by one's lack of material possessions but by how great a person's needs are). Unlike in America where conspicuous consumption lends prestige to people, Danube Swabians emphasized frugality instead.

12. Contentment - **Zufriedenheit ist der grösste Reichtum** (contentment represents the greatest wealth). But unlike material resources, contentment is more often encountered in ordinary family homes than in extravagant mansions.

13. Cravings - **Wer nichts begehrt, dem geht nichts ab - wer viel begehrt, dem mangelt viel** (a person who covets nothing, misses nothing - a person with great aspirations, has a long way to go). The notion of contentment with less, which seems out of place in America, is also accentuated in this saying.

14. Crime & punishment - **Die Galgen hat man abgeschafft, die Diebe sind geblieben** (gallows were done away with while thieves remain rampant). As firm believers in law and order, Danube Swabians traditionally favored fitting punishment of criminals over more lenient treatment that lawbreakers are generally accorded in America.

15. Defeatism - **Man muss es nehmen, wie es kommt** (one must take things as they come). In America, this common Danube Swabian saying is widely regarded as defeatist.

16. Dickering - **Bieten und Widerbieten macht den Kauf** (deals are made through offers and counteroffers). In American settings, dickering is not as common as it used to be in Danube Swabian realms. Some immigrants even tried such an approach to no avail with startled salesclerks in U. S. department stores!

17. Diligence - **Fleiss ist des Glückes Vater** (diligence is the father of happiness). Since there were no public welfare programs to speak of in traditional Danube Swabian settings, group members put a lot of faith in what was perceived as a positive correlation between industriousness and the ability to enjoy a good standard of living.

18. Divine intervention - **Wenn Gott ein Land strafen will, so nimmt er den Herren die Weisheit** (if God wishes to punish a nation, he deprives its leaders of wisdom). Adolf Hitler and Slobodan Milosevic may serve to illustrate this truism.

19. Emigration - **Besser frei in der Fremde als Knecht daheim** (it is better to be free abroad than subjected to domination at home). Not only Danube Swabians were prompted to seek a better life in America in face of oppression elsewhere.

20. Emulation - **Nicht nach den meisten, sondern nach den besten** (do not imitate the multitude but try to be like the best). In America, this may be regarded as elitism; commercially, it defies the one-size-fits-all notion.

21. Enmity - **Alte Feindschaft wird leicht neu** (old enmities revive easily). In war-torn Europe, one finds more evidence of this than in America.

22. Expertise - **Mancher will Meister sein und ist kein Lehrjunge gewesen** (many claim to be masters without having served as apprentices). This is more often true in America than it ever was among Danube Swabians.

23. Fatalism - **Seinem Schicksal mag niemand entrinnen** (no one can escape his or her destiny). The inclination to shape one's destiny is more preponderant among Americans than it has been among more compliant Danube Swabians.

24. Friendship - **Es ist nicht jeder dein Freund, der dich anlacht** (not everyone who smiles at you is your friend). Unlike in America, where mere acquaintances are often referred to as friends, friendship among Danube Swabians tended to be more profoundly based.

25. Gambling/cards - **Kart aus der Hand, willst du gewinnen** (if you want to win, stay away from card games). Playing cards was a favorite pass-time among Danube Swabians, but they normally used beans or corn kernels to keep score.

26. Gambling/lottery - **Lotterielose sind Eingangszettel ins Armenhaus** (lottery tickets add up to poorhouse admission stubs). Playing the lottery was frowned upon by Danube Swabians as a form of gambling - just as it has been in America until quite recently.

27. Good conduct - **Man muss nicht allen, doch guten Leuten gefallen** (rather than trying to please everybody, one should only be concerned about approbation by good people). In America, such an attitude might well be regarded as too narrowly selective.

28. Governing guide - **Wer regieren will, muss auch durch die Finger sehen können** (a person who wishes to govern must also be able to overlook things). Having lived in more

restrictive settings, many Danube Swabians are surprised at things that get overlooked under conditions of greater freedom in America and elsewhere.

29. Government - **Wer sich nicht verstellen kann, taugt nicht zum Regieren** (to govern, a person must be able to make believe). Orchestrating shams has never been among remarkable Danube Swabians qualities.

30. Helping - **Wer sich aufrichten will, dem soll man aufhelfen** (people trying to get on their feet, should be assisted). Many a Danube Swabian immigrant can attest to having received a helping hand from fellow Americans.

31. Hidden talent - **Begrabener Schatz und verborgener Sinn bringen niemand Gewinn** (buried treasures and secluded intelligence benefit no one). Since Danube Swabians were raised to be modest, many a gifted group member undoubtedly remained undiscovered. Being encouraged to get involved in America permits advance development of innate talents.

32. Honesty - **Ehrlich währt am längsten** (honesty is the best policy). Much lip service has been paid to this adage in different languages; however, it cannot be denied that quite a few people of various nationality, who digressed from it, achieved gains or advantages at least temporarily.

33. Human dignity - **Wer sich selbst schändet, den lobt niemand** (no one praises people who denigrate themselves). Americans are more adept in manifesting their human dignity than Danube Swabians managed to be under given conditions in their historical settings.

34. Imposition - **Besser freundlich versagen als unwillig gewähren** (a friendly refusal is preferable to an unwilling consent). The obliging nature of quite a few Danube Swabian immigrants made it difficult for them to repulse forceful salesmen in America.

35. Improvements - **Bessern ist oft bösern** (efforts to improve things often result in making them worse). In America, this is not always unintentional. Consumers' trust often winds up being abused when makers of products suddenly replace higher-priced ingredients or components with inferior substitutes, for example.

36. Injustice - **Strenges Recht ist oft das grösste Unrecht** (strict application of laws often amounts to greatest injustice). In America, laws tend to be interpreted more leniently than in most countries.

37. Insatiability - **Wer alles will, bekommt nichts** (a person who wants everything, gets nothing). Danube Swabians regarded gluttony as a primal impulse that was deemed unbecoming among civilized folks; consequently, it amazes many to see commercials designed to appeal to lower instincts. To the extent that consumers behave accordingly, it stimulates the economy notwithstanding disparaging social ramifications.

38. Learning - **Was Hänschen nicht lernt, lernt Hans nimmermehr** (skills and knowledge not acquired while young, remain elusive forever). Danube Swabian parents made every effort to enhance their children's readiness to learn. In America, head-start programs attest to similar aims.

39. Legal concerns - **Für alte Schuld nimm Haferstroh, sonst machst du nur Advokaten froh** (accept oat straw as payment for old debts; otherwise, you will only please attorneys). In contrast to many people in America, Danube Swabians ordinarily tried to avoid bringing lawyers into play.

40. Liars - **Wer lügen will, muss ein gutes Gedächtnis haben** (people who choose to tell lies must have good memories). Liars arouse less consternation in America than they used to in Danube Swabian settings.

41. Liberty - **Zu frei bringt Reu** (unrestrained liberty results in regret). Because Danube Swabians lean towards moderation, relatively few get hung up when given too much proverbial "rope" in America.

42. Lies - **Wer einmal lügt, dem glaubt man nicht, wenn er auch die Wahrheit spricht** (people caught with a lie, suffer the loss of credibility even when they are telling the truth). This is one reason, why Danube Swabians raised in traditional ways, have difficulty in sales, politics, legal affairs, etc., where the art of stretching the truth comes into play.

43. Loopholes - **Es gibt kein Gesetz, es hat ein Loch, wer's finden kann** (there are no laws without loopholes to be found). Unlike in America where much effort is spent trying to get around prevailing laws, Danube Swabians were more concerned about staying within their confines.

44. Luck - **Dem Feigen weist das Glück den Rücken** (good fortune turns its back on cowards). The American saying "nothing ventured, nothing gained" may fall into this category as well.

45. Merit - **Wer mit dem Schlechteren Vorlieb nimmt, ist des Besseren wert** (people who make do with inferior things

deserve better). Danube Swabians were taught to appreciate what they had, because only in doing so, would they be worthy of consideration for better things. In America, betterment is not contingent upon merit.

46. Mindfulness - **Frage nicht, was andere machen, acht auf deine eigenen Sachen** (never mind what others do, just tend to your own affairs). Although this may have served as a bona fide Danube Swabian behavioral guideline at one time, it is hard to imagine in today's world, how one can afford to remain oblivious of what others are up to.

47. Modifications - **Ändern und bessern sind zwei** (changes and improvements are two different things). In modern advertising, it is often suggested that mere changes entail concomitant improvements. Like alert Americans, Danube Swabians tend to know better.

48. Monetary sway - **Klingende Meinung ist die beste** (opinions with a ring to them are best). Danube Swabians never had a tendency to be as liberal with assets as Americans are apt to be in their support of all sorts of causes, including foreign aid.

49. Nourishment - **Kurze Abendmahlzeit macht lange Lebenszeit** (a light supper prolongs life). In contrast to American custom, Danube Swabians preferred to consume their main meal around noon.

50. Opportunities - **Wenn man keine Gelegenheit hat, muss man eine machen** (if no opportunity presents itself, one has to create one). In America, this can certainly be done, but in traditional Danube Swabian realms, prevailing conditions often stifled such initiatives.

51. Outlook - **Es kommt nichts Besseres nach** (nothing better follows). Contrary to Americans, who actively bring about changes in anticipation of improvements, Danube Swabians tended to be skeptical of makeovers, because results all too often only upset the status quo and made things worse.

52. People's rights - **Dem Recht ist öfters Hilfe not** (people's rights need affirmation rather often). Ready access to attorneys makes corresponding action easier in America than in most countries.

53. Performance - **Mehr sein als scheinen** (be more than you appear to be). In contrast to people who want to show off, Danube Swabians put more emphasis on actual performance than on pretense.

54. Permissiveness - **Was zähmt, das lähmt** (the taming process has a laming effect). That may explain why many American parents do not restrain their children nearly as much as Danube Swabians did theirs.

55. Pessimism - **Immer was Neues, aber selten was Gutes** (always something new, but rarely something good). Confidence tends to counteract such cynical thinking in America.

56. Phony behavior - **Vor Königen schweig, oder rede, was sie gerne hören** (be quiet in the presence of kings, or say things that they like to hear). Although America lacks true royalty, it is quite common for people to resort to similar disingenuous conduct vis-a-vis employers, bosses, public officials, etc.

57. Piety - **Der nichts kann als fromm sein, muss betteln** (begging is the fate of a person who only knows how to worship). Danube Swabians regarded begging as demeaning. Like a great many Americans, they believed that God helps those who help themselves.

58. Possessions - **Wer viel besitzt, hat viel zu streiten** (people with lots of possessions experience much contention). This tendency keeps many attorneys busy in America, but Danube Swabians were never quick to sue someone, since they were traditionally focused on trying to get along with others rather than to provoke anyone.

59. Poverty - **Scham und gute Sitten weichen der Armut** (poverty overpowers sense of shame and positive mores). By struggling to stay above poverty levels, Danube Swabians always managed to adhere to traditional cultural values.

60. Praise - **Schilt, dass du noch zu loben Platz hast** (scold in ways that still leave room for praise). Although much praise is not equally sincere in America, it is easier to come by than it used to be among Danube Swabians.

61. Priorities - **Die Alten hatten Gewissen ohne Wissen, wir heutzutage haben das Wissen ohne Gewissen** (among our forebears, adherence to one's conscience was more important than knowledge; with us today, it is the other way around). This often bewilders Danube Swabians.

62. Procrastination - **Verschiebe nicht auf morgen, was du heute kannst versorgen** (never put off until tomorrow what you can do today). Although Danube Swabians were apt to act accordingly, it cannot be entirely denied in any language that procrastination does have benefits at times.

63. Promises - **Verheissen macht Schuld** (promises obligate). One thing to which Danube Swabians had difficulty adjusting in America was broken promises by businessmen.

64. Prudence - **Hart verdient Geld geht zäh heraus** (hard-earned money is spent prudently). Among Danube Swabians it certainly used to be that way; however, in many of today's families, it seems as though only a fraction of disposable income was truly difficult to come by.

65. Relativity - **Jedes Ding hat zwei Seiten** (there are two sides to everything). While dichotomy abounds in nature, a case can also be made for the American saying that "there are three sides to everything: Yours, the real one, and mine."

66. Reliance - **Wer sich auf andere verlässt, der ist verlassen** (a person who counts on help from others will be left in a lurch). Like many Americans, Danube Swabians always regarded self-reliance as a worthwhile aspiration.

67. Religiousness - **Am Feiertag gesponnen hält nicht** (yarn spun on a holiday will not hold). Faithful observance of religious holidays was stressed in various ways among Danube Swabians.

68. Resting - **Nach getaner Arbeit ist gut ruhen** (it feels good to rest upon completion of work). Since idleness was frowned upon among Danube Swabians, the right to rest had to be earned through work.

69. Restraint - **Glück macht verrucht und Segen verwegen** (good fortune spawns atrociousness and victory gives rise to rashness). To counteract these tendencies, it is best if the triumphant think in terms of sharing their blessings as the American people did after WW II through the Marshall-Plan, for instance.

70. Righteousness - **Wer recht tut, wird Recht finden** (righteous conduct is reciprocated). This was more applicable within Danube Swabian settings than it is in general.

71. Rights - **Gnade ist besser als Recht** (being accorded mercy is better than having one's rights observed). Not many Americans would agree with this saying, which is rooted in feudalism.

72. Self-sufficiency - **Wohltat annehmen, ist Freiheit verkaufen** (obligations incurred by accepting favors, encroach upon personal liberty). This Puritan ethic was not as wide-

spread among Danube Swabians as it has been in America.

73. Shortcomings - **Was die Natur versagt, kann niemand geben** (there are no substitutes for shortcomings attributable to nature). In America, commendable efforts are constantly made to come up with surrogates anyway.

74. Slander - **Ungerechter Fluch trifft nicht** (unwarranted curses miss their targets). Righteous conduct among Danube Swabians was also rooted in their tendency to regard it as a protective shield, which was not necessarily contingent upon recognition by others; what counted above all, was that it put them at ease with their maker.

75. Smut - **Je mehr man den Schmutz rührt, desto mehr stinkt er** (the foul smell of smut is enhanced by stirring it). In contrast to some audiences in America, Danube Swabians are not likely to see entertainment value in such journalistic activity, for instance.

76. Strife - **Friede ernährt, Unfriede verzehrt** (peace nurtures, dissension ravages). Some policies of governments seem to be designed to foment controlled strife among the populace to help stimulate the country's economy.

77. Submissiveness - **Was du nicht ändern kannst, das nimm geduldig hin** (put up patiently with what you cannot change). In contrast to Americans who are admonished to speak up, Danube Swabians were taught to submit to conditions beyond their control. Accordingly, they have been less vociferous or assertive even in environments advocating freedom and democracy.

78. Talking - **Reden ist Silber, schweigen ist Gold** (talking is equated with silver while silence is likened to gold). Because Danube Swabians were never blessed with sufficient freedom in their traditional settings, it is understandable why they came to think that way. In America, keeping thoughts to oneself would be quite detrimental, since betterment of situations is often achieved through open discussions.

79. Thrift - **Gut kommt nicht von Geuden** (no estate can be built through wastefulness). Among Danube Swabians, thrift has always been regarded as a positive trait. In the United States, wastefulness is among factors that stimulate the economy; therefore, it is not considered to be unequivocally bad.

80. Upbringing - **Zucht ist das beste Heiratsgut** (good rearing is the best dowry). This concept was never as valid in America as it has been in Europe and elsewhere.

81. War - **Krieg ist leichter angefangen als beendet** (wars are more easily started than terminated). The unsatisfactory termination of WW I precipitated WW II, for example.

82. Wit - **Allzuwitzig ist unnützig** (being too witty is unproductive). While erudition is highly regarded in America, Danube Swabians tended to distrust people with formal education; however, innate wit and cumulative wisdom were esteemed.

83. Worldliness - **Der Mantel ist des, den er deckt, die Welt des, der ihrer geniesst** (a coat belongs to its wearer and the world to those who enjoy it). Americans are more apt to woo the world than Danube Swabians have been.

84. Wrongdoing - **Das elfte Gebot heisst: Lass dich nicht erwischen** (do not get caught, is said to be the eleventh commandment). Danube Swabians were taught that rules should be obeyed even if no one is watching, which largely obviated concerns about being exposed. Paradoxically, it often seems that actual acts of wrongdoing arouse less anxiety in America than the ultimate apprehension of perpetrators.

This concludes the sampling of poignant behavioral tenets embodied in the Danube Swabian mindset; along with group members' customary willingness to work hard, they constitute an integral part of the minority's cultural heritage with which constituents have enriched their host countries in Europe, the Americas, Australia, and elsewhere.

IX. ANCILLARIES

Appendix A:
Danube Swabians in the U.S.A.: A Historic Overview

By the end of the 19th Century, it was rather difficult to find additional arable land in the parts of Hungary where Danube Swabian ancestors had established homesteads during the 18th and early 19th Centuries. Meanwhile, many an offspring was prompted to migrate from such locations in the Banat, the Bacska, and the Baranya to adjacent areas like Slavonia, Syrmia and other regions if they were able to acquire land there from local Slavs or people of other nationalities.

Repeated subdividing of particular Swabian land holdings among all descendants would have made individual entities too small to support even a single family. Therefore, intact estates tended to be passed on to the oldest son whose siblings usually received money as their share of inheritances; however, since most farmers were cash-poor, heirs often had to wait for years to get what they had coming. Rarely did anyone collect interest on the money they were owed. It was not customary to even think about doing so.

Landless male descendants of large Swabian families generally had three or four possibilities for making a living:

a) Quite a few became tradesmen or artisans.
b) Many worked for other farmers as day laborers or serfs.
c) Working in factory-like enterprises such as brickyards or hemp processing plants was less common.
d) Those who sought clerical jobs were apt to lose their ethnic-German identity, as they tended to become assimilated Hungarians.

Diligent Swabian girls were coveted marriage partners especially if they had dowries coming. Many untutored girls of hard-up families wound up leaving home to work as household maids. Those with training earned a living as seamstresses, milliners, store clerks, etc., while others worked as seasonal agricultural helpers. Religious families frequently chose to send their daughters to nunneries where quite a few were trained as teachers at the Convent of Notre Dame, for example, to work at affiliated schools in the Banat and elsewhere. Since the convent records at Timisoara, Romania were destroyed during an allied bombing raid in 1944, the notes of Sister M. Leonilla Kilzer served as the primary source for a pertinent treatise by Hans Bohn. The 45-page book provides a concise overview concerning educational efforts at convents in the Banat from

1858 to 1975. It also recounts periodic struggles for existence including plights and hardships under national socialist and communist dictatorships. The ruthless eviction of the nuns from about 300 former sanctuaries in 1948 is mentioned as well: *Zur Geschichte der klösterlichen Erziehungs- und Bildungsstätten im rumänischen Banat; nach den chronologischen Notizen der Ehrw. Schulschwester M. Leonilla Kilzer* (Landshut, 1990).

Although emigration from Hungary was not officially authorized until 1903, citizens were able to visit other European countries whence they could go abroad, too. Among those looking for fresh opportunities far from home toward the end of the 19th Century were the Banat Swabians who immigrated to the United States and settled on open land in North Dakota. They can be compiled into three groupings according to times of their arrival: 1892-1893, 1897-1898, and 1903. Difficulties under which they toiled while taming new ground in a harsh climate as well as other survival aspects are treated by John M. Michels in his book, *The North Dakota Pioneers from the Banat* (Bismarck, ND, 1992).

Theresa K. Bogner Montee-Nelson was instrumental in establishing the German-Hungarian Museum at Dickinson that was subsequently relocated to Regent, ND. She also compiled a wealth of information on *The Banat German Hungarians Who Came to Southwestern North Dakota: Wiver Sach (=matters of concern to women).* The 4-volume paperback edition was published in 1998. Volume I: Introduction, Weddings, Netza (needlework), Christmas, and Kerwei (=commemoration of church consecration); vol. II: Family, Immigration, Education and Margie Smith; vol. III: Stark, New England, War, Military - CCC (Civilian Conservation Corps) and Politicians; vol. IV: Family History, Lefor - Graduations, Churches, and Obituaries. Additional information about descendants of Banat Swabians can be found in *Our Fifty Years: Regent, N.D., 1911-1961* and in *Regent Reviews, 1910-1985* (place and date of publication are not expressly given but they may perhaps be inferred from the book titles).

It appears more than likely that many Swabians who came to America from Hungary responded to advertisements by steamship and railroad companies. Budding factories in U. S. cities needed more workers, and railway officials wanted settlers along new lines to help expand operations. The fact that a person could book one-way passage from Europe to the U. S. for as little as $8.00 in 1908, for example, made the transatlantic journey economically feasible for a lot of people. Typically, the voyage lasted three weeks. Rough seas tended to prolong the duration while causing more people to become seasick. Accommodations and conditions in ship sections called "steerage" were anything but comfortable. Many poorly equipped vessels carried a lot more passengers than regulations would allow today. Consequently, long queues during mealtimes were common phenomena and so were waiting lines at sanitary facilities. Since only salt water was available for washing, vile smells prevailed in some ship areas not just from body odors.

Of the Swabians who came to the U. S. from Hungary until around 1910, three out of four were males. The majority planned to return upon saving money for a fresh start back home. It would be interesting to learn what percentage actually managed to do so. Of those who did, some came back to America to resume their quest for capital. Understandably, concerned U. S. residents asked for the adoption of legislative measures to curb attendant financial outflow. In due course of time, permitting Hungarian citizens to go abroad resulted in extra revenue for their native country as well. No less than 193,460 persons of various nationalities came to America from Hungary by 1907. Estimates of the percentage that remained or of the number who went back are not available. - My maternal grandparents Johann (1875-1919) and Anna (1878-1920) MARTIN arrived in New York on April 24, 1907 and returned to Banat-Topola in summer 1909. One of the wealthiest residents of my hometown had made his fortune in America. His surname was Martin also, but he was not related to us. As an elderly man, he used to sit on a bench in front of his corner-house and watch the world go by. My repeated attempts to speak with him were brusquely rebuffed. He seemed to prefer solitude to anyone's company.

In America, hard work was generally in the offing for the immigrants, but most Swabians were accustomed to such. However, not knowing local laws, mores, and customs in conjunction with the inability to communicate in English made them quite vulnerable to exploitation by greedy employers, cutthroat loan-sharks, dishonest politicians, swindlers, etc. They were particularly at risk where sickness or accidental mishaps were concerned since employers did not offer health insurance back then. Unemployment compensation, social security payments, or welfare benefits had not been introduced yet either. In large cities, immigrants formed mutual assistance associations that often served as social clubs as well.

Some immigrant organizations had educational goals. The "Deutsch-ungarischer Fortbildungs- und Leseverein" was founded at Cleveland, Ohio, in October 1908. By November 12, 1908, the name was changed to "Deutsch-ungarischer Gesangs- und Lese-Verein" and in 1922, the name was simplified to "Banater Männerchor" (Banat Men's Choir). Inspired by the Women's Suffrage movement, a ladies' auxiliary was founded around that time also. It was named "Banater Damen-Chor." Similar clubs were established in major cities elsewhere in Ohio as well as in other states including Illinois, Missouri, New York, Pennsylvania, and Wisconsin. Mutual German-Hungarian benefit organizations providing assistance at times of sickness or death existed at Chicago and Pittsburgh for example until the late 1950's and early 1960's, respectively. An established one in Illinois was known as "Gegenseitiger deutsch-ungarischer Krankenunterstützungsverein 'Stock im Eisen'." Since its basis of appeal was rather behind the times by the 1950's, it failed to attract Danube Swabian newcomers, which led to the organization's dissolution within about a decade.

Records in the public domain at the National Archives in Washington include lists of passenger arrivals at certain ports of entry during different eras. Among data found in these lists are entries concerning the country of which an arriving person was a subject. That information appears under the heading "Nationality." Ethnic affiliation was categorized under "Race of People." However, entries in this column are not reliable as far as arrivals from multi-ethnic countries like Hungary are concerned. Some Swabians are falsely classified as Hungarians for example while members of other nationalities are erroneously assigned to inapt cultural groups as well. Consequently, researchers will never be able to arrive at accurate tallies from such sources alone. Entries recorded after WW I prove to be even more confusing since some Danube Swabians remained citizens of what was left of Hungary while others became subjects of Romania and the Kingdom of Serbs, Croats, and Slovenes, which was named Yugoslavia after 1929. Because the Swabians residing in the latter countries could no longer be correctly called German-Hungarians or Hungarian Germans, scholars adopted the term "Donauschwaben" (Danube Swabians) as a blanket designation as of the early 1920's.

New social, political, and economic realities within the successor states of Hungary that called for readjustments in the traditional way of life produced thoughts of emigration among quite a few Danube Swabians. The literacy test that was adopted in 1917 for U. S. immigrants did not cause tremendous difficulty for Danube Swabians. However, the new immigration quota system that was based on three percent of a given nationality group's representation in the U. S. census of 1910 actually shortchanged the newly defined countries of Hungary, Romania, and the kingdom that came to be known as Yugoslavia. Thus, only 1,747 immigrants of all ethnic affiliations were admitted to the U. S. from these three countries in 1924, for example. Consequently, numerous prospective Danube Swabian immigrants were denied admission to the United States because of closed quotas. Some did not find out about cutoffs until they had arrived at a seaport from where they were planning to sail. Such was the case with my Aunt Theresa MARTIN (1904-1971) and her husband Josef HUHN (1896-1968) who wound up going to Argentina instead with their infant daughter Elisabeth (1922-1996).

Relatively few Danube Swabians returned from the U. S. to the old country during the Great Depression. The majority remained in the United States in hopes of eventually achieving a better life for themselves and their progeny. To satisfy religious needs, they attended churches that offered services in German; for socializing and entertainment most gathered at their own clubs apart from places frequented by Germans from Germany who were largely oblivious of Danube Swabians. Imperial Germany had paid little or no attention to them either for decades, but due to territorial losses following WW I, new leaders of the Weimar Republic began to show more interest in kinsmen living beyond Germany's boundaries. It became evident that chauvinist sentiments had widely replaced *laissez faire* practices that used to prevail under traditional imperial governance. Consequently, German minorities in successor states of Austria-Hungary for example were subjected to new assimilation pressures. As might be expected, Danube Swabians and kindred groups in other countries gladly accepted help from the fatherland in maintaining their ethnic identity.

During WW II, German minorities in European countries regrettably wound up as instruments of Hitler whereupon they became subject to the scorn of nazi victims. Punishments they had to endure as a consequence varied according to their countries of residence. Danube Swabians living in Yugoslavia were stripped of rights pertaining to life, liberty, property, etc., and confined to concentration camps from 1944 until 1948 where many succumbed to starvation, epidemics, and maltreatment at the hands of Tito's partisans. To circumvent calling attention to mass expulsions of Germans from Eastern Europe after WW II, non-German media have carefully refrained from relating more recent "ethnic cleansing" to what transpired then. Hungary expelled about half of the country's ethnic-Germans by 1946. Romania sent many to Russia as forced laborers in

1944/45 and forcibly relocated others to the Baragan Steppe as of 1951 to carry out an ill-conceived agricultural experiment.

Of the Danube Swabians that wound up in Germany and Austria as refugees toward the end of WW II and its aftermath, many emigrated when opportunities finally presented themselves after years of waiting. Destinations included Argentina, Australia, Brazil, Canada, France, the United States, and Venezuela. The U. S. did not officially admit German or ethnic-German immigrants until around 1953. In the meantime, millions of German *expellees* from Czechoslovakia, Poland, Hungary, and other Soviet-occupied realms were languishing along with *refugees* in overcrowded barracks and makeshift compounds throughout allied occupation zones of Germany and Austria.

In No. 104 of "Info-Dienst Deutsche Aussiedler" (September 1999), Jochen Welt, a federal official working with repatriates to Germany provided statistical data including the following:

As of 1950, there were 12,750,000 Germans registered as survivors of genocide, ethnic cleansing, and expulsion. 8.1 million of them were living in West Germany, 4.1 million in what used to be the German Democratic Republic (DDR), 430,000 in Austria, and 120,000 in other Western European countries or overseas.

The figures above included 760,000 displaced Danube Swabians that had been registered as of 1950. Their territorial distribution was as follows:

a) Of 300,000 from Yugoslavia, half were living in West Germany, 35,000 in the DDR, 100,000 in Austria, and 15,000 in other Western European countries or overseas.

b) Of 250,000 from Romania, 145,000 were living in West Germany, 60,000 in the DDR, 40,000 in Austria, and 5,000 in other Western European countries or overseas.

c) Of 210,000 from Hungary, 175,000 were living in West Germany, 10,000 in the DDR, 20,000 in Austria, and 5,000 in other Western European countries or overseas.

Between 1950 and 1998 there was an abiding influx of 3,923,951 repatriates to the Federal Republic of Germany. Of these, 426,806 (including Transylvania Saxons besides Swabians and others) came from Romania; 21,392 came from Hungary and 90,308 from areas of former Yugoslavia.

Matthias Weifert named countries with Danube Swabian groups today and provided the following corresponding data in his article "Die Donauschwaben - eine südostdeutsche Volksgruppe im und aus dem mittleren Donauraum," *Eintracht,* Jg. 79-Vol. 28 (March 17, 2001), p. 4. Approximately 220,000 are living in Hungary, 70,000 in Romania, 10,000 in Yugoslavia and Croatia. 800,000 became reintegrated in their ancestral homeland of Germany since WW II. The number of Danube Swabians in the U.S.A., including descendents of those who immigrated as of the late 19th Century, is estimated to be around 250,000. 120,000 group members are living in Austria, 50,000 in Canada, 50,000 in the Southern Hemisphere - mostly in Argentina, Brazil, and Australia. In addition, 10,000 are believed to be living in France and unnamed European countries.

In the immediate post-war years, many of the dispossessed were often without jobs, too. Survival on meager ration cards alone left many in a perpetual state of hunger. Persons with addresses of friends or relatives abroad got in touch with them hoping that they would be able to help.

Anti-German sentiments stirred up by propaganda and war efforts had also impacted Danube Swabians in America negatively. Hatred was harbored and openly expressed not only toward people who happened to be of German descent, but it was also directed against things associated with them. Sauerkraut, though already massively consumed in China by forced laborers during construction of the Great Wall for instance, was renamed "liberty cabbage." Frankfurter sausagelinks were called "hot dogs" and hamburger patties became "Salisbury steak." Many streets and towns with German appellations had been provided with English-sounding names as of WW I already. Despite constitutionally guaranteed freedom of speech in America, some people objected to the use of German in public for years after WW II had ended. As late as the early 1950's, new immigrants on Chicago streetcars were apt to have heads of indigenous commuters turn in surprise upon hearing German spoken freely.

Viewed in light of given circumstances, it took a great deal of courage, not to mention material sacrifices, for Danube Swabians in America to take action in behalf of their suffering kinsmen in Europe. They sent thousands of packages with food and clothing abroad after the war while simultaneously working toward getting U. S. immigration laws amended so that stateless ethnic-Germans would also be allowed to immigrate under quotas allotted to Germany and Austria. Corresponding efforts of the American Aid Societies for the Needy and Displaced

Persons of Central and Southeastern Europe are described by Raymond Lohne in his book, *The Great Chicago Refugee Rescue* (Rockport, ME: Picton Press, 1997).

As of 1950, the International Refugee Organization (IRO) and several religious groupings, including the National Catholic Resettlement Council, began to work with the American consulates at Salzburg, Austria, and Hamburg, Germany, in efforts to register, screen, and process ethnic-German refugees for immigration. To qualify, each applicant had to pass a medical examination and a background check in addition to having a U. S. citizen serve as a sponsor guaranteeing housing and a paying job. Transportation was chiefly provided on decommissioned U. S. troop ships, but some immigrants also arrived aboard luxury liners and by passenger aircraft. The number of Danube Swabians that immigrated from the early 1950's to the early 1960's is estimated to be 40,000. Fellow countrymen from Hungary, Romania, and Yugoslavia who were among late repatriates to Germany mostly chose to stay in the old fatherland where the economy was on an upswing yielding benefits regarding health care and pensions among others.

Judging by Danube Swabian press reports, kinsmen and their descendants that were able to remain in Hungary for example will never regain a strong awareness of their heritage. Former ethnic-German citizens of Romania willing to return permanently to that country were promised restitution of property by state authorities who valued their demonstrated diligence in enhancing the country's food supply, for example. The number of Swabian descendants remaining in Yugoslavia is statistically insignificant. Thus, the avowed aim of Tito supporters who wanted to rid the country of Germans came to pass. International condemnation of genocidal measures that were employed could have pre-empted more recent "ethnic cleansing" in Bosnia-Herzegovina, but the hushed historic event has remained voiceless in non-German world media. Pious Danube Swabians of old would have been inclined to regard the consequent breakup of Yugoslavia as divine reckoning.

Danube Swabian organizations in the United States have been represented by The Society of the Danube Swabians in the U.S.A. Affiliations at the following locations include some that may no longer be active: 1) Akron OH, 2) Aurora IL, 3) Chicago IL, 4) Cincinnati OH, 5) Cleveland OH, 6) Los Angeles (Downey) CA, 7) Mansfield OH, 8) Milwaukee WI, 10) New York NY, 11) Philadelphia PA, 12) Rock Island IL, 13) St. Louis MO, 14) Trenton NJ, and 15) Warren MI.

Canadian cities with Danube Swabian representation include Bradford, Galt, Gorrie, Kitchener, Leamington, Montreal, Niagara Falls, Queensville, Toronto, and Windsor, Ontario. The Kitchener Schwaben Club can be reached via The Canadian Schwaben Sick Benefit Association, 1668 King Street East, Kitchener, Ontario N2G 2P1. Tel. (519) 742-7979. Illustrated vignettes of a number of Danube Swabian clubs in Canada and the U. S. can be found on the web site www.donau.org/ and in "An epic document of all Germanic people on the North American continent," entitled *Heimat North America*. Written in English and German by Bert Lachner and Ernst Ott assisted by Arlene Lachner. Edward A. Michals, editor (Chicago: Landmark Books Unlimited, 1997).

Internet search engines may be employed to access web sites relating to Danube Swabians especially with regard to genealogical inquiries. The following sample URL has links to others: http://www.genealogy.net/gene/reg/ESE/dsprint.html

Johnny Weissmüller (1904-1984) was probably the best known American of Danube Swabian descent. According to a List or Manifest of Alien Passengers for the U. S. Immigration Officer at Port of Arrival, his parents Peter and Elisabeth, née Kersch arrived with their infant Johann (Johnny) in New York on January 26, 1905 aboard the steamship *Rotterdam*. Their previous residence was at Szabadfalu (German: Freidorf - now part of the City of Timisoara), Banat, where Johnny was born on June 2, 1904. Upon arrival, the family was headed for Windber, PA. The elder Weissmüller was a brickyard worker in Europe and in America he initially took a job in coal mining. Soon after Johnny's brother Peter Jr. was born in 1905 and christened at Windber on September 3, the Weissmüllers moved to Chicago, Illinois, where Johnny grew up.

As an increasingly famous swimmer, Johnny Weissmüller won 51 U. S. national championships and established 67 world records. He also won five (5) gold medals for the U. S. in the Olympic Games of 1924 (Paris) and 1928 (Amsterdam). For reasons of publicity, data concerning Johnny's actual place of birth was obfuscated so that people would regard him as a champion of outright American vintage. In some media reports, Chicago was his stated birthplace and in other accounts it was said that he was born at Windber, PA.

Between 1931 and 1947, Johnny Weissmüller played the leading role in eighteen (18) Tarzan movies that made him rich and famous, but poor investments and four failed marriages deprived him of his wealth. During the final phase of his career, he was hired to greet guests at Caesar's Palace in Las

Vegas, Nevada. Johnny had three children with Beryl Scott, the third of his five spouses. Their names were John Scott, Wendy Ann, and Heidi Elisabeth. The latter suffered a fatal accident in 1962 at age 19.

Johnny himself was hospitalized at Las Vegas in 1973 because of a hip fracture prior to two subsequent heart attacks. In 1979, throat cancer prompted an operation, and later, he experienced several additional heart attacks that eventually confined him to a clinic at Acapulco, Mexico. He also acquired a house locally, near the site where scenes of his first Tarzan-film were shot. On January 21, 1984, Johnny Weissmüller, a dazzling Americanized Danube Swabian passed away at the age of 79.

Economic success rates among Danube Swabian immigrants and their descendents have been above average; most own homes or rental property. Many among the first and second generation are college graduates and quite a few entered the professions. Of the impressive number of Danube Swabian immigrants who became millionaires, some made it in construction businesses and a few with chicken farms, but the largest segment became wealthy through real estate holdings.

Many group members started out with rundown two-family homes that were sold upon complete renovation diligently performed evenings and on weekends. Proceeds were invested in larger units with which the new owners repeated the process over and over until they had accumulated considerable equity. According to an article in a Chicago neighborhood newspaper called *Lincoln-Belmont Booster,* facelifts of houses in entire city blocks during the 1950's were largely attributable to efforts and measures taken by newcomers to America including Danube Swabians. Group members living in other parts of the country have likewise enhanced their respective environments in positive ways. - Some locations are named below in connection with clubs where many congregate.

Topics of concern to post-WW II Danube Swabian immigrants were treated in newspapers like *Der Donauschwabe* (Württemberg) and the *Nachrichten der Donauschwaben in Chicago,* among others. All articles contributed by the author eventually appeared in the anthology *Donauschwäbische Gedankenskizzen aus USA - Reflections of Danube Swabians in America: Aufsätze - Articles, 1968-1982* (Winona, MN 1983). To facilitate orientation, Danube Swabian areas of settlement in East Central Europe were identified in historic and cultural contexts. Observations about interaction between earlier fellow immigrants and newcomers were also provided, along with reassessments of contemporary states of affairs and benefits to society as a whole.

A newspaper for Danube Swabians in North America is called *Heimatbote,* published at 17 Doncrest Drive, Thornhill, Ontario L3T 4P6 in Canada, by Anton Wekerle. Telephone: 905 881 6350, Fax 905 886 3794. The Alliance of Danube-Swabians in Canada can be contacted at 7046 Brian Crescent, Niagara Falls L2J 3P5. Addresses of Danube Swabian groups in the United States of America include:

1) Akron area: German Family Society of Akron, OH, 3871 Ranfield Road, Brimfield Township, Kent, OH 44240. Tel.: 330 678-8229.

2) Chicago area: Society of Danube Swabians, 625 Seegers Road, Des Plaines, IL 60016. Tel. 847 296-6172

3) Cincinnati area: Verein der Donauschwaben in Cincinnati, 4290 Dry Ridge Road, Cincinnati, OH 45252. Tel.: 513 385-2098.

4) Cleveland area: Donauschwaben's German-American Cultural Center at Lenau Park, 7370 Columbia Road, Olmsted Township, OH 44138. Tel.: 216 235-2646. Fax 216 235-2671.

5) Detroit area: Carpathia Club, 38000 Utica Road, Sterling Heights, MI 48659. Website http://www.CarpathiaClub.com Tel. 810 781-6734.

6) Los Angeles area: Donauschwäbische Vereinigung von Südkalifornien, 12628 Vista Panorama, Santa Ana, CA 92705. Some club meetings take place at St. Stephen's Catholic Church, 3705 Woodlawn Avenue, Los Angeles, CA. Tel. 714-639-4026. Website http://www.donau.org/ also refers to affiliates in other cities.

7) Mansfield Liederkranz, 1212 Silver Lane, Mansfield, OH 44906. Tel. 419 529-3064.

8) Milwaukee Donauschwaben, N56 W14750 Silver Spring Drive, Menomonee Falls, WI 53051.

9) St. Louis area: German Cultural Society, 3652 South Jefferson Avenue, St. Louis, MO 63118. Telephone: 314 771-8368.

10) Danube Swabian Association, 127 Route 156, Trenton, NJ 08620. Telephone: 609 585-1932.

General information about Danube Swabian groups worldwide has been available from the Haus der Donauschwaben, Goldmühlestrasse 30, D-71065 Sindelfingen, Germany, where genealogy researchers known as Arbeitskreis donauschwäbischer Familienforscher (AKdFF) can be reached also. *N. B.:* Inquiries that include a couple of international postal reply coupons are more apt to be favored with a response.

Danube Swabian mementos and artifacts can be viewed at some of the clubs named above as well as at the Donauschwäbisches Zentralmuseum, Schillerstrasse 1, D-89070 Ulm, Germany. - Tel. (07 31) 9 62 54-0.

Appendix B:
Foreign Language Instruction at Winona State - An Overview: 1932-1985
Drafted by Dr. Jacob Steigerwald, staff member 1971-1992
In consultation with Ms. Marion Davis, staff member 1932-1971.
January 1986

In his book, *Winona State University: A History of Hundred Twenty-Five Years* (1985), Dr Robert A. DuFresne aptly refers to the precarious place of foreign language programs in the curriculum (cf. p. 193). A brief rundown of related developments since the 1930's should help round out the picture.

Miss Marion Davis began to teach French at Winona State in 1932. Subsequently, she also introduced courses in Spanish and some years later she offered entire programs in both languages. In addition to her teaching and administrative duties, she devoted much effort to working with foreign students over the years. After 39 years of service, she retired in 1971.

Until 1965 when newly adopted requirements by the Minnesota State Department of Education called for stronger curricula in foreign language study, Miss Davis had the difficult task of maintaining 3-year major programs in French and Spanish all by herself. As of fall 1965, Miss Joan Brown was hired on a fulltime basis as a second staff member (her last name was changed to James when she got married a few years later). Joan helped expand offerings in French and introduced courses in German at Winona State for the first time. The Spanish program was strengthened the following year when Mrs. Rhetta Speltz was hired to teach Elementary Spanish on a part-time basis as of fall 1966. A few years later, Mrs. Speltz was also teaching Intermediate Spanish.

In 1968, the academic structure of Winona State was changed from a division system to a departmental system. In order to constitute a department in the Minnesota State College System, there had to be a minimum of three fulltime faculty members in a given area. This requirement was met when Jordan Vibert Hodgson was hired on a fulltime basis as of fall 1968 whereupon augmented majors in French and Spanish were introduced and a full major in German was offered for the first time.

Jordan "Dan" Hodgson, who received his Ph. D. degree in German from Stanford University in 1973, had also completed an undergraduate major in Spanish. In addition to having served as a graduate teaching assistant at Stanford, he had gained teaching experience at Hayward, California, and at Chicago Circle. At Winona State, he became "Acting Chairman" of the newly constituted Department of Foreign Languages.

The greatest problem of the department continued to be low enrollment especially in upper division courses. This was due to several factors including the following:

1. Winona State's general education program did not include foreign language requirements after 1965.

2. The department had no established position in the college structure, which was reflected by a lack of office facilities, special equipment, library holdings, etc.

3. Since the existing majors in French and Spanish could not be immediately modified to meet the new curricular requirements established by the state in 1965, the institution's ability to attract students into its foreign language programs was considerably diminished.

Language area enrollments always appeared to be even less favorable than they actually were because "production" analysts failed to consider other relevant factors when they were assessing "output" ratios. One factor commonly overlooked in this connection relates to general courses that provide solid numerical foundations for other departments by serving different specific disciplines simultaneously, sometimes as prerequisites, in a given general area. For example, basic business and economics courses readily apply towards specialization in Marketing, Finance, Management, etc., just as general Biology courses are applicable toward in-depth studies in Zoology or Botany. However, in foreign languages there are no common lecture-type mass enrollment courses, with which a comfortable credit base can be generated for the department. In languages, specialization begins from day one! Therefore, enrollments in foreign language courses should rightfully be compared only with specialized courses of other departments and not simply across the board or in light of an overall student to faculty ratio.

The widespread tendency to apply a 19:1 student to faculty ratio in determining whether a department or program is self-supporting undoubtedly emanated from the fact that legislators find it expedient to use such a formula in arriving at a dollar amount when they are making appropriations to educational institutions in the system.

When it is pointed out to legislators that discipline areas like art, foreign languages, music, etc., are perpetually short-changed under local appropriation practices that are based on their "formula," they say that once the money has been allotted, it is up to the respective administrators at each campus how they want to divide and distribute it! However, in trying to maximize their own institution's entitlement, local budgetary decision makers usually feel compelled to assign more money to departments in which the highest tangible returns in terms of fulltime equivalencies (FTE's) can be generated. Thus, "the rich tend to get richer" while some departments periodically wind up getting little more than token support.

Being quite dedicated to their particular field or department, economically hard-pressed faculty members are sometimes prompted to yield to administrative pressures and consent to the adoption of watered down standards that ultimately prove fruitless, self-defeating, or downright irresponsible. An increase of the enrollment limit in elementary foreign language classes from 25 to 35 in 1969 on the basis of a "suggestion" by an academic dean may serve as an example of such an occurrence at Winona State. (The ideal class size recommended by the Modern Language Association is 12 to 15 students).

Fortunately, checks and balances built into the system do work! Since the acting chairperson's repeated urgent requests for additional faculty remained unfulfilled by 1970, Dr. Patricia J. Goralski, from the Professional Development Section of the Minnesota State Department of Education, found Winona State deficient in foreign language staff positions for the programs leading to certification in French, German, and Spanish. In her judgement, the three programs could not be maintained with a staff consisting of only 3.5 members. She suggested a cooperative arrangement with one of the private colleges in town to accommodate the students who were already in the unacceptable programs, and she prohibited the admission of new students to the deficient programs until they were modified and accredited.

The immediate outcome of this crisis concerning Winona State's foreign language programs was that all course offerings in French were dropped so that the entire staff contingent of 3.5 members could attend to the upgraded major and minor programs in German and Spanish. Even with the drastic reorganization, it was necessary for Winona State students to complete some of their applicable courses such as Linguistics for example at the College of Saint Teresa.

In April 1971, Winona State received a five-year provisional approval for the program leading to certification of teachers of German. Staffing uncertainties attributable to the impending retirement of Miss Davis delayed approval of the programs for Spanish majors and minors until July 1971 when the State Department of Education first had been informed of the hiring of Associate Professor Dr. Elisabeth Raab as a well-qualified replacement. Formal qualifications of Dr. Raab, better known as Sister Ricarda, included a B. E. in Elementary Education, a B. A. with a major in Spanish and a minor in French, and a Ph. D. with a major in Spanish and Latin American Studies and minors in French and Portuguese.

Family reasons prompted Mrs. Joan James, née Brown to resign as of the end of the 1970/71 academic year. Her replacement was Mr. Jacob Steigerwald, a native Danube Swabian who had a B. A. in Speech and Communication Arts (1958) from Columbia College in Chicago, a B. A. and M. A. in German (1965 and 1967) from the University of Illinois, and all but the dissertation (ABD) from the University of Cincinnati where he was awarded his Ph. D. in 1975. He was hired to teach courses at all levels of German and, occasionally, Elementary Spanish.

Upon completing only one year of teaching at Winona State, Sister Ricarda resigned in 1972 in order to accept a position at her alma mater, the College of Saint Teresa in Winona. Her replacement was Assistant Professor Charles P. Dietrick who had completed all but the dissertation toward a doctorate in Spanish at the University of Wisconsin at Madison. He also had a background of studies in German. Mr. Dietrick had barely begun to teach at Winona State when a directive came down from Chancellor Mitau's office in December 1972 prompting Winona State to help compensate for a drastic drop in enrollments elsewhere in the Minnesota State College System. Consequently, about ten local faculty members were given notices of termination of employment including Mr. Dietrick. Thus, the newly accredited major and minor programs in Spanish had to be phased out before they even had a chance to prove their viability.

In conjunction with the establishment of the External Studies Program (ESP), Mr. Dietrick was able to have his contract renewed for an additional year until 1974. However, during his second year at Winona State his "output" became part of the basis for funding the new program. Since public educational institutions get funded on the basis of the number of credits generated and not according to programs intended, administrators really have no choice but to redistribute resources in accordance with planned improvements even if it entails the weakening of one area for the benefit of another. Since the real reasons for a given state of affairs are not generally spelled out in accountants' tallies, the diminution of the size of the Department of Foreign Languages appeared to be a consequence of an unmistakable drop in its tangible output. In reality, the members of the department worked harder than ever! In order to enable Mr. Dietrick to continue to serve some of the Spanish students despite his reassignment to ESP, it was arranged to have Mr. Steigerwald serve in his place in External Studies on a part-time basis. To help generate awareness of Winona State's increased operations in Rochester, Mr. Steigerwald was even persuaded to offer an upper division German class there as an uncompensated overload.

Another reduction in the size of the Department of Foreign Languages occurred in 1973 when Mrs. Rhetta Speltz, the part-time Spanish instructor could not be offered a contract renewal because of regulations concerning tenure. If the Department's reasons for existence had been based entirely on its ability to maintain a 19:1 student to faculty "production" ratio, it would have undoubtedly suffered further declines to possible oblivion. However, the Committee on College Functions and Planning voted against allowing it to drop below two fulltime equivalency positions.

Another "justification" for the imposition of austerity measures was seen in an **anticipated** decline in enrollments which, to this date more than a decade later, has not occurred at Winona State! The misleading projection was simply based on the statistically evident lower birthrate following the baby-boom period that lasted from 1946 until 1964. Economic factors and sociological developments, such as the tendency of more older students choosing to attend college, were not taken into account and, worst of all, the departmental cutbacks that were prematurely made have never been rectified! If the Department of Foreign Languages had been enabled to grow in proportion to Winona State as a whole, it would certainly have more than the current 3.11 fulltime equivalency positions which incidentally are by no means assured either. The student body growth rate in the twenty-five year period from 1953 until 1978 was tenfold for instance as it increased from around 400 to over 4000 persons and it has continued to grow since then.

As of 1973, the effectiveness of the Department of Foreign Languages was curtailed by yet another handicap when the secretary, who also worked for the departments of Geography and Sociology, was relocated from Somsen Hall to Minné Hall. Except during office hours, no one directly connected with the department could be reached by telephone, for example. Since Mr. Hodgson's office was in a former storage room off Somsen 300 and Mr. Steigerwald's was in Somsen 125, which was a provisionally converted former classroom, some people experienced discouraging difficulty in trying to get in touch with someone from the department. Being relegated to an existence so marginally ranked for a prolonged period was bound to have a potentially negative effect on the morale of the people concerned.

In January 1974, the Department of Foreign Languages began a comprehensive revision of its only remaining major, which was rather traditional in scope. Several new upper division German courses were introduced and some of the older ones were revised or eliminated. Generally, more emphasis was placed on active language use and cultural aspects rather than literary ones. In addition, Mr. Steigerwald reintroduced Elementary French in order to help generate more credits. He taught the 3-course sequence annually from 1974 until 1978 when it was taken over by Dr. Ronald M. Mazur, a new faculty member.

Another good move in 1973-74 was the introduction of a course in "Spoken Norwegian" by Dr. Melvin O Wedul, Director of Placement Services at Winona State. The course proved to be popular enough so that it could be offered annually for over a decade now. At times, it was necessary to divide oversized classes into two sections and occasionally there was enough demand for a sequel.

Starting in 1975, a series of meetings were held concerning a closer cooperative arrangement between the foreign language departments of the three local colleges. Unfortunately, the numerous reservations expressed by various faculty members regarding different aspects of a potentially workable arrangement were largely ignored when the ill-fated official Tri-College/University agreement was put into effect as of December 1, 1977. Some of the reservations expressed aptly predicted subsequent problems connected with academic calendars, scheduling of courses, enrollment difficulties, problems of transportation, insurance coverage, office space, etc.

After the general unionization of the faculty at Winona State around 1976, carrying overloads including uncompensated ones was discouraged. At last members of less tangibly productive departments were no longer tacitly or openly expected to carry sixteen-credit loads instead of twelve-credit teaching loads per quarter to avoid being regarded as "liabilities" even by some peers. In order to enable the Department of Foreign Languages to maintain its schedule without having to start paying the two fulltime faculty members for overloads, the hiring of Mrs. Jane Ochrymowycz, a part-time staff member with a master' degree in Spanish was authorized. Initially, Mrs. Ochrymowycz taught Elementary Spanish and later intermediate courses, too.

During the 1976/77 academic year, the language laboratory in Somsen 300 was upgraded with the installation of SONY cassette recorders and additional booths so that it could simultaneously serve as a shorthand practice room. To accommodate the Department of Business Education and Office Administration (BEOA) on the third floor of Somsen Hall, classroom 301 was converted into an office complex. Half of the six offices are now occupied by faculty of BEOA and half by members of the Department of Foreign Languages. A secretary, Mrs. Shirley Flikki, was hired to serve both of these departments plus part of the faculty in Accounting. Since 1977, the language department has at last been concentrated in one area with secretarial service and ready access to modern office equipment.

When Dr. Hodgson's term as chairperson expired as of May 1977, Dr. Steigerwald was elected to succeed him as of fall quarter 1977. Around that time, plans were also finalized to put the Tri-College/University arrangement into effect, which was conceived by some as a way to expand student options; by others, it was seen as a cost cutting device. In accordance with the agreement, the first two years of French, German, and Spanish were to be offered at each of the three institutions. French majors and minors were to complete their upper division course work at the College of St. Teresa, German majors and minors were to be accommodated at Winona State, and Spanish majors and minors could satisfy their requirements at either of the private colleges.

Given staffing realities at all three institutions caused the Tri-College/University arrangement to fall short of even a good start. In addition, there were other aspects out of synchronism including the following:

a) One institution was on a semester system and the other two were on a quarter system and a trimester system, respectively, until the latter changed over to a quarter system also.

b) Class duration at the three institutions ranged from 50 to 70 minutes.

c) At one college, classes were already in session for ten days to two weeks before the dormitories even opened at the other institutions in fall.

d) No imaginable means of transportation would have allowed students to take classes in successive time periods at different institutions without getting there late or having to leave early.

In reality, the Tri-College/University arrangement has the effect of a stranglehold as it stifles the growth of the individual departments concerned; but on paper, it appears to function well enough to make its abrogation seem tantamount to asking for unnecessary added expenses.

While attending a professional meeting in 1977, Dr. Steigerwald found a way to enable Winona State students to participate in study abroad programs under Common Market provisions with Mankato State (in Mexico) and St. Cloud State (in France, Germany, Spain, and elsewhere). Arrangements were also worked out with the Regional Campus Department to offer evening courses in German and Polish in addition to Norwegian.

Off-phase scheduling of elementary language courses was experimentally introduced in an effort to achieve greater enrollment and better student retention through more appropriate class placement based on the students' respective levels of previous exposure to French, German, or Spanish. Recruitment of students was facilitated through a new department brochure which was distributed by the Admissions Office and at the spring meeting of the Minnesota Chapter of the American Association of Teachers of German. Dr. Steigerwald hosted the meeting at Winona State in April 1978.

Established related practices in the University of Wisconsin system prompted Dr. Steigerwald to adopt a retroactive credit option for foreign language students at Winona State. It rewards students for successful language study in high schools and provides an added incentive for better self-placement in accordance with corresponding achievements in the respective languages. During freshmen orientation in 1978, where the Department of Foreign Languages was represented for the first time, the latest information concerning language study at Winona State was distributed and advising services were provided.

After ten years of teaching at Winona State, Dr. Hodgson resigned as of the end of the 1977/78 academic year. His replacement was Dr. Ronald Michael Mazur who had been teaching at Michigan State University for several years. His credentials include a B. A. degree in German with a split minor in French and Philosophy from the University of Detroit and an M. A. and Ph. D. in German from the University of Michigan, Ann Arbor. At Winona State, Dr. Mazur has been teaching Elementary and Intermediate French, Polish language and culture courses, and all levels of German. As of winter quarter 1979, the Department of Foreign Languages was also authorized to hire Dr. Barbara Rusterholz from the University of Wisconsin to teach Intermediate French on a part-time basis. In having her do so, the Department was able to fully meet its Tri-College/University commitment.

Under regulations concerning tenure, Mrs. Jane Ochrymowycz, the part-time Spanish instructor could not be retained beyond the spring quarter of 1979. As of fall quarter 1979, Dr. Jacqueline Guttmann, a native speaker of French, joined the department staff to teach Elementary and Intermediate French and Spanish on a one-year fixed-term appointment with the possibility of one renewal. Another temporary department member, Mrs. Monica L. Kruse, was initially teaching Elementary Spanish on a part-time basis and later offered evening courses in German through the Regional Campus Department including off-campus classes at La Crescent, MN.

In order to be able to serve the needs of the Regional Campus Department even more fully, the Department of Foreign Languages adopted a variable-credit "Applied Foreign Language" course in 1979-1980. Thereupon, Dr. Armando Alonso was hired to teach a course in "Practical Spanish for Medical Personnel" as of spring quarter 1980. Subsequently, Dr. Alonso, a native of Cuba and Professor of Spanish at Viterbo College in La Crosse, continued to teach on a part-time basis at Winona State including course offerings at Rochester. Dr. Ahmed El-Afandi, a native of Egypt and Professor of Political Science at Winona State, was persuaded to offer a course in introductory Arabic experimentally through the Department of Continuing Education.

In 1980, a new general education program was introduced at Winona State that included an eight-credit "different culture" category. The new requirement channeled a larger number of students into foreign language classes. However, since many were primarily interested in merely meeting a requirement rather than learning a language, some tended to drag their feet which affected a few students adversely. In 1985, the eight-credit cluster was split, which led to greater flexibility in satisfying the "different culture" requirement.

When Dr. Steigerwald's three-year term as chairman of the Department of Foreign Languages ended in 1980, he chose not to run for re-election because Dean Helen Popovich refused to grant more than two credit hours annually as release time for administrative duties. In his place, Dr. Mazur accepted the nomination and was unanimously elected.

Dean Bernard O'Kelley from North Dakota who reviewed the Department of Foreign Languages in behalf of the North Central Association in 1980 indicated that the three full-time staff members were doing the work of about four and a half people. He felt that an allotment of more faculty positions to the department was a reasonable expectation in light of the services it was trying to provide. However, instead of being expanded, the department was reduced in size when Dr. Guttmann's contract was not renewed for the 1980/81 academic year. Although Winona State's total enrollment had continued to increase over the years, the Department of Foreign Languages remained limited to less than three faculty positions. It had actually experienced a diminution in size since its inception in 1968! With the reduced number of staff members, the department was no longer able to fully meet its obligations within the framework of the Tri-College/University cooperative arrangement either.

Even though classes in elementary French, German, and Spanish were increased to two and quite often even to three times the size recommended by the Modern Language Association, some students had to wait for a year or more before they could actually enroll in beginning language courses. (See minutes of department meetings dated 9/7-10/7, 1982; 10/25-11/11, 1982; and 5/5-5/11, 1983).

The Department's capacity to help attract more students to Winona State was not only reduced because of closed oversized classes and the impractical Tri-College/University arrangement, but also by the lack of a clear mission statement that might have been included in department recruitment letters and in the slide film series shown at area schools by the Admissions Office in which foreign language study opportunities were barely even mentioned.

In 1983, brand new language laboratory equipment was installed in Somsen 300. The new Telex cassette units provide full listening, recording, and playback capability in all thirty-six booths. In connection with the remodeling of Somsen Hall, which is scheduled to begin in May or June 1986, it is hoped that satellite dish antennae will be installed on the roof so that French and Spanish students will be able to receive suitable target language broadcasts from Canada and Mexico via appropriate monitors and video recorders in the language laboratory.

In 1984/85, after thirteen years of service at Winona State (and two unsuccessful previous applications), Dr. Steigerwald was granted a Sabbatical Leave for research and professional updates. His replacement was Dr. Beverly Inman, a German instructor from Iowa State. During the same year, Dr. Mazur was appointed Acting Dean of Arts, Humanities, and Social Sciences (AHSS) on a rather short notice. Miss Nancy Edstrom, part-time instructor at the College of St. Teresa, was hired to teach his scheduled Elementary French classes and Miss Inman taught some of his German classes as overloads.

During the summer of 1985, Dr. Steigerwald offered a beginning course in "Commercial Spanish" experimentally as part of a commitment under a departmental Program Incentive Grant that Dr. Mazur had worked out in consultation with the former Dean of AHSS, Dr. Jonathan Lawson.

In fall 1985, all but one of the sections in elementary French, German, and Spanish closed with about forty students in each. The breakup of the 8-credit cluster in the "different culture" category of general education requirements did not greatly affect foreign language enrollments for winter quarter 1986 either. As the end of 1985 approached, the most pressing issue facing the department related to the question of teacher certification. Until 1982, Winona State was able to have its language majors licensed (under the cooperative arrangement) through the College of St. Teresa; but when that institution made further reductions in its foreign language programs, it lost its accreditation for licensure in German. St. Mary's College is accredited for licensure in foreign languages, but it only endorses candidates who complete their professional sequence at that institution.

Winona State lost its accreditation for licensure in Spanish after 1973/74 when the major was dropped because of insufficient staff allotments. Accreditation for licensure in German was maintained for some years but eventually fell victim to further reductions in connection with repeated program reviews. Presently, there are five options open to the institution: Winona State could

1) Try to get St. Mary's College to endorse its language majors for certification, if SMC itself can maintain state accreditation for licensure.

237

2) Offer majors in one or more languages that are only intended as a supplement to other career qualifications and not for students who seek licensure,

3) Upgrade its only remaining major so that it will meet licensure requirements

4) Phase out the last remaining major and offer only "self-supporting" elementary foreign language courses, or

5) Begin to live up to expectations of a regional university by offering accredited majors in several languages.

A clear decision, and corresponding administrative support, will enable the Department to inform students, high school counselors, other educational institutions, and the general public unequivocally about the extent of Winona State's ability to help satisfy the nation's manpower needs in the foreign language area. The public confidence thusly enhanced should result in even better enrollments.

Appendix C:
Inflation Rates* and Personal Gross Income

(From W-2 Forms): 1951-1992.
*Source: "CPI Detailed Report," U. S. Department of Labor
(November 1999), p. 70-71

YEAR	% of change in CPI	INCOME in U.S. $ (excluding wife's):
1951	7.9	526.14
1952	1.9	4,496.42
1953	0.8	2,178.24
1954	0.7	1,184.30
1955	0.4	132.49 plus GI Bill stipend (PL 550)
1956	1.5	560.00 plus GI Bill stipend (PL 550)
1957	3.3	1,539.70 plus GI Bill stipend (PL 550)
1958	2.8	4,442.82 plus GI Bill stipend (PL 550)
1959	0.7	6,100.74
1960	1.7	7,381.27
1961	1.0	7,240.26
1962	1.0	6,895.53
1963	1.3	3,878.48
1964	1.3	3,114.00
1965	1.6	3,752.25
1966	2.9	3,173.84
1967	3.1	5,637.14
1968	4.2	2,229.77 + NDEA fellowship as of Oct.
1969	5.5	NDEA fellowship for doctoral studies
1970	5.7	NDEA fellowship for doctoral studies
1971	4.4	3,666.24 + NDEA fellowship till summer
1972	3.2	9,312.96
1973	6.2	11,307.68
1974	11.0	11,252.40
1975	9.1	12,519.28
1976	5.8	15,373.68
1977	6.5	15,809.56
1978	7.6	16,660.48
1979	11.3	17,902.61
1980	13.5	18,787.39
1981	10.3	21,022.70
1982	6.2	27,330.71
1983	3.2	28,011.13
1984	4.3	29,397.28 (includes summer course pay)
1985	3.6	28,005.64
1986	1.9	37,316.48
1987	3.6	39,468.48
1988	4.1	41,266,16

1989	4.8	43,293.15
1990	5.4	39,613.46
1991	4.2	41,422.25
1992	3.0	52,357.09 (included severance pay, etc.)

The cumulative total of my gross earnings in the forty-two years listed amounted to $625,560.20, which was eroded by an average inflation rate of 4.3 percent. According to projections of the 1950's when the U. S. dollar still happened to be backed by gold with a fixed price of $35 an ounce, a high school graduate was expected to earn about $258,000 in a lifetime. The figure for college graduates was $340,000.

In *Statistical Abstract of the United States: The National Data Book,* 119th Edition (Washington DC, October 1999), p. 493, the "Purchasing Power of the Dollar: 1950-1998" is depicted. Taken at a par value of 100 percent in 1982, the value of the U. S. dollar had declined to 0.713 by 1992 when I retired. In 1998, it was worth 60 cents. Accordingly, my salary in 1991 was worth around $3,000 less than what I had earned in 1982! The absurdity may serve as one indication, why not enough people with excellent potential are opting for careers in teaching.

X. REFERENCES

Annotated Bibliography

Aberle, George P. *From the Steppes to the Prairies: The Story of the Germans Settling in Russia on the Volga and Ukraine; also, the Germans Settling in the Banat, and the Bohemians in the Crimea; Their Resettlement in the Americas - North and South America and in Canada.* 4th ed. Dickinson, ND: G. P. Aberle, 1963.

Arbeitskreis Dokumentation. *Verbrechen an den Deutschen in Jugoslawien 1944-1948. Die Stationen eines Völkermords.* Georg Wildmann, ed. Munich: Donauschwäbische Kuturstiftung 1998. A spin-off in English was published by The Society of Danube Swabians in the U.S.A.: *Genocide of the Ethnic Germans in Yugoslavia, 1944-1948* (Chicago, IL, 2001). The condensed German version of a 4-volume edition represents an effort to lend a perceptible voice to the ethnic-German victims of Yugoslav genocide.

Arbeitskreis Dokumentation der Donauschwäbischen Kulturstiftung. "Das Schicksal der Donauschwaben." *Der Donauschwabe*, vol. 47, No. 49 (7 Dec 1997), p. 5. Brief depiction of the tragic fate of the Danube Swabians.

Arbeitskreis Dokumentation im Bundesverband der Landmannschaft der Donauschwaben aus Jugoslawien in Sindelfingen und in der Donauschwäbischen Kulturstiftung. *Leidensweg der Deutschen im kommunistischen Jugoslawien.* Georg Wildmann, ed. Vol. 1: *Ortsberichte über die Verbrechen an den Deutschen durch das Tito-Regime in der Zeit von 1944-1948.* Munich-Sindelfingen: Donauschwäbische Kulturstiftung, 1991. Vol. 2: *Elebnisberichte über die Verbrechen an Deutschen durch das Tito-Regime in der Zeit von 1944-1948.* Munich-Sindelfingen, 1993. Vol. 3: *Erschießungen - Vernichtungslager - Kinderschicksale in der Zeit von 1944-1948.* Munich-Sindelfingen, 1995. Vol. 4: *Menschenverluste - Namen und Zahlen.* Munich-Sindelfingen, 1994. Includes 1) locations concerned, 2) accounts of actual happenings, 3) executions carried out, names of attrition camps, and how children were affected, 4) lists known names and number of victims who perished at Yugoslav concentration camps for ethnic-Germans from 1944-1948.

Arbeitkreis donauschwäbischer Familienforscher (AKdFF). *Die Bestände der Bibliothek und des Archivs.* Josef Schmidt and Rosemarie Harjung, compilers. Sindelfingen: AKdFF,

1990. Holdings at the library and archive of the Danube Swabian family genealogists.

Arends, Shirley Fischer. *The Central Dakota Germans: Their History, Language, and Culture.* Washington, DC: Georgetown University Press, 1989. Their language and customs reflect aspects of the Danube Swabian heritage also.

Bogner, Johann Karl. *Heimatbuch der Gemeinde Banat-Topola.* [Giengen/Brenz? Germany, 1986]. Provides a historical synopsis of the village along with glimpses of ethnic-German customs as reflected in daily life. Names and addresses of surviving former inhabitants in their globally scattered locations are also given.

Bogner, Matthias. "Was waren das für böse Zeiten: Wie sich die Sieger im Herbst 1944 und danach in Banat-Topola benahmen." *Der Donauschwabe,"* vol. 20, No. 41 (11 Dec 1970), p. 5. Points up the contemptible conduct of Tito's triumphant partisans toward ethnic-Germans at Banat-Topola in 1944 and subsequently.

Bohn, Hans. *Zur Geschichte der klösterlichen Erziehungs- und Bildungsstätten im rumänischen Banat; nach den chronologischen Notizen der Ehrw. Schulschwester M. Leonilla Kilzer.* Landshut, 1990. The 45-page book is based on notes kept by Sister M. Leonilla Kilzer. Coverage spans the years 1858-1975 and is intended as a contribution toward the history of educational endeavors at convents in the Banat. Perennial struggles for existence under various political realities are also highlighted along with hardships the sisters suffered under communism upon their eviction from about 300 sanctuaries as of 1948.

Born, Joachim and Sylvia Dickgießer. *Deutschsprachige Minderheiten: Ein Überblick über den Stand der Forschung für 27 Länder.* Mannheim: Institut für deutsche Sprache, 1989. German minorities: An overview concerning the status of applicable research in 27 countries.

Braun, Katharina. "Aussiedler und Vertriebene: Zahlen zu einem Jahrhundert ethnischer Säuberung. *Der Donauschwabe,* vol. 49, No. 21 (10 Oct 1999), p. 3. Statistics concerning repatriates and expellees in the century of ethnic cleansing.

Bremer, Adolph. "Decline Hasn't Touched State University System." *Winona Daily News* (22 Oct 1981), p. 4.

---. "The Revolution on Campus." *Winona Daily News* (21 Dec 1983), p. 8.

Bresser, Michael. *The Danube Swabians: Biography of a People from Inception to Dispersal.* Philadelphia, PA: Danube Swabian Association [1984].

Brown, MacAlister. "Expulsion of German Minorities from Eastern Europe." Manuscript. Cambridge, MA: Harvard University Library, 1953.

Cammann, Alfred, and Alfred Karasek. *Donauschwaben erzählen.* 4 vols. Elwert, 1976-1979. A collection of Danube Swabian stories told by persons from every walk of life.

Das Schulwesen der Donauschwaben von 1918 bis 1944. Munich: Verlag des Südostdeutschen Kulturwerkes, 1968. Treatise concerning Danube Swabian education between 1918 and 1944.

de Zayas, Alfred-Maurice. *A Terrible Revenge: The Ethnic Cleansing of the East European Germans, 1944-1950.* John A. Koehler, transl. 1st edition. New York: St. Martin's Press, 1994.

---. *Nemesis at Potsdam: The Anglo-Americans and the Expulsion of the Germans. Background, Execution, Consequences.* Foreword by Robert Murphy. The book treats one of the greatest tragedies of WW II. It was first published at London in 1979, with several revised editions in English including one at Rockport, ME: Picton Press, 1998. Ten German editions appeared so far. The book contains over 70 photographs, maps and illustrations.

Denkschrift: 40 Jahre Donauschwaben in Österreich: Salzburg, 24.-26. August 1984. Salzburg: Haus der Donauschwaben, 1984. Commemorative proceedings from a gathering sponsored by Haus der Donauschwaben Salzburg, Donauschwäbische Arbeitsgemeinschaft Wien, Verein der Salzburger Donauschwaben, and the Verein Franztaler Ortsgemeinschaft Salzburg.

"Der donauschwäbische Leidensweg. Eine Ausstellung im Senat in Washington." *Der Donauschwabe*, vol. 48, No. 48 (29 Nov 1998), p. 7. Discussion of an exhibit in the U. S. Senate concerning the "ethnic cleansing" to which the Danube Swabians in former Yugoslavia were subjected at the end of WW II.

Dewey, John. *Democracy and Education. An Introduction to the Philosophy of Education.* New York: Macmillan, 1964.

Directory of Holocaust Institutions. Washington DC: U. S. Holocaust Memorial Council, 1988. Includes an alphabetical listing of institutions along with a geographical index as well as an activities and collections index.

Documents on the Expulsion of Germans from Eastern-Central Europe. 4 vols. Bonn: Bundesministerium für VFK, 1961. This version in English is based on a multi-volume German edition published by the ministry for refugees, etc. Edited by Theodor Schieder.

Eberl, Immo, Konrad G. Gündisch, and the Innenministerium Baden-Württemberg, eds. *Die Donauschwaben: Deutsche Siedlung in Südosteuropa: Ausstellungskatalog.* Sigmaringen: Jan Thorbecke, 1987. Guide concerning an exhibit about the Danube Swabians.

Egenolff, Franck Chr. *Sprichwörter: Schöne, weise Klugredenn, Darinnen Teutscher und anderer Spraachen Höflichkeit, Zier, höhste Vernunft und Klugheit, als auch zu ewiger und zeitlicher Weißheit, Tugend, Kunst und Wesen dient, gespürt und begriffen, Von Alten und Newen im Brauch gehabt und beschriben, in etliche Tausent zusamen bracht.* Frankfurt/Main, 1552. Reprint with an epilogue by Hans Henning. Berlin, 1967. Early German-language collection of proverbs from international sources.

Engel, Walter. *Deutsche Literatur im Banat (1840-1939): Der Beitrag der Kulturzeitschriften zum banatschwäbischen Geistesleben.* Sammlung Groos, vol. 15. Heidelberg: J. Groos, 1982. The role of cultural journals as part of the German literary scene in the Banat from 1840 to 1939.

"Enrollment Decline Seen for 1984." *Winona Daily News* (2 Oct 1979), p. 11a. At Winona State University, this prediction proved to be a foregone conclusion. - See articles by Adolph Bremer (above) and by Patrick McIlheran (below).

Evans, Gary. "State's Love for Education Has Long History." *Winona Daily News* (14 Apr 1991), pp. 6A-7A.

Fassel, Horst. *Hans Diplich: Werk und Wirkung.* Banater Bibliothek, vol. 1. Munich: Landsmannschaft der Banater Schwaben, 1994. Treats works and achievements of the Banat Swabian writer named in the title.

Flassak, Katharina Elisabeth. *Fegefeuer Balkan. Weg eines donauschwäbischen Kindes.* Sersheim: Oswald Hartmann Verlag, 1994. Autobiographic account of a Danube Swabian teacher who related her uprooting WW II childhood experiences in Tito's Yugoslavia to purgatory.

244

Folberth, Otto. "Mensch und Materie in der Bilanz der IRO." *Berichte und Informationen des österreichischen Forschungsinstituts für Wirtschaft und Politik*, vol.6, No. 279 (Salzburg: 12 Nov 1951). Austrian report concerning activities of the International Refugee Organization (IRO)

Frey, Katherine Stenger. *The Danube Swabians: A People with Portable Roots*. Belleville, Ontario: Mika Publishing Company 1982. This book is dedicated to Danube Swabian children so they may not forget.

Fröschle, Hartmut. *Die Deutschen in Kanada*. Eckartschriften, vol. 101. Vienna: Österreichische Landsmannschaft, 1987. Monograph on German-speaking people living in Canada.

Funk, Joseph M. *Willkommen! Ein Wegweiser mit den neuen Einwanderunsgesetzen für USA-Einwanderer und ihre Bürgen*. Chicago: American Aid Societies for the Needy and Displaced Persons of Central and Southeastern Europe, 1954. A guide for U. S. immigrants and their sponsors based on new contemporary legislation.

Gasteiger, Ottokar F. "Who Were the First Victims of Serbian Brutality and 'Ethnic Cleansing?' Is There a Double Standard?" *Eintracht*, vol. 77, No. 41 (12 Jun 1999), p. 2. This German-American weekly is published at Skokie, Illinois.

Gehl, Hans. *Deutsche Stadtsprachen in Provinzstädten Südosteuropas*. Mit 24 Karten. Stuttgart: Franz Steiner, 1997. German urban languages in cities of Southeast European provinces.

Geiger, Vladimir. *Radni Logor Valpovo 1945-1946*. Osijek: Njemacka Narodnosna Zajednica, 1999. A well documented work in Croatian about the forced labor camp at Valpovo, with a summary epilog in German. Death records are from books of the local Catholic parish.

Genocide of the Ethnic Germans in Yugoslavia: 1944-1948. Chicago, IL: Award Printing Corp., 2001. Published by the Danube Swabian Association of the U.S.A. in support of a German compilation from Arbeitskreis Dokumentation.

Gerescher, Konrad. *Maisbrot und Peitsche: Erlebnisbericht aus einem Vernichtungslager*. Hannoversch Münden/Scheden: Gauke, 1974. Experiences of a Danube Swabian boy in a Yugoslav extermination camp for ethnic-Germans after WW II.

---. *Unserer Hände Arbeit: 200 Berufe der Donauschwaben aus der Batschka, gesammelt und hrsg. von Konrad Gerescher.*

Hann. Münden: Gauke, 1981. Descriptions of 200 occupations that used to be carried out among Danube Swabians in the Backa/Bacska.

Gerhardt, Hans. *Heimatbuch der Heidegemeinden Heufeld - Mastort - Ruskodorf.* Munich, 1987. Monograph concerning the 18th-Century German settlements of Heufeld and Mastort in the Banat, now called Novi Kozarci. Ethnic-Germans at Ruskodorf, better known as Rusko Selo, only represented a minority locally.

Gleich, Gudrun and Wolfgang, eds. *Donau-Schwaben-Kalender 2001. Mit Bildern aus der alten und neuen Heimat.* Aalen-Württemberg: Donauschwäbischer Heimatverlag, 2000. Annual edition of a Danube Swabian calendar.

Gleich, Wolfgang. "Vertreibung nie vergessen. Ministerpräsident Dr. [Edmund] Stoiber enthüllte Gedenktafel." *Der Donauschwabe*, vol. 49, No. 15 (18 Jul 1999), p. 3. Report of the placement of a commemorative marker that is to serve as a reminder that the expulsion of 15 million Germans from Eastern Europe after WW II must never be forgotten either.

Göllner, Carl, and Heinz S. *Aufklärung: Schrifttum der Siebenbürger Sachsen und Banater Schwaben.* Bukarest: Kriterion Verlag, 1974. German literary efforts in Transylvania and the Banat, under communism.

Great Britain, Foreign Office, Historical Section. *Transylvania and the Banat.* Wilmington, Delaware: Scholarly Resources, 1973.

Gruber, Wendelin. *In the Claws of the Red Dragon: Ten Years under Tito's Heel.* Frank Schmidt, transl. Toronto: St. Michaelswerk, 1988. Title of the German original: *In den Fängen des roten Drachen: Zehn Jahre unter der Herrschaft Titos.* Jestetten: Miriam, 1986. "The diary of Father Wendelin Gruber renders an accurate account of the genocide of Danube Swabian people living in Yugoslavia." (Translator's comment inside book cover).

Guide for New Americans: An Introduction to Your New Homeland. New York: American Council of Voluntary Agencies for Foreign Service, 1950.

Hauck, Shirley A. "The Swabian Kirchweih Festival of the Romanian Banat." M.M.F.A.-Thesis: Duquesne University, 1982; 125 pp.

Hecht, L. *Les colonies lorraines et alsaciennes en Hongrie.* Nancy, 1879. Lorrainian and Alsacian colonies in Hungary.

Heilman-Märzweiler, Magdalena. *Verlorene Kindheit. Erlebnisse und Gedichte.* Freising: Scherer-Verlag. A lost childhood depicted in poems based on actual experiences of a Danube Swabian girl in post-WW II Yugoslavia under Tito and his partisans.

Hellwig, Gerhard, compiler. *Zitate und Sprichwörter von A bis Z.* Gütersloh, 1974. Quotations and proverbs in alphabetical arrangement.

Hess, Nikolaus and Michael Gross. *Heimatbuch der Banater Schwestergemeinden St. Hubert - Charleville - Soltur.* Munich: Michael Gross, 1981. Monograph regarding the three villages founded during the 18th Century by colonists from Lorraine. Upon the expulsion of the German-speaking descendants in 1945, the tripartite town called Banatsko Veliko Selo in Serbian was settled by Slavs from other parts of Yugoslavia under authority of Tito's partisans.

Hochgatterer, Anton. *Entre Rios: Donauschwäbische Siedlung in Südbrasilien.* Josef Schramm and Christoph Ursin, eds. Salzburg: Haus der Donauschwaben, 1986. An account concerning the establishment of five Danube Swabian villages near Guarapuava, Paraná, Brazil, as of 1951.

Horak, Karl. *Das deutsche Volksschauspiel im Banat. Schriftenreihe der Kommission für Ostdeutsche Volkskunde in der Deutschen Gesellschaft für Volkskunde e. V.* Vol. 14. Marburg: Elwert, 1975. Treatise about the German folkdrama in the Banat.

Horváth, Eugene. *The Banat: A Forgotten Chapter of European History.* Budapest: Sárkány Printing Company, 1931. This thin volume was published by the Hungarian Frontiers Readjustment League. It includes statistical data about different nationality group representation in various towns and villages; relevant older works about the Banat can be found in the bibliography.

Horwath, Maria. *Vier Jahre meines Lebens: Als Mädchen im Hungerlager Rudolfsgnad.* Helmut Tenz, ed. Copyright: Matthias Merkle, Heilbronn. Munich: Oberrieder & Olmanns, 1987. Describes the four childhood years of the author's confinement in a Yugoslav starvation camp for ethnic-Germans, from March 1945 until January 1948.

Hügel, Kaspar. *Werden und Vergehen der deutschen Siedlungen in Südosteuropa.* Eckartschriften vol. 116. Vienna:

Österreichische Landsmannschaft, 1991. Monograph on how German settlements in Southeastern Europe came about and eventually faced extinction.

Ilg, Gerard. *Proverbes Français, Suivis de Equivalents en Allemand, Anglais, Espagnol, Italien et Neerlandais.* Amsterdam, NY, 1960. French proverbs followed by equivalents in German, English, Spanish, Italian and Dutch.

Jordan, Sonja. *Die kaiserliche Wirtschaftspolitik im Banat im 18. Jahrhundert. Buchreihe der Südostdeutschen Historischen Kommission.* Vol. 17. Munich: Oldenbourg, 1967. Imperial economic policy in the Banat in the 18th Century when the territory was an Austrian crown colony.

Kallbrunner, Josef. *Das kaiserliche Banat und Florimund Claudius Mercy.* Veröffentlichungen, Reihe B, 11. Munich: Verlag des Südostdeutschen Kulturwerks, 1958. Treatise concerning the Banat as an Austrian crown colony under its first governor.

Koehler, Eve Eckert. *Seven Susannahs: Daughters of the Danube.* Milwaukee: Danube Swabian Association of the U.S.A., 1976. Second printing, 1977.

---, compiler. "Who are the Donauschwaben? Informational Packet of Materials Related to the Danube Swabian Experience." Milwaukee: The Danube Swabian Foundation, 1986. Spiral-bound reproductions of map drawings, book reviews, articles, bibliographic references, etc.

Krambeer, Brian. "Studies Abroad Expand Educational Experiences." *Winona Campus Life,* No. 98 (22 Jul 1985), p. 4. An interview with WSU-student Ellen Susanne Steigerwald.

Kremling, Anton and Gerda Juhasz, eds. *Die Donauschwaben in den Vereinigten Staaten von Amerika: Festschrift zur Zwanzig-Jahr-Feier des Verbandes der Donauschwaben in den USA. e. V., 1957-1977.* Cleveland, OH: Verlag des Waechter und Anzeiger, 1977. Commemorating the 20th anniversary of the Society of Danube Swabians in the United States of America.

Krischan, Alexander. *Die deutsche periodische Literatur des Banats: Zeitungen, Zeitschriften, Kalender 1771-1971: Bibliographie.* Munich: Südostdeutsches Kulturwerk, 1987. Bibliography of German periodical literature in the Banat from 1771-1971.

Kroner, Michael. *Nationale Minderheiten in Südosteuropa: Verfolgung, Assimilierung, Flucht, Vertreibung und Um-*

siedlung. Eckartschriften Heft 121. Vienna: Österreichische Landsmannschaft, 1992. Monograph on the devastating fate of national minorities in Southeastern Europe.

Künzig, Johannes, Waltraut Werner-Künzig, Gottfried Habenicht, and Michael Belgrader. *Lied- und Erzählgut der Resi Klemm aus Almáskamarás im ungarischen Banat:* Volkskunde-Tonarchiv Freiburg, 1980. 4 sound discs containing German songs and stories from the Hungarian Banat.

Lachner, Bert, Ernst Ott, and Arlene Lachner. *Heimat North America.* Ed. by Edward A. Michals. Chicago: Landmark Books Unlimited, 1997. Illustrated work, 336 pp. in English and German described by the publisher as "an epic document of all Germanic people on the North American continent."

Längin, Bernd G. *Aus Deutschen werden Amerikaner: Die Geschichte der deutschen Einwanderung in die neue Welt.* Eckartschriften vol. 126. Vienna: Österreichische Landsmannschaft, 1993. An historic overview regarding immigration of German-speaking people to the New World.

Leicht, Sebastian, Georg Wildmann, and Landsmannschaft der Donauschwaben aus Jugoslawien in Bayern. *Weg der Donauschwaben: Dreihundert Jahre Kolonistenschicksal: Graphischer Zyklus.* Passau: Verlag Passavia, 1983. Includes many drawings that illustrate the fate of the Danube Swabians as pioneers.

Lichtenberger, Jakob, ed. *Documentário ilustrado da colonização suábios danubiana Entre Rios. Bildbericht einer donauschwäbischen Siedlung in Brasilien.* [Vitória: Cooperativa Agrária Mista Entre Rios, 1976]. Bilingual (Portuguese and German) illustrated documentation of the Danube Swabian settlement established in 1951 near Guarapuava, Paraná. It encompasses five villages: Vitória (victory), Jordaozinho (little river), Cachoeira (waterfall), Socorro (help), and Samambaia (fern grove).

Liquornik, Alfred, Joseph Funk, and A. Schaefler. "General McRae." Newsletter No. 4 aboard ship (11 Oct 1951).

Lohne, Raymond. *The Great Chicago Refugee Rescue.* Rockport, ME: 1997. The book documents efforts by the "American Aid Societies for the Needy and Displaced Persons of Central and Southeastern Europe" to send food and clothing to Danube Swabians abroad and to facilitate immigration to the U. S. A.

Lutje, Peter. "Werden und Vergehen Banat-Topolas." *Der Donauschwabe,* vol. 20, No. 40 (4 Oct 1970), pp. 3 and 5. Historical synopsis concerning the village up to the expulsion of its ethnic-German inhabitants and their confinement to attrition camps.

Marin, William. *Kurze Geschichte der Banater Deutschen. Mit besonderer Berücksichtigung ihrer Beziehungen zur rumänischen Bevölkerung und ihrer Einstellung zur Vereinigung von 1918.* Verbesserte und erweiterte Ausgabe der Arbeit Unirea din 1918 *si pozi*tia *svabilor b*an*a*teni. ed. Temeswar: Facla. 1980. A short history of German-speaking people in the Banat focusing on their relations with the Romanian population.

Marrus, Michael R. *The Unwanted: European Refugees in the Twentieth Century.* New York: Oxford University Press, 1985

Maskus, Rudi. *Auch das geschah damals.- Hundert Zeitzeugen über Flucht und Vertreibung.* Gießen: R. Maskus, 2000. One hundred WW II-era witness accounts of German refugees and expellees from Eastern Europe.

---. *Die Vertreibung der Deutschen. Mit 115 Bildern: Ein fast vergessenes Kapitel der Geschichte.* 2nd ed. Gießen: Verlag R. Maskus, 1999. The expulsion of Germans from Eastern Europe, a nearly forgotten chapter of history including 115 black and white photographs primarily depicting architectural landmarks.

McIlheran, Patrick. "WSU Braces for Freshman Storm." *Winona Daily News* (1 May 1986), p. 1.

Merkl, Michael, ed. *Weitblick eines Donauschwaben: Adam Berenz. Dokumentation eines Abwehrkampfes 1935-1944, gegen nationalsozialistische Einflüsse unter den Donauschwaben Jugoslawiens und Ungarns, im Wochenblatt für das katholische Deutschtum Jugoslawiens und Ungarns: DIE DONAU.* Dieterskirch: Ein Kreis von Donauschwaben, 1968. Documentation of Danube Swabian resistance to National Socialist influences.

Merschdorf, Wilhelm Josef. *Tschakowa: Marktgemeinde im Banat. Monographie und Heimatbuch.* Augsburg: Heimatortsgemeinschaft Tschakowa, 1997. Historic portrayal of Ciacova, Banat, Romania, with emphasis on the German segment of the multi-ethnic town population.

Metz, Franz. *Die Kirchenmusik der Donauschwaben*. 1st ed. Deutsche Musik im Osten, vol. 7. Sankt Augustin: Academia, 1996. Treats church music of the Danube Swabians

Michels, John M. *North Dakota Pioneers from the Banat*. Bismarck: University of Mary Press, 1992. Provides information concerning the background and settlement patterns of German-speaking immigrants from the Banat, Hungary, who arrived in America between 1891 and 1910.

Mileck, Joseph. *Samatimerisch: Phonetik, Grammatik, Lexikographie. Geschichte der Mundart der deutschen Gemeinde Sanktmartin am nördlichen Rand des rumänischen Banats*. Berkeley models of grammars, vol. 3. New York: P. Lang, 1997. History of the German dialect of the St. Martin community in the Banat.

Müller, Karl. *Im Strom der Donauschwaben*. Munich: Baumgartner, 1994. Danube Swabian scenarios.

Nawratil, Heinz. *Schwarzbuch der Vertreibung 1945 bis 1948: Das letzte Kapitel unbewältigter Vergangenheit*. 5th ed. June 1999. Munich: Universitas, 1982. Black book about the expulsion of Germans from Eastern Europe between 1945 and 1948: A recent chapter of history yet to be appropriately ranked.

Österreichische Historiker-Arbeitsgemeinschaft für Kärnten und Steiermark. *Völkermord der Tito-Partisanen 1944-1948: Die Vernichtung der altösterreichischen deutschen Volksgruppe in Jugoslawien und die Massaker an Kroaten und Slowenen*. Sersheim: Oswald Hartmann Verlag, 1990. Genocide by Tito's partisans 1944-1948: Extermination of the erstwhile Austrian German minority in Yugoslavia and massacres of Croats and Slovenes.

Paikert, Géza C. *The Danube Swabians. German Populations in Hungary, Rumania and Yugoslavia and Hitler's Impact on their Patterns*. Studies in Social Life, vol. 10. The Hague: Martinus Nijhoff, 1967. A case study in national minorities' patterns and behavior.

Petri, Anton Peter. *Kulturgeschichtliches Wortgut in den Mundarten der Donauschwaben*. Stuttgart: Landsmannschaft der Donauschwaben in Baden-Württemberg e. V., 1965. Reflections of cultural history in Danube Swabian vocabulary.

--- and Josef Wolf. *Heimatbuch der Heidegemeinde Triebswetter im Banat*. Tuttlingen: Triebswetterer Heimatortsgemeinschaft, 1983. Monograph about Tomnatic, Banat, founded in the 18th Century by predominantly French-speaking settlers from Lorraine.

Radke, Venessa Renee. "Wahlheimat: The Resettlement of the Danube Swabians in Milwaukee." M. A. Thesis: University of Wisconsin, Milwaukee, 1995, 151 pp.

Read, Richard P. "Balkan Boundaries as Illustrated in the Former Banat of Temesvár." M. A. Thesis: Columbia University, 1926; 17 pp.

"Record Enrollment at WSU." *Winona Daily News* (24 Sep 1985), p. 3.

Regényi, Isabella and Anton Scherer. *Donauschwäbisches Ortsnamenbuch für die ehemals und teilweise noch deutsch besiedelten Orte in Ungarn, Jugoslawien (ohne Slowenien), sowie West-Rumänien (Banat und Sathmar)*. Darmstadt: Arbeitskreis donauschwäbischer Familienfor-scher, 1980. 2nd rev. edition: Schriesheim, 1987.

Reichrath, Anna. *Die Donauschwaben in Cincinnati, Ohio: Gedichte, Tätigkeitsberichte und historische Rückblicke*. Festschrift zur Zwanzig-Jahr-Feier. Cincinnati, OH: Verein der Donauschwaben, 1974. Commemorating the 20th anniversary of the local Danube Swabian organization.

Reitlinger, Gerald. *The Final Solution: The Attempt to Exterminate the Jews of Europe, 1939-1945*. Northvale, NJ: J. Aronson, 1987. The 2nd revised and augmented edition was published at New York by Yoseleff in 1968.

Réz, Heinrich. *Bibliographie zur Volkskunde der Donauschwaben*. Munich: E. Reinhardt, 1935. Reference work concerning Danube Swabian folklore.

Roch, Hans. *Donauschwäbische Heimatbilder: 12 orig. Holzschnitte*. [s. l.: s. n.], 1952. Portrays twelve original Danube Swabian woodcarvings.

Rogl, Ludwig. *Der Anteil Adam Müller-Guttenbrunns am völkischen Erwachen des Donauschwabentums*. Brünn: R. M. Rohrer, 1943. The role of the Danube Swabian writer Adam Müller-Guttenbrunn in awakening self-awareness among his compatriotes.

Rohr, Robert. *Unser klingendes Erbe: Beiträge zur Musikgeschichte der Deutschen und ihrer Nachbarn in und aus Südosteuropa unter besonderer Berücksichtigung der Donauschwaben: Von den Anfängen bis 1918*. Passau: Passavia, 1988. Deals with musical history of Germans and their neighbors in East Central Europe with particular focus on the Danube Swabians from beginnings until 1918.

Rowe, H. D. "Deadwood v. Dry Rot." *NEA Advocate*, ed. by Sheilah Vance (Nov 1981), p. 8.

Russell, Lisa A. "Language and Ethnic Identity: The Donauschwaben in Los Angeles." M. A. Thesis: California State University, Northridge, 1993; 111 pp.

Schauss, Hans et al. *Die Donauschwaben in Südkalifornien.* Whittier: Beacon Press, 1968. Describes social activities of the Danube Swabian association in Southern California.

Schechtman, Joseph B. "The Elimination of German Minorities in Southeastern Europe." *Journal of Central European Affairs* 6 (1946), pp. 152-166.

---. *European Population Transfers 1939-1945.* New York: Oxford University Press, 1946.

Scherer, Anton. *Die Deutschen und die Österreicher aus der Sicht der Serben und Kroaten.* Graz: Donauschwäbisches Bibliographisches Archiv, 1992. Germans and Austrians as seen by Serbs and Croates.

---. *Die Donauschwaben und die Deutschen im allgemeinen in den USA, in Canada, Brasilien, Argentinien, Venezuela und Australien, 1965-1975: Eine Bibliographie = The Danube Swabians and the Germans on the whole in the USA, Canada, Brazil, Argentina, Venezuela and Australia.* Danubio-Suevia, 11. Graz: Donauschwäbisches Bibliographisches Archiv, 1997.

---. *Die nicht sterben wollten. Donauschwäbische Literatur von Lenau bis zur Gegenwart.* 1959. 2nd ed. Graz, 1985. An anthology covering Danube Swabian literature from Nikolaus Lenau to the 1950's.

---. *Donauschwäbische Bibliographie 1935-1955: Das Schrifttum über die Donauschwaben in Ungarn, Rumänien, Jugoslawien und Bulgarien sowie, nach 1945, in Deutschland, Österreich, Frankreich, USA, Canada, Argentinien und Brasilien.* Munich: Verlag des Südostdeutschen Kulturwerks, 1966. A 480-page sequel to this comprehensive Danube Swabian bibliography covering the period 1955-1965 was published at Munich in 1974 and a 196-page paperback sequel covering 1965-1975 was published at Graz: Donauschwäbisches Bibliographisches Archiv, 1999.

---. "Von Serben 1916 geplant: Die 'Ethnische Säuberung' gegen die Donauschwaben." *Der Donauschwabe,* vol. 49, No. 15 (18 Jul 1999), p. 4. The author traced Serb resolve about subjecting the Danube Swabians to "ethnic cleansing" back to 1916.

"Schily für Errichtung eines Zentrums gegen Vertreibung in Berlin." *Gerhardsbote. Mitteilungsblatt des St. Gerhards - Werkes e. V. und des Südostdeutschen Priesterwerkes,* vol. 44, No. 6 (Jun 1999). Proposal by Otto Schily, head of the Department of the Interior in Germany, for the establishment of a center in Berlin to oppose population expulsions.

Schmitt, Richard. *Deutsche Redensarten: Quiz- und Übungsbuch.* Stuttgart, 1975. Exercise and test booklet on German figures of speech.

Schnur, Maria. *Unforgettable Years.* Josefine Bollmann, transl. Chicago: Bollmann, 1983. Memories of childhood years spent in a Yugoslav attrition camp for ethnic-Germans.

Schott, Arthur, and Albert Schott. *Walachische Märchen.* Hildesheim and New York: G. Olms, 1979. Romanian fairytales.

Schuster, Hans-Werner and Walther Konschitzky, eds. *Deportation der Südostdeutschen in die Sowjetunion 1945-1949.* Munich: Haus des deutschen Ostens, 1999. A publication to accompany the mobile exhibit about the deportation of ethnic-Germans from East Central Europe to the Soviet Union after WW II.

Schwicker, Johann Heinrich. *Geschichte des Temeser Banats: Historische Bilder und Skizzen.* Grosz-Becskerek: Bettelheim, 1861. Historic sketches and images from the Banat.

Schwob, Anton and Horst Fassel, eds. *Archivierung und Dokumentation: Deutsche Sprache und Literatur aus Südosteuropa. Beiträge der Tübinger Fachtagung vom 25. - 27. Juni 1992.* Munich: Südostdeutsches Kulturwerk, 1996. Proceedings from a professional conference at Tübingen regarding repositories for and documentation of German linguistic and literary works from and about East Central Europe.

Seckler-Hudson, Catheryn. *Federal Textbook on Citizenship: Our Constitution and Government: Lessons on the Constitution and Government of the United States for Use in the Public Schools by Candidates for Citizenship.* Simplified ed.

by John G. Harvey. Washington, DC: U. S. Government Printing Office, 1951.

Senz, Ingomar. *Die Donauschwaben*. Studienbuchreihe der Stiftung Ostdeutscher Kulturrat, 5. Munich: Langen Müller, 1994. This book about Danube Swabians was written as part of a planned 12-volume series covering relocation of ethnic-Germans along with German refugees, deportees, expellees, and forcible population transfers from countries in Eastern Europe.

---, Rudolf Fath, and Friedrich Fathas. *Donauschwäbische Geschichte*. Munich: Universitas, 1997. Danube Swabian history.

Senz, Josef Volkmar and Georg Wildmann. *Entwicklung und Erbe des donauschwäbischen Volksstammes: Festschrift für Josef Volkmar Senz zum 70. Geburtstag*, Donauschwäbisches Archiv. Reihe I. Schriftenreihe der ADL, vol. 10. Munich: Arbeitskreis für Donauschwäbische Heimat- und Volksforschung, 1982. Evolution and legacy of the group known as Danube Swabians, published in commemoration of the 70th birthday of J. V. Senz (1912-2001).

Simrock, Karl, compiler. *Die deutschen Sprichwörter*. Einleitung von Wolfgang Mieder. Stuttgart: Philipp Reclam Jun. 1988. Pocketbook edition of the well-known 19th Century collection of proverbial sayings in German.

Solms, Wilhelm. *Nachruf auf die rumäniendeutsche Literatur*. Marburg: Hitzeroth, 1990. A tribute to German literary creations in Romania.

Sonnleitner, Hans. *Donauschwäbische Todesnot unter dem Tito-Stern: Verbrechen in den Jahren 1944-1947. Mit einer politischen und moralischen Wertung*. Munich: Donauschwäbische Kulturstiftung 1990. With reference to victims from his own family, the author critically examines crimes committed by Tito's partisans against Yugoslavia's ethnic-Germans from 1944 to 1947.

Springenschmied, Karl. *Our Lost Children: Janissaries?* John Adam Koehler and Eve Eckert Koehler, transl. Milwaukee: Danube Swabian Association of the U.S.A., 1980. The original German version appeared as Eckartschriften vol. 65. It has the title *Janitscharen? Die Kindertragödie im Banat.* Vienna: Österreichische Landsmannschaft, 1978.

Stader, Stefan. *Auswanderer nach Südosteuropa im 18. Jahrhundert, nach der Zentralkartei der Heimatstelle Pfalz.* Schriftenreihe zur donauschwäbischen Herkunftsforschung, vol. I. Griesheim: Arbeitskreis Donauschwäbischer Familienforscher, 1978. Eighteenth Century German emigration to East-Central Europe as determined from a central data bank in the Palatinate.

---. *Familienbuch der katholischen Pfarrgemeinde Atschau = Vértesacsa im Schildgebirge, 1724-1800. Mit einer siedlungsgeschichtlichen Einleitung von Anton Tafferner.* Schriftenreihe zur donauschwäbischen Herkunftsforschung, vol. 34. Sindelfingen: Arbeitskreis donauschwäbischer Familienforscher, 1993. Catholic Church records of German inhabitants of Vértesacsa, Hungary.

Stefanovic, Nenad. *Jedan svet na Dunavu - Razgovori y komentari.* Belgrade 1997. Transl. into German by Oskar Feldtänzer: *Ein Volk an der Donau. Das Schicksal der Deutschen in Jugoslawien unter dem kommunistischen Tito-Regime. Gespräche und Kommentare serbischer und deutscher Zeitgenossen.* Munich: Donauschwäbische Kulturstiftung, 1999. Anthology concerning the fate of Yugoslavia's German minority. Selections include accounts of contemporary German and Serbian authors.

Steigerwald, Jacob. "Anregung zur Schaffung eines weltweiten Wegweisers zu donauschwäbischen Vereinen und Institutionen." *Der Donauschwabe* (24 Apr 1977), p. 5. Proposal for an international guide to Danube Swabian clubs and organizations.

---. "Auswanderung - gestern und heute." *Nachrichten der Donauschwaben in Chicago (Jan 1976),* pp. 10-11. Emigration - past and present.

---, *Banat-Topola's Schwaben: 1791-1945.* Winona, Minnesota: Translation & Interpretation Service, 1992. Monograph concerning an erstwhile Austro-Hungarian village from where the ethnic-German population was expelled by Tito's partisans and confined to attrition camps as part of "ethnic cleansing" to get rid of an unwanted minority after WW II.

---. "Bestände von Werken Adam Müller-Guttenbrunns (1852-1923) an amerikanischen und kanadischen Bibliotheken, die bis 1956 erschienen sind." *Donauschwäbische Forschungs- und Lehrerblätter*, vol. 25, No. 3 (1979), pp. 71-76. Holdings of works by Adam Müller-Guttenbrunn at American and Canadian libraries that were published before 1956.

---. "Bestandsaufnahme: Eine Generation nach Flucht und Vertreibung." *Der Donauschwabe* (9 Feb 1975), p. 3. Taking stock one generation after Danube Swabians left East Central Europe to escape communism and upon having been expelled from ancestral habitats.

---. "Bildung - ein lebenslänglicher Vorgang." *Der Donauschwabe* (7 Sep 1975), p. 9. Education - a lifetime process.

---. "Danube Swabians." *Society for German-American Studies Newsletter*, vol. 6, No. 2 (1985), pp. 12-13.

---. "Das Problem der Erhaltung der Muttersprache in den USA." *Entwicklung und Erbe des donauschwäbischen Volksstammes*, Festschrift für Josef Volkmar Senz zum 70. Geburtstag. Donauschwäbisches Archiv. Reihe I. Schriftenreihe der ADL, vol. 10. Georg Wildmann, ed. Munich: Arbeitskreis für Donauschwäbische Heimat- und Volksforschung, 1982, pp. 297-305. Discussion of problems concerning retention of fluency in one's native language while trying to become integrated into American society.

---. "Das Wunder, oder der wackelnde Kirchturm." *Der Donauschwabe* (4 Aug 1968), pp. 5 and 8. Account of a boyhood experience that included astounding aspects.

---. "Die Ausgewanderten." *Donauschwäbische Lehrerblätter*, vol. 14, No. 1 (1968), pp. 3-10. Historic conditions that enabled the Danube Swabians to maintain their national identity in the multi-ethnic setting of East Central Europe for 250 years are weighed against realities in America that result in quicker assimilation.

---. "Die Bremer Beiträger: Ihr Verhältnis zu Gottsched und ihre Stellung in der Geschichte der deutschen Literatur." Unpublished doctoral dissertation: University of Cincinnati, 1975. Deals with a group of 18th Century writers whose efforts helped pave the way toward the classical period in German literary history.

---. "Die Deutschamerikaner." *Festbuch zur 30. Jahresfeier des Verbandes der Donauschwaben in den USA, e. V., 1957-1987*. Michael Bresser, ed. Cleveland: Waechter und Anzeiger, 1987, pp. 55-56. Reprinted in *Donauschwaben in Nordamerika, in Südamerika und in Australien*, by Christian Ludwig Brücker. Munich: Donauschwäbische Kulturstiftung, 1990, p. 170-171.

---. *Donauschwäbische Gedankenskizzen aus USA- Reflections of Danube Swabians in America. Aufsätze - Articles, 1968-1982*. With a Preface by Josef Volkmar Senz. Winona, Minnesota: Translation & Interpretation Service, 1983. Includes an historical introduction, 2 map drawings, observations for further studies, and English summaries of the articles that are written in German.

---. "Ein Beispiel Elsaß-Lothringischen Kulturerbes in Banat-Topola." *Das Donautal-Magazin,* vol. 10, No. 29 (15 Jun 1986), p. 23. Discussion of a cultural vestige of immigrants from Lorraine consisting of a French enchantment for "magical transformations."

---. "Entre Rios ist eine Reise wert!" *Der Donauschwabe,* vol. 35, No. 13 (31 Mar 1985), p. 6. Impressions from a trip to the Danube Swabian settlement Entre Rios near Guarapuava, Paraná, Brazil.

---. "Ethnische Minderheiten: Stabilisierende Faktoren der amerikanischen Gesellschaft." *Der Donauschwabe* (21 Mar 1976), p. 2. Ethnic minorities are seen as stabilizing elements in American society.

---. *Exploring French, German, and Spanish.* Winona, Minnesota: Translation & Interpretation Service, 1987. This workbook can help prospective learners decide toward which language they may have greater natural leanings.

---. "In der Geburtsstunde des Donauschwabentums: Erste deutsche Gruppenauswanderung nach Amerika." *Donauschwäbische Forschungs- und Lehrerblätter,* vol. 29, No. 2 (1983), pp. 49-55. The arrival of the first group of German immigrants in America coincided with the 1683 defeat of the Ottomans at Vienna, which opened the way for ancestors of Danube Swabians to settle in Hungary along the middle Danube.

---. "Krise im Fremdsprachenunterricht in den Vereinigten Staaten von Amerika." *Donauschwäbische Lehrerblätter,* vol. 21, No. 2 (1975), p. 16-19. Illuminates perpetual problems concerning foreign language instruction in the U. S. A.

---. "Rückblick ins Mutterland." *Der Donauschwabe* (22 Feb 1976), p. 4. Comparison of living conditions in the U. S. with those in former homelands abroad.

---. "Soll unsere Jugend studieren?" *Der Donauschwabe* (4 Jan 1976), p. 3. Should young Danube Swabians pursue higher education?

---. *Tracing Romania's Heterogeneous German Minority from Its Origins to the Diaspora.* Winona, Minnesota: Translation & Interpretation Service, 1985. Eleven different groups are identified. Separate chapters are devoted to the Banat

258

Swabians, the Sathmar Swabians, and the Transylvania Saxons.

---. "Zum 25jährigen Bestehen der Vereinigung der Donauschwaben in Chicago." *Nachrichten der Donauschwaben in Chicago* (Aug 1978), p. 1-2. Commemorating the 25th anniversary of the Society of Danube Swabians in Chicago, Illinois.

---. "Zur Anpassung der Donauschwaben in ihrer neuen Umgebung." *Der Donauschwabe* (2 May 1976), p. 6. Danube Swabian immigrants adjusting to realities in the new environment.

---. "Zur Herkunft der Donauschwaben." *Nachrichten der Donauschwaben in Chicago* (Feb 1981), pp. 5-7. Background of the Danube Swabians.

---. "Zur heutigen Lage der Donauschwaben." *Donauschwäbische Lehrerblätter,* vol. 15, No. 2 (1969), pp. 4-5. An assessment of contemporary Danube Swabian affairs.

Steinmetz, Greg. "Northern Yugoslavia, 1946: According to Official History, this Ethnic Purge Never Happened." *Chicago Tribune,* section 1 (November 12, 1992), p. 11. Officials in Belgrade have yet to acknowledge criminal treatment of Yugoslavia's ethnic-Germans by Tito's partisans in the wake of WW II.

"Suddenly Ph. D.'s Are a 'Glut on the Market'." *The New York Times.* Jan 4, 1970. E9.

Tafferner, Anton. *Donauschwäbische Wissenschaft. Versuch einer geistigen Bestandsaufnahme und Standortbestimmung von den Anfängen bis zur Gegenwart.* Munich: Südostdeutsches Kulturwerk, 1974. Taking stock of sources and determining the status regarding Danube Swabian research.

---. *Quellenbuch zur donauschwäbischen Geschichte.* 4 vols: I: Munich: H. Meschendörfer, 1974; II: Stuttgart, 1977; III: Stuttgart, 1978; IV: Stuttgart: Verlag Buch und Kunst Kepplerhaus, 1982. Sources for Danube Swabian historical research.

Tóth, Ágnes. *Migrationen in Ungarn 1945-1948. Vertreibung der Ungarndeutschen, Binnenwanderungen und slowakisch-ungarischer Bevölkerungsaustausch.* Munich: Oldenbourg, 2001. This 270-page book covers migrations in Hungary between 1945-1948, including the expulsion of about half of the country's German-speaking citizens, along with population exchanges between Hungary and Slovakia, to achieve greater homogeneity.

Treuberg, Gottfried. *Nacht über den Donauschwaben, oder vertriebenes Volk.* Vienna: Schwabenverein für Wien, Niederösterreich und Burgenland, 1980. A 5-act drama that reflects the unnamed tragic fate of thousands, as it portrays the experiences of one ethnic-German family in former Yugoslavia.

Vetter, Roland. *Der donauschwäbische Beitrag zur deutschen Vertreibungsliteratur: Versuch einer Sichtung.* Bamberg: Wissenschaftliche Verlagsgesellschaft WVB, 1991. An attempt to determine the Danube Swabian share of literary coverage concerning the expulsion of millions of Germans.

Völkl, Ekkehard and Zsolt K. Lengyel. *Der Westbanat 1941-1944: Die deutsche, die ungarische und andere Volksgruppen*, Studia Hungarica, 38. Munich: Trofenik, 1991. Discourse about German, Hungarian, and other nationality groups in the Western Banat, from 1941-1944.

Walter, Elisabeth B. *Barefoot in the Rubble.* Palatine, Illinois: Pannonia Press [1997]. The story of a Danube Swabian girl who survived expulsion and Tito's attrition camps for ethnic-Germans of Yugoslavia in the aftermath of WW II just as the horrors of nazi genocide were reaching world consciousness. In 1998, the author was honored with the "Woman of the Year" award by the American Legion Auxiliary. Her book is among the selection of the Holocaust Memorial Foundation of Illinois.

Wehner, Matthias. "Erlebnisbericht Nr. 40." *Dokumentation der Vertreibung der Deutschen aus Ost-Mitteleuropa*, vol. 5: *Das Schicksal der Deutschen in Jugoslawien.* Reprint: dtv 3274. Munich: Deutscher Taschenbuchverlag, 1984, p. 256, footnote 17. Refers to the brutal killing, on November 12, of the members of Banat-Topola's Danube Swabian militia by Yugoslav partisans.

Weifert, Matthias. "Die Donauschwaben - eine südostdeutsche Volksgruppe im und aus dem mittleren Donauraum." *Eintracht*, Jg. 79-Vol. 28 (17 March 2001), p. 4. Vignette about the scattered Danube Swabian ethnic group.

---. *Donauschwäbisches Unterrichtswerk: Fächerübergreifendes Lehrbuch für Jugendliche.* Donauschwäbisches Archiv. Reihe I. Schriftenreihe der ADL, vol. 16. Munich: Donauschwäbische Kulturstiftung, 1997. Design of an interdisciplinary textbook for young Danube Swabians.

Werni, Sebastian. *Die Wojwodina 1848-1860 als nationales und staatsrechtliches Problem: Zur Geschichte der Serben und der Deutschen im ehemaligen Südungarn.* Wien: W. Braumüller, 1981. This contribution to Serb and German history examines the interim 1848-1860 status of the Vojvodina in light of state rights and criteria of nationality.

Wieden, Fritz. *Canada's Danube Swabians.* Windsor, Ont.: St. Michael's Church, 1992. Text in English and German. 96 p.

Wittje, Margaretha. *Kikinda, eine Stadt im Banat: Ein Heimatbuch der Deutschen aus Grosskikinda und Umgebung.* Peter Schwarz and Alexander Trautner, eds. Sersheim: Oswald Hartmann Verlag, 1996. Monograph focusing on the former ethnic-German residents in and around this multi-national district capital in the Vojvodina.

Wiznitzer, Manuel. *Bildliche Redensarten: Deutsch, Englisch, Französisch.* Stuttgart: Ernst Klett, 1975. German idiomatic expressions used in contexts with given concise English and French equivalents.

Wlossak, Traudie Müller as told to Margaret Farnan. *The Whip: My Homecoming.* Canberra: Golden Leaf Publishers, 1982. Reprint 1986. The story of an ethnic-German woman who returned to Yugoslavia from Germany when WW II ended, only to be confined to a concentration camp by Tito's partisans along with her two small children, until outside intervention eventually resulted in their release.

Wolf, Josef. *Deutsche Minderheiten in Südosteuropa im Umbruch: Die Volkszählungen 1990-1992.* Tübingen: Institut für Donauschwäbische Geschichte und Landeskunde, 1994. Changes involving German minorities in East Central Europe as reflected in the 1990-1992 census.

"WSU Fall Enrollment Makes New Record." *Winonan,* vol. 64, No. 4 (24 Sep 1986), p. 1.

Zülch, Tilman. "Heimatrecht und Vertreibungsächtung." *Der Donauschwabe,* vol. 49, No. 15 (18 Jul 1999), pp. 1 and 10. In this article, the author defends people's birthright and advocates banning of expulsions.

Index

a

b

220, 222, also see execution and expulsion
ethnic group, 4, 8, 10, 52, 135, 170, 172
ethnic (Gernan) minority, 5-14, 16, 30, 48, 51-55, 57, 76, 82, 110-111, 118, 135, 174, 199, 214
ethnic-German(s), vi, 6-7, 9, 10-11, 30, 35, 45, 52-60, 76, 135, 149, 215, 219-222
ethnic "kraut," 116, 221
Ethnic purge/expulsion, 57
Europe, v-vii, 2, 4-5, 8, 17-18, 23-24, 35, 46, 53, 76, 82, 84, 89, 91, 94, 101, 104, 107, 109, 116, 122, 154, 159, 170, 172, 177-178, 184, 189, 192, 207, 214, 216, 219-223
Evans, Gary, 184
Evansville, IN, 106-107
execution-style shootings, 10-11, 35
expellee(s), 8, 14, 52-53, 73, 91, 168, 219-220
expulsion(s), 8-9, 14, 52, 219-220
External Studies Program (ESP), 150-151, 229-230

f

faculty evaluations, Winona State, MN, 167-168
family growth, 123, 126-128
Festini, Justina (*1919), 23, 79, 157 (∞ Martin, Anton)
feudalism, 3, 24, 212
First Union Securities - Carl, 169
FITAFER Indústria & Comércio, Brazil, 22, 172
Fiume, Adriatic port, 18
Flikki, Shirley, 232
Florida, 187-188, 202

forced labor, 5, 10-11, 14, 30, 35, 51-53, 56, 76, 219, 221
forced relocation, 8, 13, also see expulsion(s)
foreign language instruction, 43,125, 128-129, 137, 140, 150-152, 161-163, 165-169, 174-175, 183-185, 210, 226-228, 230-237
Fort Lewis, WA, 107-109, 111-112, 117, 139-140, 187
Fort McCoy, WI, 139, 168-169
Fort Sheridan, IL, 103-104
Frammersbach, Franconia, Germany, 25
France, v, 9, 14, 17, 84, 118, 154, 156, 220-221, 233
Francis Joseph I (*1830, emperor of Austria: 1848-1916), 32, 80, 88, 158
Franconia, Germany, vi, viii, 24, 26
Frank, Anne (1929-1945), 51
Franz, a fellow refugee, 58
Frecot family, 59-60, 71, 138
freedom, 45-46, 63, 79, 90, 92, 94, 111, 113, 155-156, 208, 213, 221
French, v, vii, 2, 4, 14-15, 29, 59, 75, 81, 112, 118, 153-154, 156, 162, 166, 170, 175, 185, 226-229, 231-236
Fulbright seminar, 140, 166

g

Gakova (YU-25282),10
gallbladder (Marie's), 199
Ganghofer, Ludwig (1855-1920), 77
Gattendorf, Austria, 70

131, 139-141, 153, 169, 176-180, 182, 186-188, 192-193, 197, 202, 218, 223, 229
immigrant(s), 1-2, 13, 25, 82-83, 85, 87-89, 91, 95, 100-102, 104, 106, 126, 206, 208, 217-222, 224
immigration, vi, 18, 36, 79, 82-84, 91, 100, 216, 218, 221-223
Indústria de Aços Laminados Ltda. (INDAL), Sâo Paulo, Brazil, 22, 172
Indústria Metalúrgica "Jota eMe" Limitada, 22, 172
infantryman, 104, 107-108, 116, 139, 187
inflation, 65, 101, 153, 163-164
Ingolstadt, Germany, 170-171
injustice, 12-13, 208, also see criminal conduct
inn, 17, 19-23, 34, 36-44, 48, 50, 58, 92, 94
Innsbruck, 122, 156
Instituto de Filología Hispanica, 139, 149
Instituto Mexicano de Cultura Internacional, 139, 170
Inter Faculty Organization (IFO), 167-168, 183
International Refugee Organization (IRO), 84, 222
Islam, 23
Israel, 84
Italian, 31, 45, 89, 99, 119, 122, 202
Ito, Lance (Judge), 6

j
Jajce, Bosnia, 5, 12, 51
Jans, Joseph M., 176-177, 180-181
Jefferson County, CO, 193, 199, 225

Jews, 20-21, 46, 48, 60, 95
Jim Carson - code name, 154
John Paul II, (*1920), 184
John Wiley and Sons, 186
Jonika, Wanda (*1937), 200 (∞ Martin, Hans)
Joseph II (1741-1790), 14
Julitz, John, 202
Jung, Jackie & Bob, 176
Juville, France, 15

k
Kafka, Franz (1883-1924), 159
Kanász, István, 44, 76
Kanász, András, 44
Kane, John (Jack), 183
Kapitaen, Brigitte, 34, 107, 202 (∞- Day, Bill)
Kapitaen, Erich (1962-1983), 34
Kapitaen, Joe, 107, 188
Kapitaen, Marianne, 34
Kaplan, Sheila, 166
Karageorgevich, Paul (1893-1976), 79 (Regent)
Karátsonyi, Counts of, 29
Kardelj, Edward, 7
Kardos, Gergö, 40
Kardos, János, 19-20, 34, 37-42
Kardos, Maris, 40
Kardos, Victoria (+1924), 34 (∞ Steigerwald, Josef)
Käthe (+1998), 36 (∞ Barba Andreas)
Kathreinfeld/Ravni Topolovac (YU-23212), 29
Kati - Hungarian girl, 62
Kennedy, John F. (1917-1963), 45
Kentucky, 104-107, 111, 115, 133-134
kidney stone pain, 167, 189
Kiesinger, Kurt (1904-1988), 155

Sigmaringen, Germany, 30-31

Sigmundfeld/Lukicevo (YU-23261), 30

Silva, Abimael Ruiz da (*1949), 200

Silva, Marcelo (*1983), 200

Silva, Mariane (*1987), 200

Simonsen family, 134

Simpson, O. J., 6

Sindelfingen, Germany, 26, 155, 225

Sister Ricarda (Elisabeth Raab), 229

skin graft on my finger, 198

Skokie, IL, 93, 119, 122, 124, 139, 176, 179

Slavonia, 10, 215

Slav(s), 5-9, 14, 52, 55-57, 215

Slovakia, 95, 189-190

Slusarska, Marzena, 188-193, 199 (∞2 Steigerwald, Carl J.)

Slusarski, Adam (*1950, 191

Slusarski, Bogdan (*1962), 191

Slusarski, Eduard (1935-1998), 191, 199

Slusarski, Jurek (*1975), 191

Social Turner Hall, Chicago, IL, 90, 101, 117

socialist, 4, 73, 138, 216

Society of Danube Swabians, IL, 225

Society of the Danube Swabians, U.S.A., 222

Souderton, PA, 107

Soujanc Street, 37-38

Southeastern Europe, v, 222

Soviet Union, 8, 11, 30, 35, 53, 76, 169, also see USSR and Russia

Soviet zone of Austria, 78

Soviet(s), 73, 75, 78-79, 220

Spacil, Claus (*1971), 34

Spanks (soldier), 104-105

Speltz, Rhetta, 226, 230

Spessart forest, 24-26, 183

Springer, Anna (1878-1920), 15, 17-19, 38, 87, 217 (∞ Martin, Johann)

Springer, Elisabeth (1891-1937), 17, 35 (∞ Binder)

Springer, Katharina (1892-199?), 16-17, 20 (∞ Martin, Mathias)

Springer, Leonard (1855-1901), 17

Springer, Marianne (1896-198?), 17 (∞ Potwen, Peter)

Springer, Nikolaus (1903-1995), 30

Springer, Rosalia (1900-1994), 17 (∞ Rossmann)

sputnik launch (1957),125

Srebrenica, 10

Sremska Mitrovica, 10

SS military units, 9

St. Hubert, 14-15, 27, 35-36, 56, also see Banatsko Veliko Selo

St. Louis, MO, 222, 225

St. Paul, MN, 150, 185

St. Peter the Apostle Church, Philadelphia, 17

St. Peter Square, Rome, 122

Stalin, Joseph (1879-1953), 14, 79

StampTech, Brazil, 22, 172

Stark, Thomas F. 173, 183

starvation, 5, 9, 11, 14, 19, 35, 51-52, 54, 86, 219

Statendam (ship), 122

Statue of Liberty, 87

Stefczak, Bob 134

Steigerwald forest, 26, 155

Stein, Karl of Charleville (*1931), 58, 61-62
Steinmetz, Greg, 57, 76
Stewart of MD, 104-105
student to faculty ratio (WSU), 151-153, 227, 230
Sunset West subdivision - SW of Denver, 192
Supply Records Specialist, 116
Swieton, Irena (*1937), 191 (∞ Slusarski, Eduard)
Syrmia, 10, 215
Szapak, Maria, 120
Szeged, 1, 65-66, 69, 71

t

Tacoma, WA, 108
taking stock, 204-205
Tarzan movies, 223-224
Tasi tizedes-ur, 68
The Church of Jesus Christ of Latter-day Saints, 24, 114, 174, also see Mormon(s)
Theisz, Magdalena (1905-1983), 102, 128, 143, 177 (∞ Holecsek/Holt, Frank)
Theisz, Marie (1916-1984), 158 (∞1 Giel, ∞2 Stein)
Theisz, Peter (1907-1977), 154
Third Reich, 48, 75
Timisoara, Romania, 215, 223
Tisza River, 1, 22, 65
Tito, Josip Broz(ovic), 1892-1980: vi, 6-7, 9-12, 14, 16, 25, 30-31, 35, 51-53, 56-57, 59-60, 62, 76, 79, 110-111, 118, 122, 199, 204, 219, 222
Tito's partisans, 12, 16, 30-31, 35, 52-53, 56, 76, 219, also see partisans
Tkacz-Weber, Hilda, 35, 202
Tkacz-Weber, Linda, 35

tolonc-ház, viii, 66-67, 69, 75
Tomnatic/Triebswetter RO-1974), 14, 58-60, 62, 71
Töröktopolya, 1, also see Banat-Topola
Torontáltopolya, 1, 29, also see Banat-Topola
torture, 35, also see executions
Translation & Interpretation Services, 139, 169, 187
Transylvania Saxons, 134, 174, 220
Treaty of Trianon, France, 1
Trenton NJ, 222, 225
Tri-centennial Anniversary of German Settlement in America, 170
Tri-College/University arrangement, 162-163, 166,174, 231-235
Triebswetter, 14, also see Tomnatic (RO-1974)
Trieste, Italy, 31, 122

u

U. S. Army, vi, 97, 102, 104, 108, 117, 122
U. S. Army language school, 108
U. S. immigration laws, 82, 100, 218, 221-222
U. S. zone, Austria, 75, 78-79
U.S.A./United States, vi-vii, 12, 16, 22-23, 32, 35-36, 56, 81-82, 84, 90, 93, 100, 106, 109, 111, 120, 157, 160, 168, 171-172, 178, 182 189, 204, 213, 215-216, 219-222, 224
Uncle Sam, 83, 106-107
United States Armed Forces Institute (USAFI), 111
University of Chicago, 150

280